What Has Religion Studies in Africa Been Up To?

What Has Religion Studies in Africa Been Up To?

Relevant Themes and Topics

Edited by
Jaco Beyers

WIPF & STOCK · Eugene, Oregon

WHAT HAS RELIGION STUDIES IN AFRICA BEEN UP TO?
Relevant Themes and Topics

Wipf & Stock
An Imprint of Wipf and Stock Publishers
199 W. 8th Ave., Suite 3
Eugene, OR 97401

www.wipfandstock.com

PAPERBACK ISBN: 978-1-5326-6803-6
HARDCOVER ISBN: 978-1-5326-6804-3
EBOOK ISBN: 978-1-5326-6805-0

04/03/23

Contents

List of Illustrations and Tables

List of Contributors

Jaco Beyers (editor), associate professor of Religion Studies at the Faculty of Theology and Religion, University of Pretoria

Molly Manyonganise, research associate with the Faculty of Arts, Culture and Heritage Studies, Department of Religious Studies and Philosophy / Georg Forster postdoctoral research fellow, Alexander von Humboldt Foundation, University of Bamberg, Catholic Theology Institute, Bamberg, Germany / research associate in the Department of Religion Studies, Faculty of Theology and Religion, University of Pretoria, South Africa; Zimbabwe Open University, Harare, Zimbabwe

Lillian Mhuru, associate of the Department of Public Law in the Faculty of Law, Zimbabwe Open University, Harare, Zimbabwe

Elijah Elijah Ngoweni Dube, postdoctoral fellow in the Department of Religion Studies, Faculty of Theology and Religion, University of Pretoria.

Joel Mokhoathi, senior lecturer in the Department of Religion Studies, University of the Free State

Lerato Mokoena, senior lecturer of Religion Studies at the Faculty of Theology and Religion, University of Pretoria

Pieter Verster, professor of Religion Studies at the University of the Free State, Bloemfontein, South Africa

Margaret Makafui Tayviah, professor of Religion at Kwame Nkrumah University of Science and Technology, Kumasi, Ghana

Beverly Vencatsamy, research associate at University of South Africa, Pretoria, South Africa

Johan Strijdom, professor of Religion Studies and Arabic at the University of South Africa, Pretoria, South Africa

Lee-Shae Salma Scharnick-Udemans, senior researcher at the University of Western Cape, Cape Town, South Africa

George Ossom-Batsa, associate professor of Biblical and Mission Studies in the Department for the Study of Religions, at the University of Ghana, Accra, Ghana

Ben-Willie Kwaku Golo, senior lecturer at the Department for the Study of Religions, University of Ghana, Accra, Ghana

Research Justification

THIS BOOK, ENTITLED *WHAT Has Religion Studies in Africa Been Up To? Themes and Topics*, provides a coherent overview of topics and themes under discussion from various parts of Africa on Religion Studies. The purpose of the book is to provide a collection of perspectives from various parts of Africa on what scholars in Religion Studies are currently engaged with, whether it refers to topics or methodology. Each chapter is written from the perspective of a scholar working within a particular context on a particular theme or topic related to Religion Studies.

Several methodologies have been implemented in each contribution to the book. Each contribution applies a different methodology for the purpose of investigating a specific topic or research theme. In general, the majority of contributions follow a method of critical literature review as applied to a specific field.

The book is not intended to provide an exhaustive list of all possible topics and themes addressed in current research in Africa. From a decolonized perspective, the book gives voice to African scholars to exhibit their scholarly work as related to Religion Studies. Topics addressed range from curriculum design and pedagogical approaches in teaching Religion Studies, the relation between religion and culture in an African context, religion and health, religion and gender, interreligious relations in Africa, religion and ecology, and religion and mission.

The target audience of the book is academic scholars who are interested in Religion Studies. Related fields such as Theology, Education, Health Sciences, and Humanities may also find the book helpful. Furthermore, the book is accessible to scholars from other academic disciplines outside of the mentioned disciplines.

The book contains original research and contributions have not been plagiarized from existing publications.

Jaco Beyers
Editor

Introduction

AFRICA HAS BEEN LABELLED as being "notoriously religious"[1] as well as "incurably religious."[2] This emphasizes the important role that religion plays in Africa. The geographical context of this book is Africa, although the topics under discussion do not only relate to Africa. To not study religion would be a grave mistake if trying to understand and generate the meaning of events in Africa. The question can be asked if it is truly religion that we are interested in when claiming that we study religion in an African context. Is there a difference between religion and culture in Africa? This book wants to highlight these kind of probing questions as to what are scholars really busy with when studying religion.

The book is divided into six parts dealing with categories relating to studying religion. In Part I three contributions deal with the matter of Religion Education. In the first chapter Jaco Beyers deals with challenges that a department of Religion Studies encounters at an institute of tertiary education. Some of the most prominent challenges are the definition and demarcation of the field of study. The matter of intercultural communication is of growing interest especially in a multicultural environment such as Africa is. In the second chapter Beverly Vencatsamy deals with the same matter of challenges experienced at an institute of tertiary education. Her contribution deals with the matter of adjusting content to reflect a local context as well as the matter of perspective—religion from humanities and/or theological perspectives. In the third chapter, Lee-Shae Salma Scharnick-Udemans investigates the possible prospects

1. Mbiti, *African Religions*, 1.

2. Parrinder, *Religion in Africa*, 235.

of introducing the element of religion and social media in Africa into tertiary education.

Part II of the book deals with interreligious relations. In chapter 4 Pieter Verster deals with the theoretical considerations on the desirability and neccessity of dialogue between religions. He highlights six guiding principles necessary for dialogue. In chapter 5 Margaret Makafui Tayviah deals with a specific case of interreligious dialogue, namely between Christian and Muslim communities in Africa. She highlights the possibilities for cooperation between communities as way of stimulating dialogue.

In Part III on Socio-Economic Matters Ben-Willie Kwaku Golo deals in chapter 6 with the matter of development in Africa. The socio-economic development and environmental concerns in Africa are combined and discussed from a religious perspective.

In Part IV on Methodology Johan Strijdom deals in chapter 7 with an assessment of the analysis of the concepts of rituals, gender, and race in African indigenous religion as discussed by David Chidester, a prominent scholar of Religion Studies in Africa. Chidester's suggestion is that in order to understand concepts in the studying of religion, concepts must receive theoretical depth.

Part V deals with cultural studies. In chapter 8 Molly Manyonganise and Lillian Mhuru addresses the influence of indigenous knowledge systems on the way in which COVID-19 is treated in Africa. This view incorporates the perspectives of religion, culture, and health. In chapter 9 George Ossom-Batsa deals with the matter of life and death as viewed from the Krobo tribe in Ghana. This contribution discusses from an anthropological view the way in which life and death is viewed in Africa. A valuable contribution is made with the discussion of several rituals pertaining to life and death.

In Part VI the influence of Christianity on the continent is discussed. It starts off with chapter 10, where Elijah Elijah Ngoweni Dube gives an historic account of the growth of Christianity in Zimbabwe. He focuses in particular on the growth of the United Baptist Church. In chapter 11 Joel Mokhoathi deals with the burning matter of the reception of Christianity in Africa from a theological perspective. He discusses the matter from the perspective of the relation between religion and culture. In the final chapter 12, Lerato Mokoena deals with the way in which rituals function in an African context. She uses the Christian Holy Communion as point of reference indicating how the meaning of symbols function.

She applies the insights to the use of Holy Communion during the COVID-19 pandemic.

This book serves as a non-exhaustive showcase of what different scholars from across the African continent are contributing to the field of knowledge in Religion Studies. As part of the larger postcolonial project, this publication gives an opportunity to scholars to voice their opinion.

Part I

Religions and Education

Chapter 1

Challenges of a Department of Religion Studies at a University in Africa

Jaco Beyers

Introduction

The discipline of religion studies, often referred to as "religious studies," engages with a wide range of topics. Each researcher has their own perspective, method of doing research, and epistemology used for interpreting data gathered on the field related to religion studies. When investigating what religion studies scholars in Africa are focusing on in their research, some trends can be observed. The question as to what constitutes religion is constantly an important question. Since a definition of religion in an African context differs from other contexts, it remains an important task to define concepts. Besides providing clear definitions, it is also necessary to explain the choice of words: why "religion studies" and not "religious studies"?

When discussing research performed in religion studies as an academic discipline at tertiary institutions in Africa, there appears to be two variables at play: religion and cultural context. Africa is a large continent with multiple cultures and religions. The communication of knowledge about religion often entails communicating about a religion stemming from a foreign culture, such as would be required when communicating about Christianity, Islam, Judaism, Buddhism, or Hinduism to name only a few. Studying these religions would require knowledge of the culture of origin of the religions as well as the cultures into which these religions are introduced. This leads us to the matter of intercultural communication and how it effects the study of religions in Africa.

This contribution wants first to explain the use of the name religion studies or religious studies, followed by an excursion into what religion is. Thirdly, a description of the status of the study of religion in an African context follows. In a next section five principles that may be considered as a guide in what the study of religion in Africa ought to look like is presented. Consideration is then given to the place of intercultural communication in education and the challenges faced by intercultural communication. This contribution then ends with a conclusion.

Religion Studies or Religious Studies

The traditional way of referring to the study of religions is "religious studies."[1] The discipline known as the "science of religion" was introduced during the twentieth century and is mostly used in the English-speaking world, in particular in the USA. Since the word "science" is considered to have too much baggage to be used indiscriminately for a discipline of scholarship, the term "science of religion" has been substituted by "religious studies." The discipline science of religion existed parallel to religious studies.

Jonathan Z. Smith[2] argues that there is in fact no definite difference between religion studies and religious studies. His argument[3] is that traditionally the difference between religion studies and religious studies is that of "being religious" as opposed to "doing religion," or formulated differently by Smith,[4] that "academic study of religion is not religious." The term "religion studies" is a recent addition to the existing list of titles used for the academic study of religion. "Religion studies" is especially used to refer to the study of religion from an educational perspective.

To make the explanation of Smith clear, the difference between religious studies and religion studies can be explained semantically.

1. Compare the concise description of the origin of the name in Beyers, "Quest," 2.
2. Smith, "Religion and Religious Studies," 231–44.
3. Smith, "Religion and Religious Studies," 231.
4. Smith, "Religion and Religious Studies," 231.

"Religious" in religious studies is an adverbial description of the nature of the study, emphasising the manner in which the study will be conducted. This can easily lead to the perception that a biased understanding will be the result, as would be the case of studying religion at a seminary or theological faculty. With religion studies, "religion" is used as a noun indicating the object to be studied, as would typically be found in the humanities.[5] Smith[6] indicates that this distinction is in fact superficial as it would imply an incorrect or outdated assumption that theological studies uses an intact canon when approaching studying religion and that human sciences are objective and free of values. The perception can even exist that theological approaches are not scientific. Donald Wiebe[7] indicates how the terms "religion studies" or "religious studies" were used interchangeable in the history of the development of the discipline. In this contribution the decision has been made to use the name religion studies in order to reflect the most current state of the discipline.

There appears to be no specific preference for one particular term, "religion studies" or "religious studies," as is proven by the interchangeable use by several institutions in Africa. To avoid any complication and compromise some institutions even formulate the name of the field uniquely.[8] Compare the names of some departments in the following institutions of higher education in Africa:[9]

5. Compare in this regard Smith's ("Religion and Religious Studies," 232) argument on the religiously motivated study of religion as opposed to the scientific study of religion, or the teaching about as opposed to the teaching of religion.

6. Smith, "Religion and Religious Studies," 233.

7. Wiebe, "Religious Studies," 99.

8. Upon inquiry with several institutions in Africa it appears as if the majority of lectures on religion studies are presented in English. In such cases no translation for the word religion is required. For example, in Zimbabwe the technical name for the discipline in the Shona Language is 'Zvidzidzo ZveChitendero' which is translated into English as the study of religion. Even in Portuguese speaking countries in Africa the search is on for an expression reflecting an African way of understanding. For example, the name Studies of Religion tries to avoid the hegemonic term Science of Religion in an attempt at avoiding reducing the approach to science as privileged mediation considering the plurality of ways of knowing in Africa. In Tanzania, I have been informed, there are efforts to enhance Swahili as academic language, as is the case at the University of KwaZulu Natal (UKZN) in South Africa promoting IsiZulu as academic language when it comes to the study of religions.

9. This list does not pretend to be exhaustive. Many private universities are not listed here as are church sponsored institutions. Also, religion specific courses such as would be presented by Christian seminaries and Muslim universities are not reflected here. The purpose of the list is to illustrate the alternating use of the descriptors

- Department of Philosophy and Religious Studies—Kenyatta University, Kenia and Department of Philosophy and Religious Studies—University of Nairobi, Kenia
- Department for the Study of Religions—University of Ghana
- Department of Religion Studies—University of Pretoria, South Africa
- School of Religion, Philosophy and Classics—University of KwaZulu-Natal, South Africa
- Department of Religious Studies and Arabic—University of South Africa
- Department of Religion Studies—University of the Free State, South Africa
- Department for the Religion and Cultural Studies—University of Nigeria
- Religious Studies is presented as a course at several universities in Nigeria (e.g. Babcock University; University of Benin; University of Ibadan; University of Jos)
- Department of Philosophy and Religious Studies—Cameroon Christian University
- Department of Theology and Religious Studies—University of Botswana
- Department of Religion and Theology—University of Namibia
- Department of Philosophy, Religion and Ethics—University of Zimbabwe
- Department of Religious Studies—University of Zambia
- Courses in Religious Studies are presented at several universities in Malawi (e.g. University of Malawi, Chancellor College; Catholic University of Malawi; Malawi Adventist University; Mzuzu University; Malawi Assemblies of God University)
- Department of History, Philosophy and Religious Studies—The Open University of Tanzania and the School of Theology and Religious Studies—St John's University of Tanzania

---

"religion" and "religious" in the title of departments dealing with the field of study.

- Programmes on Religion and Religious Studies are presented at several universities in Uganda (e.g. Kyambogo University, Makerere University, Kampala University, Bugema University
- Programmes on Religion and Religious Studies are presented at several universities in Rwanda (e.g. University of Rwanda and Catholic University of Rwanda)
- Department of Religions—University of Benin
- Programmes in Religious Studies—University of Gambia

The diagnostic interpretation of the status of religion studies reveals that there is in fact an upsurge in interest in religion. This renewed interest can be ascribed to several reasons. The reasons for the growth in importance of studying religion is indicated by Smith[10] as the result of religion moving into the public sphere and the renewed interest in studying religion at a secular or public university. The report by Norris and Inglehart[11] emphasizes the prominence of religion in poor and destitute communities as would be the case in many communities in Africa. Religion is still prevalent in Africa as will be discussed below.

The prominence of academic study of religion in Africa can be ascribed to the intense impact of religion on society in Africa. It can also to a large extend be regarded as the remnant of the colonial heritage where the modernistic mind of knowing and labelling everything drove scholars to investigate and analyze all phenomena, including religion, in Africa. This endeavour took hold in the scientific study of religion now evident at universities established in Africa.

For Wiebe[12] it is important to note that religion studies has as a task to investigate religion as a social phenomenon, shedding the theological cloak that might be suspected to be worn by the researcher. The purpose of religion studies is to reach an academic and critical understanding of religious traditions without creating the perception of nurturing faith.

Studying religion at the University of Pretoria, South Africa,[13] is done from a non-confessional and unbiased position. Religion studies

10. Smith, "Religious Studies Whither," 407–8.

11. Norris and Inglehart, *Sacred and Secular*, 53.

12. Wiebe, "Religious Studies," 99.

13. As this is the academic home of the author of this contribution, it would only be fair not to generalize about all institutions presenting religion studies in Africa, but to refer to that which is known to the author.

at the University of Pretoria is, in line with the description by Wiebe,[14] not a faith-based study of religion as theology and religion education would attempt. There is no instruction in religion but only teaching about religion.[15] Without the confessionally bound position associated with seminaries, the scope of studying religion academically is broadened to include a wide variety of possible approaches and connections. It is in this regard that Wiebe's[16] comment that it is impossible to define religion studies as an academic discipline must be understood. Benson's[17] description that the connectedness of religion studies consists of "disciplines gathered around the complex phenomenon of religious belief and practice" proves to be helpful in understanding the interconnectedness of topics and themes surrounding religion studies as is evident from the diverse topics found in the contributions in this publication. This interconnectedness is also evident from the combination of disciplines (e.g., philosophy, culture, sociology, linguistics, and theology) in the different departments studying religion.

It would be irresponsible to assume that all scholars in the study of religion share the same understanding of what constitutes religion. A brief overview of possible understandings of the concept of religion is therefore necessary.

What Is Religion?

It would only be fair to start off by explaining what it is that is studied when we declare that we study religion and religions. Readers from different contexts might have different ideas as to what constitutes religion. We need to clarify what we mean with the concept of religion.

By tracing the origin of the word "religion" we are able to gain a clue as to the intended meaning of the word. The word comes from the Latin noun *religio*. The root of the noun might be traced to several possible verbs: *re-ligare*, "to connect," as was used by Augustine;[18] and *religere*,

14. Wiebe, "Religious Studies," 99.
15. Wiebe, "Religious Studies," 100.
16. Wiebe, "Religious Studies," 98.
17. Benson, "Religious Studies," 92.
18. Urban, "Religion der Urgeschichte," 88.

"to follow closely," as was used by Cicero.[19] Sundermeier[20] adds another possible root, namely *relegere*, meaning "to engage again," alluding to the interaction between humans and the supernatural. The noun "religion" then refers to the passive connection between humans and gods as well as the active participation by humans in worshipping gods.[21] Two constitutive elements are present. To have religion, there needs to be humans whose attention and focus is directed to something outside of themselves, to something impossible to define, but accepted to be supernatural.

Jenny Daggers indicates how the word "religion" was not originally filled with the same meaning attached to it today. Up until the early medieval period Christianity utilized the word "religion" as only referring to Christianity. All other forms of what is today regarded as religion were labelled as "sects" or "law."[22] During the late medieval period Christianity started using the word "religion" to refer to worship and commitment to monastic life.[23] Only Christianity would be able to lay claim to be religion or true faith. For long the differentiation between religions was between orthodoxy (=Christianity) and heresy (=all other religions).[24] During the fifteenth century Roger Bacon claimed Christianity was superior to other sects as it possessed the true revelation of the single true God.[25] During the fifteenth century the ideas of Cardinal Nicolas of Cusa brought about a change in the understanding of religion. For Cusa all humans worshipped the same God, thus all possessed religion. Since not all people subscribed to the belief in the Trinitarian God, they were considered heretics. There may be only one religion but it is expressed in multiple rites of worship.[26] As Cusa argued for a single religion, the implication was that many religions may exist.[27]

There are scholars who deny the right of existence of the concept of religion. There is no such thing as religion. Religion is, based on the

19. Urban, "Religion der Urgeschichte," 88.
20. Sundermeier, *Was ist Religion*, 27.
21. Urban, "Religion der Urgeschichte," 88.
22. Daggers, *Postcolonial Theology*, 8.
23. Daggers, *Postcolonial Theology*, 8.
24. Daggers, *Postcolonial Theology*, 15.
25. Daggers, *Postcolonial Theology*, 16.
26. Daggers, *Postcolonial Theology*, 17.
27. Daggers, *Postcolonial Theology*, 17.

argument presented by Daggers, a purely Western construct. Asad[28] points out that in premodern writing there is no evidence of a separation between sacred and profane. The practice of religion is just as active in the private as the public sphere.[29] Asad's[30] explanation is that scholars such as Emile Durkheim took the typical form of primitive religion and turned it into the concept of the sacred as a universal essence. The concept of the sacred originated from the research by anthropologists and was under the influence of comparative religion developed further and only later on taken over by theologians.[31] The concept of the secular was only later introduced after contact with non-Christian religions encountered in the non-European world.[32] "Secular" was then an epithet to indicate falsity and otherness in comparison to the one religion, namely Christianity.[33]

Religions differ and therefore it is difficult to establish one definition covering all forms of expression of religion. The Austrian-born philosopher Ludwig Wittgenstein[34] and later Ninian Smart[35] indicated that the interrelatedness of religions can best be explained in terms of family resemblances. Religions exhibit similar characteristics binding them into groups without identifying them with one another. In this sense it is simultaneously impossible to define religion but also necessary to attempt a definition nevertheless. Several definitions of religion emanated from research done in the past. John Ferguson[36] lists seventeen different definitions of religion. Cox[37] categorizes these seventeen definitions into five useful categories, namely theological, moral, philosophical, psychological, and sociological. Cox[38] indicates that it is more useful to categorize

28. Asad, *Formations of the Secular*, 30.

29. Asad, *Formations of the Secular*, 183.

30. Asad, *Formations of the Secular*, 30.

31. Asad, *Formations of the Secular*, 31.

32. Asad, *Formations of the Secular*, 32.

33. Asad, *Formations of the Secular*, 33.

34. Wittgenstein, *Philosophical Investigations*, 31–32. Wittgenstein uses the word "game" and indicates how the similarities between different games causes the different games to be categorized together under one name, namely "game." The similarities is based on what he refers to as "family resemblances."

35. Smart, *Concept and Empathy*, 46.

36. Ferguson, *Religions of the World*, 13–17.

37. Cox, *Introduction*, 3–7.

38. Cox, *Introduction*, 7.

the definitions and work with the perspectives on religion than to evaluate the usefulness of individual definitions.

In spite of identifying working definitions, it remains difficult to define religion.[39] For Smith the inadequate existing multitude of definitions is an indication that the term should be discarded as it has become unusable. For too long, Smith argues,[40] Western culture has prescribed the way in which religion should be perceived and defined, as well as the relations between religion and other disciplines. Western researchers have over centuries labeled, named, and explained religions, so to speak, domesticated the concept. The methods for studying religions are also due to historical Western scholarly processes. As Chidester[41] summarizes, religion is a modern invention, a Western construction, a colonial imposition or an imperial expansion.

Smith presents a solution as how to deal with the problem of transposing the (Western) concept of religion onto world religions. Smith's[42] suggestion is to discard the term "religion" altogether. His argument is that the term is misleading, confusing, and unnecessary. The term hampers the understanding of people's faith and traditions. This hampering is caused by our attempt to conceptualize the faith and traditions into what we refer to as "religion."

Smith[43] suggests that it is more appropriate to talk about "cumulative traditions" than to refer to them as "religion." Traditions have contexts and history. The concept of religion tends to call to mind a structured system of beliefs. There are more words available to label the phenomena that Western minds over time have so diligently labeled.[44] Smith suggests the terms "piety," "reverence," "faith," "devotion," and "God-fearing" as alternatives. Terms also worthy of inclusion are "spirituality," "religiosity," and "witchcraft." These terms do not necessarily call to mind an organized structured system, but do belong within the same domain. Chidester[45] suggests that related terms should include concepts such as superstition and magic, heresy and infidelity, secularism and irreligion. The point

39. Smith, *Meaning*, 17.
40. Smith, *Meaning*, 52.
41. Chidester, "Beyond Religious Studies," 75.
42. Smith, *Meaning*, 50.
43. Smith, *Meaning*, 53 (footnote 2)
44. Smith, *Meaning*, 52.
45. Chidester, "Beyond Religious Studies," 76.

Chidester argues is that the scope and interdisciplinary approach to the study of religion should be expanded.

The value of Smith's and Chidester's diagnosis is that it reveals the bias with which religion in Africa is academically studied. A Western-biased concept such as religion is studied at an institution of tertiary education, which has historically been determined by Western principles of education on the African continent. Africa can be many things to many people, but being exclusively Western is not one of them. In postcolonialism, it is necessary to reconsider the hermeneutics governing teaching and research.

The problem arises that should the concept of religion be completely discarded, the discipline of religion studies might lose focus as to what ought to be studied. The result might be that we end up studying everything as Chidester[46] points out. Religion studies is not anthropology or theology. Where anthropology focuses on studying human behavior in all its forms from a purely humanistic point of view, religion studies concentrates on the spiritual behavior of humans, without studying the transcendence to which human spiritual attention is directed. This is the area of interest to theology.

The study of religion should include the congealed traditions communities historically inherited from the past and apply to their own current needs. The separate belief systems and their relations should still fall within the scope of religion studies. The value of Smith's analysis is that he creates awareness that studying a religion is not complete without taking notice of the religiosity or cumulative tradition underlying the religious expressions. Studying religion should therefore still include the study of religions, but as indicated by Smith also include the study of religiosity underlying religious expressions. Chidester's suggestion of expanding the field as to include related terminology should also form part of the study of religion.

As to a working definition, the explanation of Edward Farley[47] as to what religion is proves to be useful for the sake of our discussion here:

> Religion is not an entity or a field of entities but an aspect of human experience which has specific historical and cultural expressions. Religion as religiousness is the individual human being's response to what it discerns to be the most comprehensive

46. Chidester, "Beyond Religious Studies," 79.

47. Farley, *Fragility of Knowledge*, 66.

> powers of its environment. Religion as historical tradition is the corporate and symbolic expression of that discernment rendered into forms of repetition, transmission, institution.

Farley emphasizes that religion takes on multiples cultural expressions as humans become aware of the transcendental. It is precisely these multiple cultural expressions that the study of religion is concerned with. Krüger, Lubbe, and Steyn[48] indicate that there are three general characteristics of all expressions of religion in Africa: the belief in a supreme being, the spiritual realm, and the sacred community. These characteristics become evident when a short explanation of religions in Africa is presented.

According to Credo Mutwa,[49] the African understanding of religion is based on an understanding of a division of reality into different spheres. Spirits reside in the spiritual realm and can be summoned to act in the visible world, the world of the living. The ultimate God—supreme being—resides in everything and everywhere and is impossible to comprehend or see.[50] God created souls when he created himself. According to African understanding, humans possess a soul as well as a self, referred to as the *ena*.[51] The *ena* is not immortal but over time grows into a human being and can exist long after the death of a body.[52] When the human body dies, the *ena* returns to the invisible world known as the "Land of Forever-Night," where it continues to exist until all human memory of the individual dissipates when the *ena* enters a state of non-being.[53] The task of the *ena* is to present human problems to the gods and request assistance for human relatives. It can be mistaken that the *enas* are worshipped in African societies, but in fact, according to Mutwa,[54] it is the *enas* that worship humans as the *enas* are dependent on humans for food in the form of animal sacrifices. As gifts in return the *enas* implore the gods to bestow blessings on humans in the form of wealth, protection, and good fortune.[55]

48. Krüger, et al., *Human Search*, 32–35.
49. Mutwa, *Indaba*, 560.
50. Mutwa, *Indaba*, 561–62.
51. Mutwa, *Indaba*, 568.
52. Mutwa, *Indaba*, 569.
53. Mutwa, *Indaba*, 570.
54. Mutwa, *Indaba*, 570.
55. Mutwa, *Indaba*, 570.

An African understanding of religion emphasizes the importance of a dual worldview with a holistic and causal understanding of interaction between the spiritual and visible realms. Religion is part of the social fiber to such an extent that religion is not something people do, but something people are. In the study of religion in Africa, the interaction of African traditional religions with other religions, especially Islam and Christianity, forms part of the field of study.

The Status of Religion Studies in Africa

An endeavor to investigate the status of the study of religion in Africa is as exciting as daunting. Any survey of the teaching and learning of religion studies in Africa risks being a study ad infinitum as the field (geographically as well as academically) is just too vast and fast changing. A lot has been published[56] on religion studies in Africa. It is best to categorize the huge amount of publications. Many publications approach religion studies from a particular religion's perspective (e.g., Christianity, Islam, Baha'i, African traditional religions). Many contributions focus on the relation between religions and violence, social matters (e.g., gender), health matters (e.g., HIV), or law. Some contributions address religion studies in a specific geographical region. The article by Clasquin[57] for example presents a valuable overview of religion studies in Southern Africa. Some write about religion studies from a specific perspective and context such as education (compare Smit and Chetty[58]).

What makes the current contribution unique is that it presents perspectives stemming from different academic institutions in Africa on the topics currently being researched from a religion studies perspective. The goal of this contribution is not to try and prescribe or suggest what a curriculum on religion studies in Africa must look like, but rather to establish the principles that would guide the process of creating a curriculum relevant for religion studies in Africa.

56. Smit and Kumar, *Study of Religion*; Omenyo and Anum, *Trajectories of Religion in Africa*; Blakely et al., *Religion in Africa*; Ejizu, *Readings on Religion*; Green et al., *Religion, Law and Security*; Asamoah-Gyadu et al., *Studies of Religion in Africa.*

57. Clasquin, "Religious Studies," 5–22.

58. Smith and Chetty, "Reflecting on a Decade," 134–56.

Africa is a large continent. Dick[59] states that one of the biggest problems in the process of Africanization is that there is "no pure and essential African identity." Africa has been influenced for so long by other cultural, religious, and political elements that it has become difficult to speak of that which is essentially African. To talk of something as typically African is misleading as there does not exist one uniform or homogenous entity constituting Africa. Africa is a continent filled with diverse cultures and various expressions of religion. Just as diverse as the geographic scenery of Africa are the languages and cultural, religious, and political structures on the African continent.

Africa has been labeled as being "notoriously religious"[60] as well as "incurably religious."[61] This emphasizes the importance that religion plays in social life in Africa. Mbiti[62] based his statement on his observation that "religion permeates all the departments of life so fully that it is not easy or possible always to isolate it." This statement by Mbiti already gives an indication of an African understanding of religion. There is no separation between religion and other spheres of existence. Religion has to do with everything. The implication is that an expanded definition of what constitutes religion is necessary. Religion no longer only entails beliefs and rituals, but the "stuff of religion"[63] includes so much more. This increases the difficulty of delineating religion from culture. As Mbiti[64] states: "a study of these religious systems is, therefore, ultimately a study of the peoples themselves in all the complexities of both traditional and modern life." To study religion in Africa would then imply studying the people of Africa, in all environments. Such an endeavor would border on the fringe of anthropology, bringing the matter of interdisciplinarity to the fore.

Africa has been the arena where several large communities of faith have interacted. According to research by the Pew-Templeton Global Religious Futures project,[65] Africa has had substantial populations of Islam, Christianity, and African traditional religions for quite some time.

59. Dick, "What is wrong with Africanization?," 382.

60. Mbiti, *African Religions*, 1.

61. Parrinder, *Religion in Africa*, 235.

62. Mbiti, *African Religions*, 1.

63. Here is referred to the statement by David Chidester "Material Culture."

64. Mbiti, *African Religions*, 1.

65. http://www.globalreligiousfutures.org/regions/sub-saharan-africa.

It is peculiar that in recent research[66] the secularity of African communities has also been emphasized, leading to the conclusion that Africa is not as religious as previously been claimed but that signs of secularization are also evident in Africa.[67]

What does this say about studies of religion on the African continent? If the assumption is that Africa has always been religious and we discover different conclusions, how does it impact on the study of religion?

In terms of the status of religion studies in Africa, Clasquin[68] already stated in 2005 that it is an exaggeration that it is all well with religion studies. The reason is that there are only a few academic institutions in Africa presenting religion studies as an academic discipline. This may be contested as the list presented earlier may indicate. The list, however, only presents a quantitative survey and is not the result of a qualitative investigation. The amount of institutions presenting studies on religion in Africa does, however, testify to the prominence and eagerness to know something about the role of religion in society.

It cannot be denied that there is a growing interest in studying religion in Africa. This statement is based on a synchronic observation and does not reflect a diachronic investigation as to how interest in studying religion has grown or declined over a period of time. Some perspectives as to what the study of religion in Africa may need to consist of is presented now. These are not prescriptive but merely assertions based on an interpretation of current developments in Africa.

What Are the Principles Guiding Us in Determining What Religion Studies in Africa Should Be Studying?

The study of religion is contextual (historical as well as geographical). Studying "the stuff of religion" should always make sense in a local context but should also align with international trends of studying religion. No department of religion or religious studies comes into existence out of the blue without a preceding history and a given context. The historic development and context will determine the purpose of the study of religion. Some important principles necessary to heed in establishing a curriculum for religion studies in Africa might include the following:

66. Compare Van der Toren et al., *Is Africa Incurably Religious?*
67. Van der Toren, "African Neo-Pentecostalism," 77.
68. Clasquin, "Religious Studies," 18.

Acknowledging a Post-Colonial Context

The Africa of the future is different than the Africa of the past. Africa is facing a future with a diminishing influence of colonialism on human interaction and thought. Compare Sugirtharajah's[69] distinction between "postcolonial" and "post-colonial." The hyphenated form refers to a historical period succeeding the period of colonialism. The unhyphenated form refers to a theory and approach by the colonized to the ruling knowledge systems introduced by the colonizers and an attempt at restoring the past while questioning neocolonizing tendencies. It is clear that "postcolonial" refers to a certain methodology of inquiring and responding. This approach has the purpose to investigate and critically analyse all structures of power, dominant systems of thought, and ideologies. The goal of postcolonialism is to give recognition to perspectives of marginalized people, cultures, and religious entities that once were regarded as being inferior.

Religion studies should conceptualize its academic role as the avenue for enabling the once-marginalized voices to take up their rightful place in expressing thoughts on religion in society. Scholars of religion should also participate in the social debate on identifying instances where communities are still being marginalized and silenced due to the heritage of colonial structures or the introduction of neocolonial influences. The postcolonial mindset becomes a new frame within which religion can be studied as a truly transformed discipline.

Interdisciplinary and Ecumenical Possibilities

Studying religion does not take place in a vacuum. The interconnectedness of religion to related fields has already been alluded to earlier and is to a certain extend already evident in the way in which religion or religious studies is presented at academic institutions. The interdisciplinary relations should, however, be expanded to indicate the extended spheres in society relevant to the study of religion. The way in which the study of religion engages with society can contribute to the understanding of the relevance and effect of religion on society. In this regard the connections with sociology, law, arts, ecology, and health sciences are already an indication of possibilities.

69. Sugirtharajah, "Charting the Aftermath," 8.

Religion studies also does not need to focus on the effect of one religion on society. Interreligious relations are a matter of burning importance to the study of religion. The way in which different religions can collaborate on addressing matters of social interest and concern is an indication of the positive role religions can have on society when working together.

Social Engagement

When and how religions engage with matters of social interest and concern illustrates the impact religions can have on the well-being of society. Religions ought to take the lead in addressing ecological concerns and protecting the environment. Working towards social cohesion and harmony is possible if religions focus on the impact of values and ethics directed towards how society is governed and expects members of society to conduct themselves.

Treating the other as one would expect to be treated is not only a golden rule of behavior, but also an expression of tolerance and positive reciprocity. Shared ethics will contribute to the eradication of corruption and contribute to social well-being. An emphasis on ethics will also ensure the protection of human rights, allaying homophobic and xenophobic fears.

Religions can play a role in assisting society to rebuild itself. Religion can do research on sustainable development and contribute to the retaining of human dignity while investigating possibilities of creating livelihood responsibly.

The Effect of Secularization

As has already been alluded to earlier, Africa has not been spared the effects of secularization. The different definitions explaining the secular can be captured in five categories identified by Stefan Paas. Paas[70] identifies five categories or secularization paradigms into which the understanding of the secular can be divided: differentiation, rationalization, privatization, pluralization, and individual loss of faith.

70. Paas, "Post-Christian," 6.

- Differentiation: According to this understanding, secularization is understood to refer to a process separating spheres. Religion is detached from the spheres of politics, education, economics, jurisprudence, and science. The spheres of religion and state are separated and end up as independent entities or as compartments.[71]
- Rationalization: Through a rational process of seeking meaning and explaining reality in scientific terms, belief in magic was destroyed, leaving the world disenchanted and demystified.[72] The previously unknown in the world is now explained rationally based on science, leaving the world devoid of mystery and supernatural beings.
- Privatization: This understanding of secularization implies that religion has lost its influence on society.[73] Religion has become an individual and private matter. Religion is now a subjective and selective activity for those who still want religion present in their lives. The social relevance of religion is on the decline and will eventually disappear.
- Pluralization: This theory on secularization holds that there are many ways to attain meaning. Meaning can be provided either by religion, atheism, or secular humanism. There are multiple options available that can contribute to religious meaning. Charles Taylor[74] indicates that a belief in God is no longer the only option, but has become an option alongside many other possibilities for providing meaning.
- Individual loss of faith: The most common way of explaining secularization is to argue that people are becoming less religious. This is evident from declining number of people attending religious events.[75]

Religion can easily be relegated to be viewed as a mere mundane social activity with spiritual meaning only for some. The study of religion at a secular or public university may become a study of human behavior. The separation of the spheres of state and religion results in an education system purified from religious influence. The study of religion in Africa will also need to study the phenomenon of decline in interest in religion.

71. Compare Dobbelaere, "Meaning and Scope," 606.

72. Compare the theory of Max Weber in Weber, *Sociology of Religion*, 125.

73. Paas, "Post-Christian," 8.

74. Taylor, *Secular Age*, 2–4.

75. Paas, "Post-Christian," 9.

Technology

Since the identification of the emergence of the Fourth Industrial Revolution by Klaus Schwab,[76] technology has become the driving force behind society. The way people relate and interact with reality has been relegated to technological mediums. Africa has not been spared the dehumanizing effect[77] of a technologically driven realty. The way in which technology affects human relations and even the way humans perceive the supernatural will be worth investigation through the study of religion. On the effect on the understanding of religion by the Fourth Industrial Revolution pursuing technology several publications have seen the light.[78]

These five principles discussed here will guide the study of religion in the immediate future. The principles do not prescribe a curriculum to the academic study of religion, but do indicate directions in which development of the study of religion may lead. The study of religion is not only the conveying of knowledge to students of religion, but the study of religion also asserts influence on society at large. The way in which the research on matters pertaining to religion is disseminated is important. In the process of teaching and learning about religion, it will benefit those involved to take note of the intricacies of intercultural communication.

Intercultural Communication

Intercultural communication implies a context of diversity and a need for equity. To communicate across cultures assumes that there are different cultures at play. A relation with that which does not belong to oneself—the stranger—is construed as a polarized relation between oneself and the other. The relation with the other as object outside of oneself has been problematized by the German sociologist Georg Simmel.[79] For Simmel[80] the "other" is a member of a system of group formation, but not strongly attached to it or accepted by the other members of the system. To communicate with the other implies a willingness to acknowledge the

76. Schwab, *Fourth Industrial Revolution*, 1.

77. Schwab, *Fourth Industrial Revolution*, 1.

78. Compare Van den Berg, *Engaging the Fourth*; Stahl, *God and the Chip*.

79. Simmel, *Sociology of Georg Simmel*.

80. Compare in this regard the research in Rogers, "Georg Simmel's Concept, 58–74; and Rogers and Steinfatt, "Intercultural Communication."

existence of the other. In the relation with the other a perceived hierarchical arrangement of relations might exist.

The problem with culture is that, as Liu, Volčič, and Gallois[81] state, "Culture defines a group of people, binds them to one another and gives them a sense of shared identity." While culture may be an identity marker, it has the function of emphasizing exclusivity. Culture has the ability to alienate and demarcate boundaries between people.

For a very long period in time colonial powers considered the existence of the other in Africa and Asia as inferior, subhuman, and not worthy to communicate with. This has changed with the end of colonialism[82] and the emergence of national independence and autonomy across Africa and Asia. The changed political order brought about a reconfiguration of social relations as well as a change in communication patterns amidst cultural diversity.

It is precisely the sociological research by Simmel on the relation with the stranger that Rogers[83] and Liu, Volčič and Gallois[84] indicate gave rise to the creation of the contemporary discipline of intercultural communication as a field of study. As a definition of intercultural communication, the explanation of John Sniden[85] proves to be helpful:

> Intercultural Communication involves the sharing of information across different cultures and social groups, including individuals with different religious, social, ethnic and educational backgrounds. It seeks to understand the differences in how people from a variety of cultures act, communicate, and perceive the world around them.

Coexistence in a multicultural environment is not only challenging but also exciting. It is necessary that meaning is conveyed across cultural boundaries in such a way that the message remains intact while the manner of communication conveys reciprocal respect. The everyday process of communication opens up avenues of discovering knowledge about oneself as well as about the other.

Multiculturality in Africa did not commence with globalization. Through colonialism many foreign cultures were indeed introduced to

81. Liu, et al., *Introducing Intercultural Communication*, xv.

82. Compare Zulu, "Language, intercultural communication," 305.

83. Rogers, *Georg Simmel's Concept*, 58.

84. Liu et. al., *Introducing Intercultural*, xv.

85. Sniden, "Importance of Intercultural."

Africa. But even prior to the colonial age, Africa consisted of different cultures, each with their own traditions and language. Africa does not present a homogeneous uniform outward expression. Africa has many faces. The challenge of intercultural communication is part of everyday existence in multicultural communities across Africa, but it is exacerbated in an education environment.

Challenges of Intercultural Communication in Education

Education represents a specific focus area for intercultural communication. Issues related to the field of education include language, epistemology, and identifying relevant content.

Language

Although many countries in Africa may have only one official language, the reality is that regions contain multiple local languages and dialects. Languages may be considered to belong to different levels of importance based on social stratification. Some lingual hegemony may exist in some cases. This creates a challenge as to the choice of a language of instruction in an education environment. The happy middle would assume a language that everyone understands and that, although it may not be the mother language, would be acceptable to all. Quite often the happy medium is a remnant of colonial influence, as would be the case with French in countries in central Africa, English in the southern parts of Africa, and Portuguese in southwestern and southeastern parts of Africa. The influence of Islam bringing Arabic as vernacular to Africa can also not be ignored, especially in eastern and northern Africa. These languages introduced to Africa were under colonial times considered to be the logical language of choice for instruction as mastering the language was a sign of civility and scholarship. Part of this heritage may remain in some areas in Africa. Not only the language of instruction but the duplication of an education system prevalent in Europe may also influence the way in which tertiary education is conducted in Africa.

The mode of instruction in a multicultural and multilingual education environment is important. To identify a lingua franca among multiple official languages may be essential for successful communication across cultures.[86] The use of English in a South African education environment serves as an example. English may for practical considerations be a good choice as mode of instruction, but English is perceived as a road to exclusivity as it is the language of the educated[87] and the language providing access to the economy.[88] It is true that English gives access to academic resources, as textbooks may be more available in English than in local languages. In this sense English does provide access to good education. The result, however, may be the degradation of local languages and possible demise of local cultures.[89] The educated will now possess a foreign language as tool to communicate their knowledge to communities they come from. This creates alienation between the educated and their cultural homes.

The corrective is to consider utilizing local languages as modes of instruction besides English. This is possible when, as Potgieter and Athonissen[90] suggest, an African renaissance fuels the need for African languages in education. This leads to investigating the plausibility of mother tongue education.[91] By using multiple languages as mode of instruction improved communication may be the result.

The choice for multiple or a single language as mode of instruction should be measured against the effectiveness of the pedagogical process. In many instances, as Antia[92] mentions, discussions on multilingualism are to align policies with national programs of transformation. Intercultural communication should be aware of the need for a balance between single or multilingualism. The educational needs of learners need to take priority in a decision.

Epistemological Diversity

In a post-colonial Africa few useful remnants of the colonial era remain. Of these the most noteworthy may be an education system. Besides being

86. Potgieter and Anthonissen, "Managing Multilingualism," 131.

87. Potgieter and Anthonissen, "Managing Multilingualism," 131.

88. Potgieter and Anthonissen, "Managing Multilingualism," 144.

89. Potgieter and Anthonissen, "Managing Multilingualism," 146.

90. Potgieter and Anthonissen, "Managing Multilingualism," 146.

91. Compare the results and considerations of African languages as mode of instruction in Potgieter and Anthonissen, "Managing Multilingualism," 148–51.

92. Antia, "Modelling Multilingualism," 158.

an effective system, the education structure in Africa unfortunately adopted the European epistemology that goes along with the infrastructure. The result is that not only the form but also the content of education is still much determined by European influence. The Western modes of interpretation and understanding and the way of conducting science remain part of the way of education in Africa. The rationality as well as humanity of Africans are subjected to the result of Western superiority over against a denigrated African-oriented epistemology.[93]

Epistemology[94] can best be described as the theory of knowledge, investigating the origin, nature, scope, and limits of human knowledge. It is concerned with qualifying beliefs as knowledge by investigating the truth of beliefs. The sources of knowledge are investigated to determine from whence we acquire knowledge: is it from reason, observation, memory of orally transmitted traditions,[95] or testimonies by the wise elders? This would be responses to the question: what do we know and how do we know what we know? It also includes the critical investigation into when something can be considered as justified and truthful, and therefore qualify as knowledge.

African epistemology has been degraded by the West as being irrational and unscientific.[96] The reason is that the knowledge Africans presented appeared to be determined too much by emotion, religious beliefs, intuitions, and myths and therefore unworthy for academic pursuit.[97] The result is that African ways of creating knowledge are frowned upon or, worse, ignored. A challenge for intercultural communication would be to consider ways in which African views on creating knowledge could be made part of the education system. Ndubuisi[98] suggests three ways in which an African epistemology can be considered, namely intuitive knowledge, religious knowledge, and mythological knowledge. Etta[99] identifies the categories of wholistic, intuition, perceptual, mystical, rational, ancestral, communal, ontological, individual, and God's

93. Compare Ndubuisi, "Appraisal of African Epistemology," 296.

94. Compare the definitions of epistemology in *Encyclopedia Britannica* and Wikipedia.

95. Compare Etta, "Reality of African Epistemology," 279–312.

96. Ndubuisi, "Appraisal of African Epistemology," 297.

97. Ndubuisi, "Appraisal of African Epistemology," 297.

98. Ndubuisi, "Appraisal of African Epistemology," 309–13.

99. Etta, "Reality of African Epistemology," 295–303.

knowledge. These represent sources from where knowledge can be generated in an African context.

This does not mean that knowledge is less rational or scientific. The place of origin of knowledge according to an African epistemology is less in the mind of the scientist than in the traditions and culture surrounding the scientist. As Ndubuisi[100] states, knowledge is not in the mind or intellect only, but in the whole being of existence—knowledge is felt, experienced, reasoned, thought, and intuited.

In Africa reality is not compartmentalized but holistically considered to be part of a whole. The invisible and spiritual world is distinct but not separate from the visible world.[101] Looking through religion as a lens, reality is interpreted and made sense of. The transcendental is used to make sense of the material and experienced world.[102] Spiritual beings and elements reveal knowledge of reality to humans; therefore religious knowledge forms part of the epistemic process.

Africans try and make sense of their existence via mythical consciousness.[103] The value of myths is that they convey knowledge far beyond the grasp of the human mind. Such knowledge would refer to explanations of the origin of everything, including the Supreme Being and evil, as well as the stages of life.[104] By acknowledging the validity of indigenous knowledge, the base of knowledge is broadened to include more than what Western-oriented science allows access to. Myths allow access to parts of reality to which Western science does not.[105] Knowledge of reality cannot be limited to what Western science provides access to.

Generating and conveying knowledge needs to be culturally sensitive of the sources of knowledge. Intercultural communication needs to heed epistemology.

Content

The African view of religion makes the Western definitions of religion difficult to apply to an African context. If religion is everything and

100. Etta "Reality of African Epistemology," 309.
101. Etta, "Reality of African Epistemology," 309.
102. Etta, "Reality of African Epistemology," 309.
103. Etta, "Reality of African Epistemology," 311.
104. Etta, "Reality of African Epistemology," 311.
105. Etta, "Reality of African Epistemology," 312.

everywhere, there cannot be a separation between spheres of existence as a Western interpretation of reality or worldview suggests. In generating and conveying knowledge as part of the education process in studying religion, an African context would demand an African epistemological understanding of the place and role of religion in society.

The sources of knowledge mentioned in the previous section would become the places to search for the content of what forms part of the curriculum of the study of religion. Studying religion in Africa cannot ignore the place of myths and rituals, nor the transmittance and role of oral traditions. The complexity of the matter can be illustrated with a metaphor. When the church father Tertullian asked the critical question "What does Jerusalem have to do with Athens?," he tried to indicate that Greek philosophy is not relevant to the understanding of Christianity. In the same vein we might ask the question: what does Rome, Tübingen, or Edinburgh have to do with Nairobi, Accra, or Pretoria? Now the reference is to how the traditional classical study of religion relate to an African context of studying religion. Does the structure as well as the content making up the content of European education institutions apply to a different cultural environment? The answer is dual: yes and no.

Of course, the foundation of the traditional studies of religions is important to understand the origin of content and methodology. But the foundation is merely the foundation. From there building on top of the foundation must be undertaken in a unique localized format. In this sense globalization and localization are balanced. If one of these two should be overemphasized, the building project will be at risk. Without a deep (historically) rooted foundation the project will be superficial and unstable. Without a building resembling a local style the project will be irrelevant and uninhabitable for those seeking shelter in the study of religion.

The study of religion in Africa can only have an impact if it is relevant to a local context and Africans can relate to it. For example, the relation between technology as part of the contemporary context of Africa creates a unique challenge as it requires new interpretation of how technology mediates the relations between a spiritual and material world.

In the study of religion, a curriculum informed by epistemological considerations is essential to the understanding of beliefs and practices associated with religions.

An additional problem is the question as to who may teach. This sounds like a silly question as the education system determines that an academically qualified person is permitted to present instruction at a tertiary institution of education. But the question points towards two matters: on the one hand, should only Africans be allowed to teach on religions in Africa, and secondly, should the teacher be a scholar or a religious practitioner? At the root of both questions lay the concern as to whether teachers should present insider versus outsider perspectives. In the academic process of teaching and learning the learning activity is guided by pedagogical principles. By adhering to the pedagogical principles, the question as to who may teach becomes irrelevant. The process will teach. The one doing the teaching follows the pedagogy and through the process knowledge is conveyed.

Intercultural communication demands diversity and inclusivity.[106] These two concepts, however, do not have in mind to destroy any culture and have all cultures compromised to fall in with one consensus culture. Multiculturalism carries the threat of conflict and adversity. By acknowledging diversity, the first steps towards equality is given. By including perspectives from different cultures, the study of religion is presented as a non-threatening academic endeavor during which there is learning about and from one another.

Conclusion

A department of religion or religious studies at a university in Africa encounters several challenges. The field of knowledge to be addressed needs to be defined. What is considered as religion is contextually determined. The method of study and interpretation (epistemology) has to be clarified.

Religion is not foreign to Africa, although the concept is not endemic to Africa. It is only relatively recently that Africans can acknowledge that that which they and their ancestors have been practicing for so many centuries is what is called "religion" by people from other continents. To engage with the academic study of religion in Africa poses several challenges. The education system in Africa may still be filled with remnants of colonial elements, including the formal structure of teaching (e.g., sitting in a lecture hall in rows listening to a monologue by an "expert," writing tests assessing the ability to recall facts). The content may reflect the thoughts and ideas on religion of people not indigenous to the African continent. A balance between the traditional classical roots of the

106. Compare Liu et al., *Introducing Intercultural*, 200.

study and the local contextualized content is necessary in order to make the study viable and relevant.

Studying religion in Africa should be contextual and locally relevant just as much as it should be internationally aligned with research. The African scholar should have agency in determining who lectures what content in which manner in an academic environment. Only when religion is presented as a relatable concept can Africans contribute to the study of religion, and make no mistake, Africa has indeed something to contribute to the understanding of religion.

Bibliography

Antia, Bassey E. "Modelling Multilingualism: Modelling Rationales for Language Policies." In *Multilingualism and Intercultural Communication: A South African Perspective*, edited by Russell Kaschula et al., 157–80. Johannesburg: Wits University Press, 2017.

Asad, Talal. *Formations of the Secular: Christianity, Islam and Modernity.* Stanford: Stanford University Press, 2003.

Asamoah-Gyadu, J. Kwabena, Mary A. Nyangweso, and Hassan Juna Ndzovu, eds. "Studies of Religion in Africa". Supplements to the *Journal of Religion in Africa.* Leiden: Brill, 2022.

Benson, Thomas L. "Religious Studies as an Academic Discipline." In *Encyclopaedia of Religion*, 14:88–92. Eliade, Mircea. New York: MacMillan, 1987.

Beyers, Jaco. "The Quest for the Understanding of Religious Studies: Seeing Dragons." *Verbum et Ecclesia* 37/1 (2016) http://dx.doi. org/10.4102/ve.v37i1.1607.

Blakely, Thomas D., et al. *Religion in Africa: Experience & Expression*. Monograph Series of the David M. Kennedy Center for International Studies at Brigham Young University 4. London: J. Currey, 1994.

Chidester, David. "Material Culture." In *Vocabulary for the Study of Religion*, edited by Robert A. Segal and Kocku von Stuckrad. Leiden: Brill Online, 2016.

Chidester, David. "Beyond Religious Studies? The Future of the Study of Religion in a Multidisciplinary Perspective." *Journal for Theology and the Study of Religion* 71/1 (2017) 74–85.

Clasquin, Michel. "Religious Studies in South(ern) Africa—An Overview." *Journal for the Study of Religion* 18/2 (2005) 5–22.

Cox, James L. *An Introduction to the Phenomenology of Religion*. New York: Continuum, 2010.

Daggers, Jenny. *Postcolonial Theology of Religions: Particularity and Pluralism in World Christianity*. London: Routledge, 2013.

Dick, Archie L. "What Is Wrong with Africanization?" *Information Development* 30 (2014) 382–83.

Dobbelaere, Karel. "The Meaning and Scope of Secularization." In *The Oxford Handbook of the Sociology of Religion*, 599–615. Oxford: Oxford University Press, 2011.

Ejizu, Chris J. *Readings on Religion and Culture in Africa.* Port Harcourt, Nigeria: M and J Grand Orbit Communications, 2016. ISBN: 9789785420869.

Etta, Emmanuel E. "The Reality of African Epistemology." *International Journal of Innovative Science, Engineering and Technology* 6/10, 279–305.

Farley, Edward. *The Fragility of Knowledge: Theological Education in the Church & the University*. Philadelphia: Fortress, 1988.

Ferguson, John. *Religions of the World: A Study for Everyman*. Cambridge: Lutterworth Educational, 1978.

Green, M. Christian, T. Jeremy Gunn, and Mark Hill, eds. *Religion, Law and Security in Africa*. Papers from the annual conference of the African Consortium for Law and Religion Studies held in Rabat, Morocco, in 2017. Stellenbosch, South Africa: Conference-RAP, 2018.

Krüger, Jakobus S., Gerrie J. A. Lubbe, and H. Chrissie Steyn. *The Human Search for Meaning: A Multireligion Introduction to the Religions of Humankind*. 2nd ed. Pretoria: Van Schaik, 2009.

Liu, Shuang, Zala Volčič, and Cindy Gallois. *Introducing Intercultural Communication: Global Cultures and Contexts*. Los Angeles: Sage, 2015.

Mutwa, Credo. *Indaba, My Children: African Tribal zhistory, Legends, Customs and Religious Beliefs*. Edinburgh: Payback, 1998.

Ndubuisi, Christian A. "Appraisal of African Epistemology in the Global System." *Alteration* 20/1 (2013) 295–320.

Norris, Pippa, and Ronald Inglehart. *Sacred and Secular: Religion and Politics Worldwide*. Cambridge: Cambridge University Press, 2004.

Omenyo, Cephas Narh, and Eric B. Anum, eds. *Trajectories of Religion in Africa: Essays in Honour of John S. Pobee*. Studies in World Christianity and Interreligious Relations 48. Amsterdam: Rodopi, 2014.

Paas, Stefan. "Post-Christian, Post-Christendom, and Post-Modern Europe: Towards the Interaction of Missiology and the Social Sciences." *Mission Studies* 28 (2011) 7–9.

Potgieter, Anneke, and Chirstine Anthonissen. "Managing Multilingualism in Education: Policies and Practices." In *Multilingualism and Intercultural Communication: A South African Perspective*, edited by Russell Kaschula et al., 131–56. Johannesburg: Wits University Press, 2017.

Rogers, Everett M. "Georg Simmel's Concept of the Stranger and Intercultural Communication Research." *Communication Theory* 9/1 (1999) 58–74.

Rogers, Everett M., and T. M. Steinfatt. *Intercultural Communication*. Prospect Heights, IL: Waveland, 1999.

Schwab, Karl. *The Fourth Industrial Revolution*. Geneva: World Economic Forum, 2016.

Simmel, Georg. *The Sociology of Georg Simmel*. Translated by Kurt H. Wolff. New York: Free Press, 1950.

Smart, Ninian. *Concept and Empathy: Essays in the Study of Religions*. London: MacMillan, 1986.

Smit, Johannes, and Pratap Kumar. *Study of Religion in Southern Africa: Essays in Honour of G.C. Oosthuizen*. Leiden: Brill, 2005.

Smith, Jonathan Zittell. "Religion and 'Religious Studies': No Difference at All." *Soundings: An Interdisciplinary Journal* 71/2–3 (1988) 231–44.

———. "Religious Studies: Whither (Wither) and Why?" *Method & Theory in the Study of Religion* 7/4 (1995) 407–14.

Smith, Wilfred Cantwell. *The Meaning and End of Religion*. Minneapolis: Fortress, 1991.

Sniden, John. "The Importance of Intercultural Communication Training to the Global Workforce." ATD blog, 2021. https://www.td.org/insights/the-importance-of-intercultural-communication-training-to-the-global-workforce.

Stahl, William A. *God and the Chip: Religion and the Culture of Technology*. ProQuest EBook Central, 1999.

Sugirtharajah, Rasiah S. "Charting the Aftermath: A Review of Postcolonial Criticism." In *The Postcolonial Biblical Reader*, edited by Rasiah S Sugirtharajah, 7–32. Cornwall: Blackwell, 2006.

Sundermeier, Theo. *Was ist Religion: Religionswissenschaft im theologischen Kontext*. Gütersloh: Gütersloher, 1999.

Taylor, Charles. *A Secular Age*. Cambridge: Harvard University Press, 2007.

Urban, Otto H., "Religion der Urgeschichte." In *Handbuch Religionswissenschaft: Religionen und ihre zentralen Themen*, edited by Johann Figl, 88–103. Innsbruck: Tyrolia, 2003.

Van den Berg, Jan-Albert, ed. *Engaging the Fourth Industrial Revolution: Perspectives from Theology, Philosophy and Education*. Bloemfontein: Sun, 2020.

Van der Toren, Benno. "African Neo-Pentecostalism in the Face of Secularization: Problems and Possibilities." In *Is Africa Incurably Religious?*, edited by Benno Van der Toren et al., 76–84. Regnum, 2020.

Van der Toren, Benno, Joseph B. Bangura, and Richard E. Seed, eds. *Is Africa Incurably Religious?* Regnum, 2020.

Wittgenstein, Ludwig. *Philosophical Investigations*. Translated by G. E. M. Anscombe. Oxford: Basil Blackwell, 1953.

Wiebe, Donald. "Religious Studies." In *The Routledge Companion to the Study of Religion*, edited by John R. Hinnells, 98–124. London: Routledge, 2005.

Weber, Max. *The Sociology of Religion*. Translated by Ephraim Fischoff. London: Methuen, 1966.

Zulu, Nogwaja S. "Language, Intercultural Communication and Literature." In *Multilingualism and Intercultural Communication: A South African Perspective*, edited by Russell Kaschula et al., 301–12. Johannesburg: Wits University Press, 2018.

Chapter 2

Changes, Challenges, and Choices

Teaching Religion at the University of KwaZulu-Natal

Beverly Vencatsamy

Introduction

Religious studies is a relatively recent academic discipline in South Africa. Even the University of Cape Town's Department of Religious Studies, which is perhaps the oldest in South Africa, has only existed since 1967.[1] Therefore, it is not surprising that in 1980 Harold Turner, known as the founder of religious studies, observed that "Religious Studies is still at a rudimentary stage of its development."[2] When religious studies scholar Michel Clasquin offered his overview of the discipline in 2005, he claimed that this view was no longer the case.[3] His analysis highlighted two factors that contributed to developments in religious studies: one which he described as positive—the policy in South African schools that expanded the space for religious studies education—and one the effects of which he believed remained to be seen—the mergers of various

1. Clasquin, in his "Religious Studies," 11, puts in a disclaimer that the former University of Westville disputed this idea.

2. Clasquin, "Religious Studies," 11.

3. Clasquin, "Religious Studies," 8.

South African universities.[4] These changes arose when universities across the country began questioning the financial viability of the seemingly more minor disciplines within the humanities framework. In addressing the changing South African landscape, religious studies disciplines have had to reposition their teaching strategies to align themselves with an interdisciplinary space within the humanities. To some extent, this repositioning of religious studies has contributed to its continued existence as an academic discipline.

It must be stated at the outset that not much research has been conducted on religious studies in South Africa, including the curriculum design or pedagogy within South Africa. Using my experience as a lecturer in religious studies as a case study, I will attempt to shed some light on the lesser-known effects of the mergers, at least as they relate to the universities that combined to form the University of KwaZulu-Natal (UKZN), and consider other challenges such as the "crisis" in humanities,[5] the context of South Africa, and the COVID-19 pandemic. This chapter considers some of the trajectories of religious studies at UKZN as a discipline and questions whether interdisciplinary collaborations may allow religious studies to re-envision itself in the present in order to secure its future.

Religious Education in South African Schools

In 1994, the African National Congress (ANC) won South Africa's first democratic election, bringing an end to apartheid and the era of white minority rule. The country's new constitution declared that all children had the right to basic education. As South Africa began reconfiguring the curriculum and the entire education system post-1994, religious education was introduced in schools in 2001 to educate students on religion and religious diversity.

The Revised National Curriculum Statement published by the Department of Education in 2002 states:

> religion education contributes to the wider framework of education by developing in every learner the knowledge, values, attitudes, and skills necessary for diverse religions to co-exist in a multi-religious society. Individuals will realize that they are part

4. Clasquin, "Religious Studies," 5.

5. Nussbaum, *Not for Profit.*

> of the broader community and will learn to see their own identities in harmony with others.[6]

Within this framework, South Africa's new education policy for teaching and learning religion became inclusive,[7] allowing students to acknowledge their existence in the broader South African community and accept their identities in accordance with others. To deviate from the enforced Christian indoctrination of the apartheid era, the policy on religion education proposed teaching and learning outcomes centered on religious diversity that promoted an empathetic understanding of religion and allowed students to critically reflect on religious identity and difference.[8] While the promulgation of South Africa's policy on religious education was delayed until 2003,[9] the National Policy on Religion in Education later excluded confessional and sectarian religion from public schools. However, the policy made provision for the teaching of religious studies as an academic subject, to be done fairly and equitably.[10]

As such, many students are still skeptical about job opportunities a degree in religious studies may afford them. Clasquin's hope that the introduction of religious studies education in schools would positively affect student enrollment for religious studies degrees at university level has unfortunately failed to reach the desired outcome, as the subject at school level is subsumed as a chapter in the Life Orientation curriculum and does not receive much attention in the crowded curriculum, certainly not enough to be considered a "teaching subject" on the same level as history, geography, or one of the languages.

The Humanities in Higher Education Institutions

As far back as 1964, with the publication of Plumb's *The Crisis in the Humanities*, debates have been ongoing regarding the causes of and solutions to the supposed decline of the humanities at higher education institutions (HEIs). Plumb argues that the humanities have become too specialized, the curriculum has become fragmented and incoherent, and

6. Department of Education, "National Curriculum."
7. Chidester, "Religion Education," 264.
8. Chidester, "Religion Education," 264.
9. Van der Walt, "Religion in education."
10. Van der Walt, "Religion in Education."

the perception that has persisted is that the humanities have become increasingly irrelevant in a world dominated by modern science.[11]

Declining enrolment numbers in undergraduate degrees have also contributed to this crisis, lending itself to the global call for concern for the "dying humanities." This has led to several interventions modeled on the neoliberal approach that favors economic growth, such as the corporatization of HEIs. In the early 2000s, this led to what is known as the "mergers phase" of universities and other tertiary institutions in South Africa. This decision, mandated by the Department of Education, was taken in order to reduce the number of institutions established by the apartheid regime and to redistribute resources to traditionally underresourced institutions. To this end, historically black universities merged with historically white universities to create new institutions, one of which was the University of KwaZulu-Natal, and the total number of higher education institutions in South Africa decreased from thirty-six to twenty-one.

Matters did not magically improve. In 2011 the Academy of Science of South Africa (ASSAf) released its *Consensus on the State of the Humanities in South Africa*. Presenting a dismal view, it identified three key findings:

1. There is a crisis in the humanities reflected in declining student enrollments, falling graduation rates, and decreasing government funding within institutions of higher learning.
2. The evolution and administration of government policy in the post-apartheid period have systematically benefited science, technology, engineering, and mathematics (the STEM disciplines) to the exclusion and detriment of the humanities disciplines in the country.
3. The humanities within institutions of higher learning are in a state of intellectual stagnation and, singular innovations notwithstanding, they have remained in this moribund condition for more than fifteen years.[12]

One of the critical recommendations of the ASSAf study was to advance the idea of a broad-based humanities curriculum, ideally within an interdisciplinary program for undergraduates, thereby exposing all university students to some study of the humanities. The report clearly

11. Arndt, "Two Cultures."

12. ASSAf, *Consensus*, 15.

articulated the strengths of the humanities and social sciences in South Africa, stating that critical thought and asking fundamental questions to gain insights into various challenges affecting humanity lies at the heart of these.

Recognizing this, the South African Department of Basic and Higher Education adopted the approach identified by Ball,[13] who called for education to be geared towards creating "flexible generalists"—by equipping people with the necessary knowledge, skills, and values, enabling them to adjust willingly to numerous career changes and contribute to life through their personal development and the world. This shift in thinking is from education for employment to education for employability, from developing the ability to do a specific job to adapt acquired skills to new working environments.

South Africa's education systems have developed key learning areas committed to lifelong learning in response to changing global trends and as a survival mechanism amidst the alarming unemployment rate in the country. Guidelines set out by the South African Qualifications Authority (SAQA) state that when learners are aware that there are clear learning pathways that may provide access to and progression within education, training, and career paths, they tend to be more inclined to improve their skills and knowledge base to improve their employment opportunities. This ensures improved success in the global community.

The South African education system comprises different National Qualifications Framework (NQF) levels. The NQF is a formal system of principles and guidelines by which records of learners' achievements are registered to enable the national recognition of acquired skills and knowledge. This integrated system encourages lifelong learning. Adopted by SAQA in 2008, it recognizes that the educational system of any country is inextricably linked to the labor market. In clearly and publicly outlaying the NQF levels, job seekers can now attain jobs closely related to their course of study. This also enables potential employees to understand the minimum educational requirements necessary to be employed in various positions.

Compounding the (perceived) crisis in the humanities was—and still is—the significant unemployment rate in South Africa, even among those with university degrees. According to the *Quarterly Labour Force Survey* (*QLFS*) of the first quarter of 2021, the official unemployment rate

13. Ball, "Life Long Learning."

was 32.6 percent. Among those aged between fifteen and twenty-four years, the unemployment rate stands at over 63 percent. Given the graduate unemployment rate of 40.3 percent for those aged between fifteen and twenty-four and 15.5 percent among those aged between twenty-five and thirty-four years, it is unsurprising when many first-time entrants to university (including parents and guardians) ask "What job can you get with this degree?" before they ask what the degree is about.

Religious Studies at UKZN: A Merger

UKZN was officially established on the 1st of January 2004 as a result of the merger between the University of Natal and the University of Durban-Westville. The former, founded in 1910, was granted its independent university status in 1949 due to its rapid growth in numbers and opportunities for research. The latter was established for the Indian community in the 1960s, and later became a crucial site in the anti-apartheid struggle. With the formation of UKZN, a new School of Religion and Theology was formed out of the School of Theology from the University of Natal and the School of Religion and Culture from the University of Durban-Westville. Under this new banner, theology was to be offered at the Pietermaritzburg campus, and religious studies would move from the Westville campus to Howard College (Durban campus). In 2012, in response to ASSAF recommendations and in line with neoliberal agendas, UKZN underwent a significant reorganization—with the introduction of the suggested "college model." This saw the introduction of four colleges in place of multiple faculties—Humanities; Agriculture, Engineering, and Science; Health Sciences; and Law and Management Studies. Each college comprises several schools made up of disciplines. Religious studies now falls under the School of Religion, Philosophy and Classics, which accommodates these three disciplines plus that of theology and ethics. Religious studies have now been contextually influenced, and new modules and courses have been designed to address societal changes. Motivated by two critical elements in religion, i.e., lived religion and experiential learning, an interdisciplinary approach to the study of religion locates itself in issues students can easily recognize. This is a distinctive trait currently as universities streamline their productivity outputs to become more competitive to survive the global higher education environment.[14]

UKZN: A Case Study

In foregrounding the University of KwaZulu-Natal as a case study, this approach is particularly useful when there is a need to obtain an in-depth analysis of an issue or phenomenon in its natural context. The aim is to provide insight into how the religious studies curriculum at UKZN has been restructured to attract students and assert its value within the echelons of higher education.

The Bachelor of Arts Major in Religion

The current major in religion has four compulsory modules out of eight, and electives as corequisites at the same level. The compulsory modules and electives at level 1 serve as prerequisites for level 2, and the compulsory module and elective at level 2 are prerequisites for entry into level 3. This structure aligns itself to the basic format of the Bachelor of Arts (BA) major at UKZN.

In an attempt to grow the religious studies discipline at the University of KwaZulu-Natal and acknowledge that a degree in religious studies is not the first choice for many students, collaborative discussions were held with various disciplines and faculties across UKZN, permitting students to take religion modules as electives or service modules. From a religious studies perspective, modules and activities therein were developed as an interdisciplinary learning tool, enabling students to consciously articulate disciplinary, career, and existential expectations across the disciplines, aligning themselves with South Africa's ongoing social transformation. The development of the religion curriculum within the new context also aided in understanding some of the discipline's challenges—the least of which was the need to adapt courses to be information-laden instead of deep learning, which recognizes the complexity of religion and understanding the role of religion in society.[15]

As such, the Bachelor of Arts major in religion is currently structured as follows:

14. Troiani and Dutson, "Neoliberal University."
15. Baker and Dinham, "New Interdisciplinary Spaces."

Semester 1	**Semester 2**
Level 1	
RELG101: Introduction to Religion (16C) **Aim**: To introduce students to the academic study of religion by exploring the history of religious traditions and examining the beliefs and traditions of these religions.	**RELG106: Religion and Conflict (16C)*** **Aim**: To understand how religion as a resource can be used in addressing conflict both socially and politically, nationally and internationally.
Level 2	
RELG203: Sociology of Religion (16C) **Aim**: To provide students with social scientific competencies to reflect on religion with respect to popular culture, media, gender, sexuality, as well as religious preferences and practices more generally.	**RELG217: Religion and the Media (16C)*** **Aim**: To understand the role of religion in media and how media uses religion to influence the perceptions of people.
Level 3	
RELG308: Research Methodology in Religion and Culture (16C) **Aim:** This module aims to bring together a broad understanding of qualitative and quantitative methods of research taken from the social sciences and applied to the study of religion and culture.	**RELG309: Method and Theory in Religion and Culture Studies (16C)** **Aim**: The module introduces students to some critical methodological and theoretical issues in the study of religion.
RELG306: Colonialism, Post-Colonialism and Religion (16C)* **Aim**: To enable students to gain insight into the historical conditions for the development of colonialism, colonization, its strategies and its impact on indigenous religions and culture.	**RELG311: Religion and Human Rights (16C)*** **Aim**: To understand how religion is used to foster human rights advocacy and as a contributing factor in denying human rights in areas of conflict
Core Modules * **Electives**	

Table 1. Structure of the Bachelor of Arts major in religion[16]

16. University of KwaZulu-Natal, College of Humanities, Handbook, 2021.

Elective modules may change from year to year depending on staff availability and to allow for a general rotation of modules. While the discipline offers a variety of electives that students may register for, the rotation helps to keep these modules active. This is our offering for 2022, narrowed down to accommodate online teaching amid the pandemic. All modules are weighted at sixteen credit points.

While every attempt is made to attract students as religion majors (Figure 1), many students are still sceptical about the job opportunities a degree in religious studies may afford them. The Religion Department has seen a fluctuation in the number of students pursuing undergraduate degrees in religious studies over the past decade. However, while the modules remain widely popular among undergraduates, the fluctuation and drastic decline in 2020 and 2021 could be related to the economic crises caused by the pandemic. Students prefer to enroll in degree programs that will allow more employment opportunities. The module and student data in Figure 1 below were extracted from statistics generated by the Institutional Intelligence Department at UKZN.

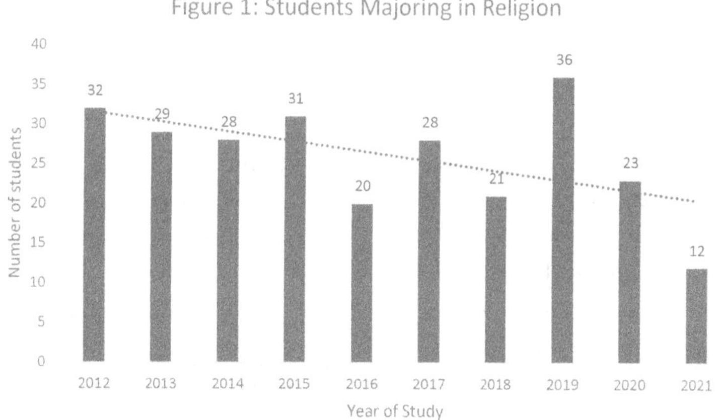

Figure 1: Students majoring in religion[17]

Although the discipline generally attracts a large number of students in part because of the exploration of a wide variety of themes, the situation is somewhat different when considering the number of students electing to take the core modules (see Figure 2):

17. Data supplied by Institutional Intelligence at UKZN, 2022.

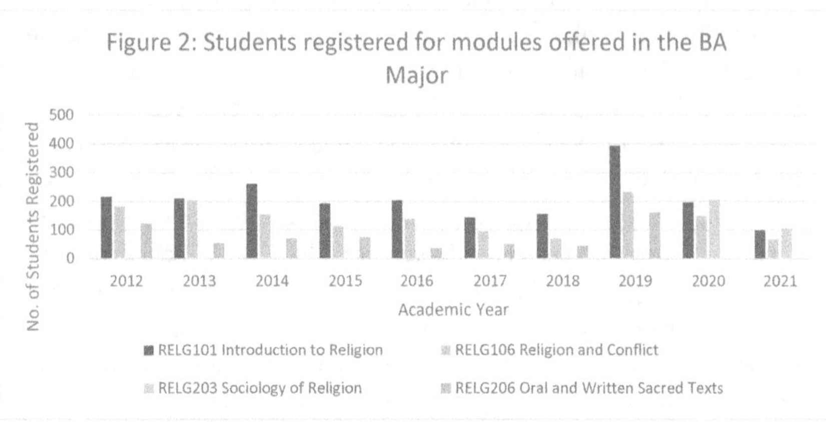

Figure 2: Students registered for modules offered in the BA major[18]

This graph depicts the number of students who opt to take the core modules as electives but do not advance further into the major program. As a comparison, the first-year elective RELG 106: Religion and Conflict is included in the graph to show that while at the first-year level, the discipline attracts a fair number of students in both RELG 101, which is offered in semester 1, and RELG 106, offered in semester 2 in each year. However, these numbers do not necessarily filter towards the second-year or the third-year levels.

The third-year modules are designed to introduce students majoring in religion to the world of research. Hence, two research methodology modules are offered that are not popular as electives and two comparative religion modules that may serve as electives. It is important to note that while the credits allocated to electives are necessary for the completion of any degree program, many students opt to take these additional modules in years 1 and 2 and focus on their majors in their third/degree year. Again, this could equate to students who are structuring their curriculum to align with specific career paths.

The Students

Acknowledging that a degree in religious studies is not the first choice for many students, but recognizing the need to grow the discipline

18. Data supplied by Institutional Intelligence at UKZN, 2022.

nevertheless, it is essential to delve deeper into the student profile at UKZN and their needs.

Because most of these students will have been exposed to religious studies in the subject of Life Orientation at secondary level, it is assumed that students enter the religion lecture halls with a basic knowledge of religion other than the one they themselves practice. However, for many it is their first engagement with the academic study of religion.

The religious studies discipline at UKZN caters for a diverse student population. While 80 percent of South Africa's population identify themselves as members of a Christian denomination, the location of UKZN is a fusion of different cultures and religious beliefs. The classes include students from various religious traditions such as Christianity, Islam, and Hinduism—noting here that Durban has one of the largest Hindu diasporas in the world. The majority of students, however, come from the African traditional religious groups—it is vital to be cognizant that while students here may fall wholly under the African traditional umbrella, others form part of the association with the African Independent Churches, which is an amalgamation of Christianity and African traditional religion. Given the diversity of the student population at UKZN and curriculum orientations, the approach to teaching religious studies is motivated by two critical elements: lived religion and experiential learning. From a sociological perspective, lived experience may be understood as religion expressed and experienced in the lives of individuals. It emanates from the specific rather than the general and focuses on what happens to religion within specific contexts. Religious studies modules in this framework begin with a broader understanding of core religious beliefs and practices, inclusive of brief historical analyses, before contextualizing the same principles within the South African context. To make religious studies relevant to the students, they are introduced to the historical aspects of how adventitious world religions entered South Africa and how some of the rituals and practices have been adapted to their new context. However, this may not necessarily apply to a religion like African traditional religion, which finds its origins in Africa, thus the adaptation of this religion and its links with Christianity and Islam becomes a central theme for inquiry. In terms of experiential learning (pre-COVID), students were encouraged to apply certain theoretical principles to a religious event not affiliated with their own they had attended, as part of an assessment in the introductory module. In other instances, this learning is usually effected through group work in tutorial settings and open-ended discussions within the formal lecture setting.

When delving deeper into the theoretical framework of any religion module, students are able to realign their thinking with the more academic study of religion. This offers them the opportunity to recognize the various ways in which religion can be defined and the emotional, social, and functional features that contribute to this new understanding, allowing them to make meaning of their personal beliefs and the world around them.

This is evident in the responses from a simple exercise in the introductory module at first year, where students were asked to "write a short paragraph in which you formulate your own understanding of the concept religion." In the absence of in-person tutorials, the activity was set up via the online learning platform Learn2022, which is similar to Moodle. The students responded via a chat session, and while students did not engage with each other on this platform, a discussion was held during the formal lecture.

The following student responses via the chat on Learn2022 are included below:

> Student 1: Simply religion is a system of beliefs that a group of people live by and follow. It provides structure and moral guidance to one's life. Religion comprises practices, rituals, events, and something sacred that unifies its followers/adherents. In addition to unification, it can be used to justify class, gender, and colonial forms of discrimination. Often religion is used as a comfort for people, providing a constant in their life as well as to help explain questions about the unknown that we may have, for example, origin, death, afterlife. Religion provides security and hope in people's lives.
>
> Student 2: I understand religion as a sort of comfort. When you're going through a lot, your first instinct is to pray and after that you feel weight lifted because there's a superior being who heard you and you believe will help you get through any situation. I also see religion as a system that keeps people in line and behave because now with certain beliefs that religion has, the do's and don'ts make people refrain from doing certain things to not sin or go against the "laws" of one's belief system.
>
> Student 3: My understanding the concept of religion is one that has been an integral part of human socialization since almost the beginning of time and it refers to a system of beliefs and practices that a group of people share in reverence of

> a Divine entity, which could be a God, Goddess or a number of deities. But the role that it plays in one's life is so significant that it not only prescribes its adherents with an identity but also standards and guidelines to which they need to uphold to fulfil that identity and help secure them peace in the afterlife. That "peace" being either heaven, paradise or nirvana.

These responses are interesting as the students only had one formal lecture on "What Is Religion?" and were already able to identify and relate to the emotional, social, and functional aspects of religion in their definitions.

Curriculum Models

Given the diversity of the student population at UKZN and curriculum orientations, it begs the question of how students assign meaning to their own experiences. Furthermore, how do we as educators reflect on the curriculum and its delivery to augment the student's construction of this meaning? Schubert[19] identifies four curriculum traditions, posited within a religious studies context.

1. *Intellectual traditionalists* are grounded in a European worldview that values classical texts to forge ideas and disciplinary knowledge. This perspective requires an in-depth knowledge of the subject, which moves beyond the details of the text to the intuitive and imaginative to make it come alive in the classroom. While classical texts are essential in the study of religion, they need to be contextualized to meet the current needs of the students and society. This allows one to generate specific themes/ideas within religion for example religion and conflict. The aim is to create space for students to ask questions and grapple with ideas they cannot question within religious institutions.
2. S*ocial behaviorists* emphasize empirical evidence and rely on the systematic and strategic planning of the curriculum. Identifying different behaviors to assist students to be successful often involves reference to successful individuals and their attributes. Here the *loci* of authority are external, both in the scholars who conduct the analysis

19. Schubert, "Character Education."

and the examples of successful people.[20] This offers little value to the religious studies discipline, as students are encouraged to construct their own critiques of religious figures and their philosophies.

3. The *experientialists* hold that lifelong learning, interpersonal skills, knowledge and values are critical features of their perspectives. Powerful learning is best achieved through genuine interest and concerns found in a progressive curriculum. Teaching is viewed as interdisciplinary, fulfilling a more profound human interest. The how to learn is more important than the *what* to learn. This integrated perspective promotes the learning of skills, and the study of new bodies of knowledge becomes associated with growth and meaning. Within religious studies, this may include involving students in aspects of community engagement where students experience situations first-hand, connecting them with the outside world instead of only reading about them in the prescribed content.
4. For *critical reconstructionists*, the values highlighted in the curriculum and the instruction thereof is aimed at social reconstruction and organized within a progressive curriculum where it addresses social injustices and human suffering.[21] This type of curriculum structure considers students' social, cultural and political context of students; the intended learning outcomes hold the same value for each student. Situated within the critical theory framework, educators teach or reproduce the inequities in their particular socioeconomic setting, which are later addressed. In creating an awareness of the injustices, students are motivated to become activists within their own learning experience. This thus speaks to the very nature of religious studies as a discipline.

Curriculum Model at UKZN: An Interdisciplinary Approach

Ensor[22] identifies two discourses that have shaped the curriculum restructuring methods in higher education in South Africa—the credit exchange and the traditional disciplinary discourses. The credit exchange, which is widely considered more flexible in academia's response to globalization,

20. Lee, "Curriculum Paradigms."
21. Schubert, "Character Education."
22. Ensor, "Contesting Discourses."

allows students to select their modules according to their interests and needs, therefore determining their own curriculum, making it interdisciplinary. This particular discourse applies to students who take religion modules as electives. Within this discourse, it is assumed that students are competent to do this, and the modules they choose should prepare them for participation in the workplace. The traditional disciplinary discourse, which is more dominant in the science and humanities faculties, aims to organize modules along clear pathways. This allows students to achieve apprenticeships in discipline-related domains. Here the students are assumed to need guidance in structuring their curriculum, emphasizing vertical progression, as in the BA major in Religion.

The curriculum is set within UKZN's critical constructionist framework, and it aligns with the institution's mission and vision to be the premier university of African scholarship, striving for academic excellence and critically engaging with society. Much of the teaching and learning occurs within Schubert's notion of experiential learning. Because religion starts from religious text/orality, the classic textual beginnings and the core scholarly writings are the grounding theory for the modules.

Strengths of the curriculum as per the disciplinary discourse are that the core texts and religious theory form an essential aspect in grounding students who register for the major. This prepares them to analyze information from a critical perspective. At the same time, it allows for the choice to specialize in a specific religion (e.g., Hinduism or Islam) or select modules according to comparative religion and different interests that could complement their other significant modules (e.g., environment, gender, media). This comparative basis of religion provides students with a broader understanding of the pluralistic society we live in and how each religion conditions the community concerning different issues. It motivates students to think beyond their immediate faith and cosmology to the different experiential factors of other students who represent the plural society—bearing in mind that this can be an emotive and subjective process at times.

This model, however, is not without weaknesses. For those taking religion modules as electives to fulfill the credit requirements, the significant problem is that they do not have a grounded knowledge of religion theory and so often are ensnared by the subjective and faith-based concept of practicing religion rather than benefit from the intended critical learning objectives of the module.

Many students enroll for the religion modules as they have no other alternative or assume religion is an easier, more viable option. We are often presented with a scenario where students are not passionate or interested in the disciplinary opportunities the program could offer them. Once students take our modules, they realize that religion is an exciting and crucial element of society that is implicitly and explicitly inherent in aspects of culture, politics and gender therefore offering them an opportunity to see the world through a different lens.

Stream-Based versus Comparative Modules

For a broader overview of all the modules, in terms of the set curriculum, the module offerings are divided into two approaches: a) *stream-based* modules that are historical and deal with specific religions such as *Hinduism in South Africa* and *Islamic institutions in South Africa*; and b) *comparative* modules focusing on social issues which include modules such as *Religion and Conflict*, *Women in Religion and Culture*, and *Religion and Human Rights*.

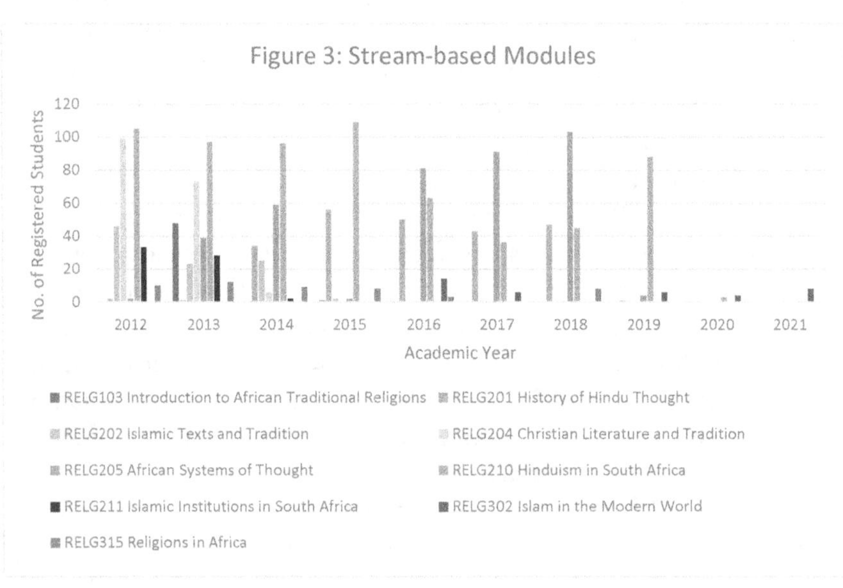

Figure 3: Stream-based modules[23]

23. Data supplied by Institutional Intelligence at UKZN, 2022.

Figure 3 visibly depicts the decline in student enrollments in our stream-based modules. While these modules are offered as electives and thus accessible to all students, the common trend across all these religion-specific modules is that it tends to draw students from that particular religious group. This could be ascribed to the fact that students prefer to draw on their existing knowledge of the religion. Thus, their engagement with it on an academic platform may offer them an opportunity to present a critical awareness of religion in their social setting. The third-year modules focusing on Islam have become fairly popular with the international students.

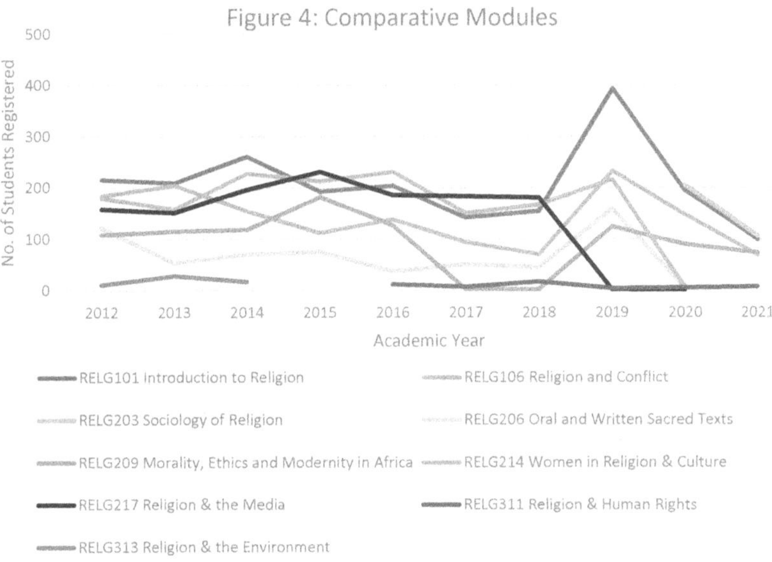

Figure 4: Comparative modules[24]

The findings depicted in Figure 4 above illustrate the growing popularity of the comparative religion modules offered at UKZN from the humanities reconfiguration in 2012 to 2021. The statistics clearly show that first- and second-year level modules attract more students due to the eclectic mix of themes it explores.

The comparative study of religion offers an alternative approach to studying one religion at a time, as in our stream-based modules. Comparative religion studies provide the primary theoretical approach to

24. Data supplied by Institutional Intelligence at UKZN, 2022.

studying religion in this program. Students tend to find the comparative study of religion more appealing as it directly relates to their lived reality instead of being based solely on historical aspects.

Because the comparative modules are also theme based, students can investigate how the various religions engage with each issue. Many students enter the program intrigued by what courses such as religion and conflict offer. The comparative approach offers the potential to gain an objective perspective on religions. By engaging with the dominant religious traditions in our immediate society, students can situate each religion relative to others. While a personal understanding of one's own religious beliefs should not be overlooked, a comparative approach can enhance one's perceptions, particularly when questions about religious practices and rituals go unanswered in the home environment.

Returning briefly to the NQF levels, the table below indicates how the levels differ for each year of study, using skills 1 and 6 as exemplars:

NQF Level	Year of Study	Skill 1: Scope of Knowledge	Skill 6: Accessing, Processing & Managing Information
5	1	Knowledge of the main areas of one or more fields, disciplines or practices, including understanding the key terms, concepts, facts, principles, rules and theories of that field, discipline or practice.	An ability to gather information from a range of sources, including oral, written and/or symbolic texts, to select information appropriate to the task and to apply basic processes of analysis, synthesis and evaluation to that information
6	2	Detailed knowledge of the main areas of one or more fields, disciplines or practices, including an understanding of and an ability to apply the key terms, concepts, facts, principles, rules and theories of that field, discipline or practice; knowledge of an area or areas of specialization and how that knowledge relates to other fields, disciplines or practices	An ability to evaluate different sources of information, to select information appropriate to the task and to apply well-developed processes of analysis, synthesis and evaluation on that information

7	3	Integrated knowledge of the main areas of one or more fields, disciplines or practices, including an understanding of and an ability to apply and evaluate the key terms, concepts, facts, principles, rules and theories of that field, discipline or practice; detailed knowledge of an area or areas of specialization and how that knowledge relates to other fields, disciplines or practices	An ability to develop appropriate processes of information gathering for a given context or use; an ability to independently validate the sources of information and evaluate and manage the information

Table 2: NQF levels[25]

Aligning teaching and learning strategies to NQF levels develops the skills required for the job market. This allows students to apply the knowledge gained from religion modules to other disciplines and develop their critical thinking skills. Even if the study of religion does not assure employment, studying in the religion discipline facilitates employability.

It is evident that the religious studies modules can develop skills generally, and through a comparative approach, specifically: both these skills sets are crucial as it allows students to appreciate the complexity of religious cultures and communities. The comparative nature of the modules creates the space for students to encounter diverse religious belief systems that will add to their understanding of various cultures and societies and develop an awareness of the multifaceted influence of religion on our history and political and economic sectors. These skills also allow them to ask complicated and often uncomfortable questions about religion in a safe space without fear of reprisal, and to organize and critically analyze information drawn from a wide range of sources, instead of a single textbook. The students are given an array of readings in the form of journal articles, book chapters, and blogs as the course content, which are regularly updated to be relevant both contextually and to the students' learning experience.

25. Source: https://www.saqa.org.za/docs/misc/2012/level_descriptors.pdf.

Concluding Remarks

Religious Studies in 2022 and Beyond

Although the number of students registering for the religious studies modules is relatively acceptable for the size of this discipline, there has been a decline in students in the past three years. While the latter is undoubtedly related to the COVID-19 pandemic and the introduction of remote teaching and online learning, it is not anticipated that that numbers will return to the pre-COVID levels, given the economic effects of the pandemic. Therefore, it is critically important that we take stock of where we are and what can be done to improve the popularity and value of religious studies for our students.

While statements about the crisis in humanities continue to refer to declining enrollments, it seems that an interdisciplinary approach to the study of religion could be a way of ensuring continuity of the religious studies discipline, albeit in an altered state.

In the quest to continue the religious studies discipline within academia, we need to be mindful that we are inevitably reimagining the discipline itself in offering interdisciplinary modules. In reconstructing the discipline, we have to be cognizant of how the fundamental boundaries of religious studies have changed over the last few years and will continue to change. There is a fear that we may be pushing undergraduate students into interdisciplinary studies before they can fully grasp their disciplines. Learning basic skills of each discipline while simultaneously acknowledging their differences is challenging for any student and takes time. This may be of more significant concern at an institution such as UKZN, which caters to students from the lowest socioeconomic communities, further compounded by the fact that the medium of instruction varies amongst the high schools in these communities, and noting that South Africa has eleven official languages. Thus, students often struggle to understand the meaning of religious concepts.

Another concern relates to the integrity of the discipline and the staff involved. These changes directly impact on the academics' areas of specialization and training and the need to preserve academic freedom while resisting the takeover of curricula and departments by administrative powers. Questions may also arise about the quality and value of the education we are now delivering in light of diluting our modules.

Conclusion

Religious studies departments worldwide have faced numerous threats of closure for decades, with the powers that be citing that the discipline itself is not a financially viable option. In response, these departments have restructured their curriculums and pedagogies to be contextually relevant, and assert their value in developing well-rounded students; the University of KwaZulu-Natal is no exception.

The attraction of comparative, theme-based modules necessarily lead to a discussion of interdisciplinarity. The relocation of the religious studies discipline at UKZN was centrally located in the same vicinity as the other humanities disciplines. This encouraged what was perhaps an inevitable move towards interdisciplinary collaboration. Religious studies has now been contextually influenced, and new modules and courses have been designed to address societal changes. Motivated by two critical elements in religion, that of lived religion and experiential learning, an interdisciplinary approach to studying religion locates itself in issues students can easily recognize. This is a distinctive trait currently as universities streamline their productivity to become more competitive to survive the global higher education milieu.[26]

This reflection is only the beginning of deeper ideological issues that may influence our thoughts and actions towards structuring a more fully integrated and interdisciplinary field of study.

Bibliography

Arndt, David. "The Two Cultures and the Crisis in the Humanities." *Forum on Public Policy*. 2007. Accessed January 28, 2022. https://files.eric.ed.gov/fulltext/EJ1098521.pdf.

ASSAf (Academy of Science of South Africa). *Consensus Study on the State of the Humanities in South Africa: Status, Prospects and Strategies.* Pretoria: ASSAf, 2011.

Baker, Christopher, and Adam Dinham. "New Interdisciplinary Spaces of Religions and Beliefs in Contemporary Thought and Practice: An Analysis." *Religions* 8/2 (2017). doi:10.3390/rel8020016.

Ball, Christopher. "Life Long Learning for the 21st Century." Keynote address at the 21st Improving University Teaching Conference. Nottingham: Trent University, 1996.

Chidester, David. "Religion Education in South Africa: Teaching and Learning about Religion, Religions, and Religious Diversity." *British Journal of Religious Education* 25/4 (2003) 261–78. doi:10.1080/0141620030250402.

26. Troiani and Dutson, "Neoliberal University."

Clasquin, Michel. "Religious Studies in South(ern) Africa—An Overview." *Journal for the Study of Religion* 18/2 (2005) 5–22.

Department of Education. "National Curriculum Statement Grades 10–12, Life Orientation." 2002. Accessed January 21, 2022. http://education.pwv.gov.za/DoE_Sites/FET_folder/FET_schools/ncs/default.htm.

Ensor, Paula. "Contesting Discourses in Higher Education Curriculum Restructuring in South Africa." *Higher Education* 48/3 (2004) 339–59. https://www.jstor.org/stable/4151521.

Lee, John Chi-Kin. "Curriculum Paradigms and Perspectives of Life and Spiritual Education: Contrast and diversity." *International Journal of Children's Spirituality* 25/3–4 (2020) 175–86. doi:10.1080/1364436X.2020.1853369.

Nussbaum, Martha. *Not for Profit: Why Democracy Needs the Humanities.* Princeton: Princeton University, 2010.

Stats SA. "Quarterly Labour Force Survey (QLFS); 1st Quarter 2021." 2021. http://www.statssa.gov.za/?page_id=1854&PPN=P0211&SCH=72943.

SAQA. *The South African Qualifications Authority Level Descriptors for the South African National Qualifications Framework.* 2012. https://www.saqa.org.za/docs/misc/2012/level_descriptors.pdf.

Schubert, W. H. "Character Education from Four Perspectives on Curriculum." In *The Construction of Children's Character*, by A. Molnar, 17–30. Chicago: University of Chicago, 1997.

Troiani, Igea, and Claudia Dutson. "The Neoliberal University as a Space to Learn/Think/Work in Higher Education." *Architecture and Culture* 9/1 (2021) 5–23. doi: 10.1080/20507828.2021.1898836.

Van der Walt, Johannes L. "Religion in Education in South Africa: Was Social Justice Served?" *SouthAfrican Journal of Education* 31 (2011) 381–93. http://sajournalofeducation.co.za/index.php/saje/article/view/543/259.

Chapter 3

Prospects and Potential for the Study of Religion and Digital Media in (South) Africa

Lee-Shae Salma Scharnick-Udemans

Introduction

The presence of religion in diverse digital spaces can be traced to the earliest days of the Internet. Consequently, scholarly interest in religion's digital dynamics and dynamism has been consistent since the early to mid 1990s. Leading scholars of digital religion Campbell and Evolvi[1] describe four evolutionary "waves" or phases in the development of the field. In the first and second waves scholarship was focused on identifying the phenomenon of digital religion and tried to make sense of digital practices in light of questions of how religious communities and individuals respond to the opportunities and challenges that digital media affords. The third phase reflected the evolution and expansion of digital media technology and practices by emphasizing "the embeddedness of the Internet in everyday life and its impact on non-digital venues."[2] The fourth and current phase notably nuances and broadens the scope of digital religion studies. In acknowledging the continuity of online/offline space, identities, and practices as well as the entanglements

1. Campbell and Evolvi, "Contextualizing Current Digital Religion."
2. Campbell and Evolvi, "Contextualizing Current Digital Religion," 5.

between religion and other intersections of oppression and privilege, this wave pays attention to "existential, ethical, and political aspects of digital religion, as well as issues of gender, race, class, ethnicity, sexuality."[3]

The interdisciplinary and intersectional scope of digital religion is exemplified in this current phase of research and development. At the very least the study of religion and digital media combine the study of religion and the study of media; however, given the vast and diverse ways in which digital religion is engaged and expressed, the field intersects with a variety of different disciplines including politics, history, international relations, gender, sociology, anthropology, education, and language studies. Scholars of religion, in particular, may find this interdisciplinary orientation refreshing since it undermines secularist impulses to separate religion from other domains of public and private life. The interdisciplinary scope of religion and digital media studies engenders greater creative and critical license in conceptualizing the making and meaning of religion as conceptual framing, lived experiences, material expressions, and subjectivity within the dynamics of digitality. In terms of intersectionality, the politics of digitality reproduces existing intersections of power and marginalization but also presents a context wherein novel expressions of individual characteristics and identity frames are constructed, curated, circulated, and contested.

While the study of digital religion flourishes in the Global North, it appears that its study in Africa is still in its infancy. As I wrote this chapter, the timing of the second edition release of *Digital Religion: Understanding Religious Practice in Digital Media*[4] felt fortuitous since, as with the first edition, it is positioned as an introduction to the field in its current state. Despite having tracked a pattern of epistemological, contextual marginalization and near absence of African scholarship and perspectives from the so-called mainstream corpus of religion and media, I was hopeful that there would be at least one contribution that features research from the African continent.[5] Unfortunately, I was disappointed but not surprised to find none.[6] The first six chapters reflect themes that have shaped the field and include religion, ritual, identity, community,

3. Campbell and Evolvi, "Contextualizing current digital religion," 7.

4. Campbell and Tsuria, *Digital Religion*.

5. For more see Scharnick-Udemans, "Gender Perspectives," 145–63; and Scharnick-Udemans and Hackett, "Introduction," 1–13.

6. Africa is nominally mentioned twice in the bibliography of one chapter in Campbell and Tsuria, *Digital Religion*.

authority, and embodiment. Twelve thematic case studies enliven and effuse these chapters with a range of provocative, empirically grounded examples. A further three chapters that center on theory, ethics, and theology conclude the revised version of this important text. In studying the text I found much resonance with African contexts. The strategic utility and value of this text for any scholar of religion and digital media is as obvious as it was intended to be. While the authors by no means claim the text as exhaustive, it reads as both informative and instructive and offers both historical and contemporary views of the field, its development and scope. Furthermore, the text imbues a sense of authority and ownership, especially in the recollection of the founding myth of the field.

The editors reflect on the early history of digital religion studies when the tiresome work of justifying this new intellectual terrain was a regular activity that scholars would need to undertake in order to convince colleagues of its scholarly merit. They recall the moment when the status of digital religion studies as a legitimate field of inquiry with the study of religion was conferred. It took place at the book launch of the first edition at the 2012 annual American Academy of Religion conference, "where key chapter contributors presented their work to a packed, standing-room crowd of more than 100 scholars." The editors recall a shift in the kinds of questions that were asked by those in attendance. Instead of being asked to account for why the study of religion and digital media was a worthy endeavour, questions of how the relationships between religion and digital media could be understood and its meaning for the study of religion and society were raised. This meeting was a truly transformational experience for the field and the scholars who have committed their resources and energies to its development. Campbell and Tsuria report, "Several participants and chapter authors described this as the moment when they first felt their work was legitimated and lauded by the academy."[7]

The omission of African scholarship from these kinds of discipline-defining texts and experiences cannot be dismissed as oversight. Indeed, the constitution and operation of the field of religion and digital media reflect the historical and epistemological "silo-izing"[8] of Africa, Africans, and African scholarship by the Global North. African media scholars Schoon et al., in exploring African digital experiences as epistemic sites of knowledge production, explain that as in many other disciplines,

7. Tsuria and Campbell, "Introduction to the Study," 1–2.

8. Waisbord, "My Vision," 32.

"methods and intellectual approaches drawn from the West are seen as sacrosanct, while approaches and concepts emerging from the Global South are deemed to have a lower ontological density in the hierarchical ordering of knowledge."[9] It is beyond the pale of this essay to discuss in detail the historical and political underpinnings of the contextual and representational asymmetry that continues to define the enterprise of knowledge production and circulation in the academy, and especially as it relates to the development of digital religion studies. The purpose, however, of sharing the above vignette is, on the one hand, to suggest that the exclusions emphasized by the second edition of *Digital Religion: Understanding Religious Practice in Digital Media* not be dismissed as innocent despite the absence of nefarious intent and, on the other, to emphasize the importance and urgency of the emphasizing and developing digital religion studies in Africa.

In addition, it is important to convey that while African perspectives and scholarship have been excluded in this particular authoritative text, Africans have been producing work on the topics related to digital religion and deploying digital research methods in their research. Digital religion scholarship suggests a divergence between the fields of religion and media, which presumes a longer history of media and deploys a more expansive definition of mediation and mediaization, and digital religion studies, which claims a later genealogy aligned with the subfield of religion and internet studies. Scholarship from the Global North appears to most often assume the latter genealogy. On the contrary, this chapter aligns with the work of Becker and Cabrita,[10] who argue against tendencies in scholarship that seek to prescribe a binary or evolutionary approach to the study of media, ostensibly differentiating between old and new, electronic and digital, and instead suggest that "old and new media coexist on a single spectrum of media practice in Africa." This orientation to the study of religion and media in Africa is especially valuable given the disparate ways in which media technology, infrastructure, and consequently media access have developed across the continent, is useful because it embraces how media culture has unfolded with the particularity of African locations, cultures, and institutional contexts and highlights its entanglement with the historical and contemporary socio-political conditions that characterize the media landscape and produce its publics.

9. Schoon et al., "Decolonising Digital Media Research," 4.

10. Becker and Cabrita, "Introduction," 2.

There are few extended studies that are intentionally framed as digital religion.[11] However, based on my experience as a scholar of religion and media in South Africa, topics within the purview of digital religion are becoming more popular and the field is beginning to burgeon. The increase in critical scholarly attention focusing on religion's digital dynamics reflects both the interests and concerns of a generation of emerging academics, many of whom are experienced with and enthusiastic about the research opportunities that digital media present, and an eagerness from more seasoned colleagues to consider the implications that the enfolding and entanglement of online/offline might mean for more established topics, subjects, and debates within the study of religion and theology more broadly. Following African media scholars,[12] it is necessary to state upfront that while this chapter advocates for the development of the study of religion and digital media in Africa, its agenda is not predicated on a radical dismissal of conceptual and methodological approaches from other parts of the world, nor is it anchored in "a localized research agenda of separatism."[13] Therefore, while building on existing concepts, theories, and approaches including that from the Global North it does so from an intentionally South African perspective by offering insight from local scholarship and interactions with digital media and religion. In doing so, I hope to encourage colleagues from other regions on the continent to do the same when working out and through religion's digital dynamics.

The first part of this essay explores the scope of digital religion studies and its associated methods. The second part of this essay explores scholarly studies on religion and digital media that are focussed on South African contexts and highlights how scholars in the region have responded to the possibilities that a focus on digitality and religiosity might yield. This section also offers empirical examples that emphasize the scope of research topics that are available to scholars interested in pursuing the possibilities that digital media may yield for the study of religion in South Africa in particular and Africa more broadly, questions related to research ethics, and discussion of what the digital turn may mean for the study of religion in Africa.

11. See Faimu and Lesitaokana, "New Media," as this edited volume offers some insights with a focus on Christian-oriented case studies.

12. Schoon et al., "Decolonising Digital Media Research."

13. Atton and Mabweazara, "New Media and Journalism," 670.

Scoping the Field

Scholars agree that digital religion is not a singular phenomenon but rather a framework for articulating and understanding religion's dynamic interactions with digital media. In the past two decades scholars have described, categorized, and theorized what is known as the "material turn"[14] in the study of religion. Material religion as an empirical, theoretical, and epistemological orientation to the study of religion deliberately expands the scope of the study of religion beyond a focus on the interiority of belief to the ways that religion is materially, concretely, or even physically manifested and mediated through objects, feelings, and sensory experiences as well as bodily performances. Strijdom[15] explains ". . . (T)hat this shift in research emphasis, from beliefs to practices, from ideas to material things, though not abandoning interest in the former, profoundly challenges the modern, secular location of religion in the interior, private sphere of the individual by re-situating religion explicitly within the public sphere." The deliberate re-situation of religion in the public sphere reminds us that the focus on materiality requires that we pay critical attention to the conditions and orientations of power and authority, whether epistemological, racial, political, cultural, technological, economic, or gendered. A material orientation emphasizes religion's entanglements with public culture and upholds religion's essentially mediated character, which predates the history and development of modern technology.[16]

A material approach to the study of digital religion supports a non-binary view of the online/offline and reinforces the socio-political scope of the fourth wave. Furthermore, given religion's diverse expressions within digital culture, narrow, universalist definitions of religion fail to capture the complexities of the features and functions of religion in public culture. A material approach to the study of religion encourages the contextualized construction of second-order definitions of religion that are critical and creative, historically informed, contextually grounded, and analytically rigorous.

The study of digital religion requires an understanding of the Internet, along with its material and conceptual analogues such as mobile

14. See Houtman and Meyer, "Things"; Strijdom, "Material Turn"; and Chidester, *Religion: Material Dynamics*.

15. Strijdom, "Material Turn," n.p.

16. Morgan, "Mediation or Mediatisation."

technology devices, applications, and social media, as contexts and spaces where religion is creatively constructed, curated, circulated, and contested by a number of diverse and variously motivated communities, individuals, organizations, and corporations. Furthermore, digital religion scholarship presupposes that the legitimacy of these sites as locations for the encounter of and engagement with religion is taken as seriously as conventionally located religious institutions, practices, and expressions. Digital religion is underwritten by a fundamental tenet of Internet studies that speaks to the continuity between online/offline. Miller and Slater[17] articulated this point particularly well in the early days of Internet studies: "We need to treat internet media as continuous and embedded in other social spaces, that they happened within mundane social structures and relations that they may transform but they cannot escape into a self-enclosed cybernian apartness." The continuity and embeddedness of the Internet have far-reaching implications including the potential for offline consequences with the potential to cause irreparable damage and harm. Within these contexts religion may emerge as a nexus of both agreement and acrimony. Once more this underscores the need for serious and sustained scholarly attention to be directed at the relationship between religion, digital media, and the cultures it produces.

Located at the intersection of new(er) media technologies, religion, and digital culture, definitions of and approaches to the study of digital religion should ensure that the scope of the field, its foci and methods are deliberately porous and flexible, reflecting the character of digital media as well as the interdisciplinary character of the field and its scope for intersectional inquiry. Digital religion is defined more by what it features and how its functions than by what it "is." Campbell[18] suggests a spectrum of topics and approaches to the study of digital religion. This includes what could be considered the study of how religious communities and individuals engage with the Internet. It extends to the study of how religious beliefs and practices are expressed through digital practices and affordances and it can involve what is considered implicit religion. "Implicit religion" refers to "how some forms of contemporary practice or meaning-making can take on religious-like qualities to the extent that beliefs and practices associated with them can be defined as exhibiting a family resemblance to religion." When applied to the study of digital

17. Miller and Slater, *Internet*, 5.

18. Campbell, "Surveying Theoretical Approaches."

religion, this might involve casting technology as an implicit religion and implies that the practices involved in its usage have religious-like attributes and meaning for those who use it. As will be shown in the following section, practices of online shaming may feature as implicit religion on South African social media platforms.

As noted earlier, digital religion may very well follow a genealogy that differs from mainstream religion and media scholarship. However, three main theoretical approaches borrowed from this sibling or perhaps parent discipline shape the study of religion and digital culture. These include theories of mediatization of religion, mediation and religion, and the religious-social shaping of technology. Despite the siloing of African scholarship in the mainstream religion and media corpus, these theories have been appropriated and developed in the scholarship of African scholars of religion, and scholars of religion in Africa, to understand older forms of media. They may present theoretical inroads to the exploration of the new forms of mediatization and mediation that reflect the heterogeneity of religion and digital media on the African continent.[19]

For example, I have argued previously[20] that the utility of mediatization of religion as a concept and theory, developed in the Northern European context, is diminished in relevance for South African religion and media scholarship due to an overemphasis on the socio-cultural processes that place media in a position of power over religion, and an implicit dismissal of the politics that play a critical role in regulating the ways both religion and media interact and operate within the public culture. I argued that the particularities of the South African context determine a definition of the mediatization of religion that is cognizant of the manner in which religion and media have both been reconfigured by the post-1994 nation-building efforts.

The rise of digital communication and technology has provisioned innovations not only to topics of research that we engage in but also to the ways in which we conduct our research. In the following section digital religion research methods and orientations are explored.

19. For more please see Meyer, *Aesthetic Formations*, and Meyer and Moors, "Religion, Media."

20. Scharnick-Udemans, "Biographies."

Digital (Religion) Research Methods

Digital religion studies methods are significantly shaped by the field of digital research methods, which includes a diversity of approaches to the constitution and conceptualisation of digital methods. Tsuria et al.[21] suggest three lenses for understanding digital religion methods: environments, tools, and frames. These lenses provide a useful framework for outlining what scholars are doing when they say they are studying digital religion. A focus on the environment highlights the importance of the continuity of online/offline and suggests that researchers should locate the research on this continuum by asking questions regarding where the research takes place, where the data is located, and from where it is extracted. When conceptualizing digital methods in terms of the use of tools similar questions about the origin of the tools are asked. Non-digitally[22] born tools such as surveys and interviews can be easily transformed into digital tools. Additionally digital research tools include the use of applications for video and voice recording interviews and the use of analytical and research software that enable the relatively fast and accurate production of data of large quantities of digital information. This includes the digital tools developed for the filtering and processing of what is known as "big data." Digital research methods include the online availability of offline archives that were previously only available to those who could physically access them. Empirical research involving human participants that may have been strictly bound to time and space and perhaps deterred by material conditions including issues of safety and costs is now open to the possibilities that digital communication offers. The third perspective that shapes digital research is framing, which according to Tsuria et al.[23] "informs the researcher's world view and one's methodological approach." The frame is determined by the researcher's theoretical and philosophical orientation to the digital and in this case religion. It refers not only to how information is derived and organized but also to how and why it is imbued with particular meanings. The frame is essentially defined by the methodological orientation of the project and directs the methods.

21. Tsuria et al., "Approaches to Digital Methods."

22. The author prefers the use of the less offensive terms "digitally born" and "non-digitally born" due the derisive overtones of the term "native," which is popular in Western literature.

23. Tsuria, et al., "Approaches to Digital Methods."

In reviewing the literature Tsuria et al.[24] have determined three methods that predominantly feature in digital religion studies. These include textual analysis, interviews, and ethnography. All of these methods require that notions and practices of text, interview, and ethnography are reconceptualized within the context of digital environments, tools, and frames. Given the ways in which the field of digital religion is developing, a level of intellectual ingenuity and flexibility is needed to reimagine the ways that online/offline research methods are much like the online/offline worlds, "bridged, blended, and blurred."[25]

Two recent master's theses by emerging religion-and-media experts at the University of the Western Cape illustrate how three perspectives on digital research methods in the study of digital religion may be understood in practice. Ashleigh Petersen,[26] in a study of a mediated court testimony that she conceptualized as a narrative of clergy sexual abuse, explored the YouTube comments sections attached to each video testimony in order to assess how social media users affirmed or contested patriarchal religious understandings of gender and power through their engagement with the videos. The derivation of the data from the comments sections as its point of origin determines the location of this study in a digital environment. In terms of digital tools, Petersen deployed the use of a specifically developed tool, ATLAS.ti qualitative data analysis software, a digitally born tool, to sort the data and develop the principle codes that undergirded the analytical engine of the research project. In a study of Muslims and Islam on public broadcasting in South Africa Sakeenah Dramat[27] was able to use YouTube to conceptualize and produce a digital archive for a non-digitally produced and circulated television program broadcast by the national public broadcaster. The program is aired on a weekly basis and older episodes were until recently[28] not available for public viewing or reviewing. The multidisciplinary scope of digital media research particularly as it relates to the study of religion is most evident when witnessing the ways in which Dramat and Petersen adopt framing in their research. Both studies regard media as legitimate sites of knowledge about religion. Dramat's approach to the digital data,

24. Tsuria et al., "Approaches to Digital Methods."

25. Campbell and Evolvi, "Contextualizing Current Digital Religion," 5.

26. Petersen, "He Asked Me To."

27. Dramat, "Representations of Islam."

28. It is worth mentioning that in the past the broadcaster has started to upload selected episodes to YouTube.

while more tool based, is informed by theories of the mediatization of religion as well as decolonial approaches to the study of Muslims and Islam. Petersen's work is framed by digital formations of public culture as well as African feminist approaches to the study of Christianity.

In this section I reference scholarly studies on religion and digital media that are focused on South African contexts and highlight how scholars in the region have already responded to the possibilities that a focus on digitality and religiosity might yield. I follow and extend Campbell's three general categories of digital religion research to organize the discussion as follows: firstly, the use of digital media by religious communities and individuals; secondly, the expression of religiosity through digital practices and affordances; and thirdly, implicit religion. After each section I offer empirical examples that emphasize the scope of research topics that are available to scholars interested in pursuing the possibilities that digital media may yield for the study of religion in South Africa in particular and Africa more broadly.

The Use of Digital Media by Religious Communities and Individuals

Maria Frahm-Arp conducted an in-depth study on social media usage in three mega Pentecostal Charismatic Christian Churches in South Africa. The shape and character of Pentecostal Christianity are diverse and varied and Frahm-Arp explains that these churches share a focus on prosperity theology, ". . . that promises to move believers from the margins of economic success and material prosperity to lives of triumphant attainment of all the goods of the world."[29] The study focused on the hitherto under-explored and theorized demographic of South African Christians identified as black and middle class. A content analysis was deployed to explore the churches' Facebook accounts along with the Twitter pages of two of the three church leaders. Frahm-Arp illustrates a mixed-methods approach to the study of religion and digital media. While the study took place in digital environments afforded by social media and utilized data derived therein, Frahm-Arp also employed in-person empirical methods including site and participant observation and semi-structured interviews. The study is well located within the political economy of South Africa and provides an incisive view of the political unease as well as the

29. Becker and Cabrita, "Introduction," 256.

responses of the churches (or lack thereof) that defined this particular moment.[30] The focus of this analysis was on the messages of the leaders to the congregants during this time and the congregants' responses to these messages. The findings of the study contest dominant assumptions perpetuated in scholarship on Pentecostalism in Africa that infer that media usage is mainly functional and show that the churches under discussion intentionally albeit differentially use social media "to shape the religious experience of believers, provide a space of testimonies, and offer new devotional material and channels for political engagement."[31]

TikTok is a social media application that is centered around short videos. It has been touted as the fastest growing social media platform in the world. There are a reported one billion users,[32] of whom only 4 percent are active content creators, also known as "TikTokers." TikTokers have access to a number of specialized tools to enhance their content, including filters and an enormous music library, to develop stylized video content that showcases any aspect of their lives, identities, and interests. The application is fully interactive and allows for creators and followers to interact in a number of different ways including, commenting, liking, downloading, sharing, participating in trends, or producing duets.[33] Farren Watt (@farrenwatt) is a minister in the Dutch Reformed Church of South Africa and has been listed as one of the top five promising TikTok creators in South Africa. She is twenty-six years old and serves a community in a small fishing town, Lamberts Bay, on the west coast of South Africa. Watt has a TikTok following of over sixty thousand followers, an impressive number for the Southern African region. Watt certainly does not present as the conventional image of a minister, particularly one from the notoriously conservative Dutch Reformed Church, but she is intent on breaking stereotypes related to the vocation of religious service.[34] A lifestyle article makes the following claims about Watt's appearance: "Being a member of the clergy does not mean that Farren Watt cannot

30. The study took place between 2015 and 2016, a year or so after Jacob Zuma, the third president of South Africa, took up a second term of office, and coincided with a particularly turbulent time in the socio-political and economic landscape of South Africa.

31. Frahm-Arp, "Pentacostalism," 277.

32. Stokel-Walker, "TikTok Boom."

33. For an explanation of the features of the platform please see https://influencermarketinghub.com/what-is-tiktok/.

34. Africa, "Top 5 TikTok Creators."

have long flowing curls and red lips and wear heels that would give other people a fear of heights."[35] Watt shares a diversity of content on TikTok, from a night out with her fiancé to snippets from the church council meeting. She generally communicates in her first language, Afrikaans, is known for her candor, and while she shares parts of her sermons, videos of herself, and the community in worship and participates in church fundraising events such as bazaars, she also provides hair and makeup tips and features her ever-growing shoe collection as a backdrop to many of her videos. According to Watts the purpose of her page is to show her followers that even though she is a religious leader she lives a "normal" life. In another media article about Watt's use of TikTok, the journalist claims, "Young pastor has another pulpit, TikTok",[36] and it is precisely this formulation of TikTok as a pulpit, as articulated through the example of Watt, that highlights how religion's dynamic entanglements with digital media are not only changing the nature of the medium but also of the message and its meaning.

Socio-cultural anthropologist Marleen de Witte suggests that in religion and media literature "African traditional religion is generally thought of outside of the context of modern mass media and the public sphere."[37] The constitutive diversity of the continent, indigenous African religions, as well as the histories and institutional orientations and operations of local media institutions determine the extent to which this statement is an accurate reflection of current media trends. According to de Witte the lack of attention to African traditional religions in the literature may be understood as three-pronged. First, it is partly shaped by the rural bias of scholarship of indigenous religions in Africa, secondly, by issues of local media censorship in various contexts may play a role; and thirdly, by wariness on the part of traditional practitioners and leaders to adopt or engage modern media technologies. While relationships between traditional religions and electronic forms of media including television and radio have been fraught, digital media reveals an alternative trajectory.

African traditional practitioners, healers, and leaders have a visible presence on various digital media platforms, including websites and social media, notably Instagram and TikTok. While the digital presence of *sangomas* has steadily risen as the popularity of these platforms

35. Micheals, "Young Pastor."

36. Micheals, "Young Pastor."

37. De Witte, "Media Afrikania," 207.

have increased, it was during the lockdown seasons of the COVID-19 pandemic in South Africa when digital presence of African traditional practitioners was firmly established. Media reports[38] shows that social distancing and other protocols of the pandemic forced African indigenous healers to transform the ways in which they do their work. This led to the development and the formation of online directory systems[39] and a number of online stores where traditional religious objects and medicines may be purchased. Furthermore, there has been an increase in profiles and pages on social media that reveal the identity and services of the African traditional practitioners. The presence of African traditional religion on digital media platforms reveals a younger generation and more urban demographic of practitioners. These pages are not only service based, but many are pedagogical in orientation and used to inform and educate their audiences on various beliefs and practices. The pages are also used to share snippets of live events, including revealing selected aspects of certain rites and rituals, and some traditional practitioners will also conduct question-and-answer sessions using the tools that platforms provide. In addition practitioners may use the platform to highlight various other aspects of their lives, including their domestic and professional lives, personal interests, food preferences, and fashion choices. For example, Gogo Dineo Ndlanzi has a following of over one hundred thousand users and links her Instagram page directly to her website, where she is described as "pre-eminent and pioneering sangoma who has successfully merged the sacredness of African spiritualty and modern thinking. She is a celebrated spiritual teacher life coach, African story teller, actress, writer, dancer and trained facilitator."[40] She uses Instagram as a virtual diary of her life and presents all of her roles and functions in addition to her personal lifestyle preferences on her social media.

Frahm-Arp's study and the examples of Watt and Ndlanzi, respectively, represent the diverse ways in which the use of digital media by religious communities and individuals takes place, the various platforms on which they are utilized, and the different messages they choose to impart.

38. Schutz, "Traditional Healers Zoom In."

39. The site gogoonline.co.za is one such example.

40. Gogo Dineo, "Introduction."

The Expression of Religious Identity, Beliefs, and Practices through Digital Media Practices and Affordances

In a study of twenty Christian dating websites in South Africa Sofka F. John explores how the religious identity and preferences of daters constitute key data in algorithmic matchmaking processes.[41] This study foregrounds the silent power and pervasiveness of the algorithm, a "quiet and opaque object employed to process and turn into capital the massive data that are continually generated from our digital life and practice."[42] Underwritten by essentially commercially motivated intentions, John claims that not only do these religious dating sites reinforce heteronormativity and patriarchy but they also entrench these attitudes through pitching notions of love, romance, and God's will for relationship within the confines of niche understandings of Christian sexual ethics based on conservative scriptural interpretation and born-again discourses of morality. Through the practices and affordances that enliven these dating sites, including the completion of surveys, the submission of profile statements, photographs, and for some the eventual public testimony of Godly romantic success, heterosexual Christian men and women are able to express various aspects of their religiosity especially as it relates to the dynamics of intimate relationships. John shows how through the utilization of biblically derived tropes of providence and predestination these media sites are sacralized as mediators and facilitators of heavenly and holy plans for romantic relationships. As affordances of new media technology these sites have deliberately constructed a sense of authority that certain Christian daters find legitimate. This study highlights that even though the algorithm represents a technologically predetermined framework into which personal and sociological data is fed, site users are still able to exercise agency when determining what information they choose to share with the site and they choose to present themselves. Since these sites clearly represent a niche in the market of online dating and matchmaking, they represent spaces where religious beliefs, especially those about love and intimacy and the correct Christian ways in which to seek out and develop intimacy with potential partners, are articulated in a setting that is not considered traditionally religious.

41. John, "Computing Cupid."

42. John, "Computing Cupid," 86.

In South Africa Muslim women content creators[43] feature significantly and are leaders in the genre of digital lifestyle content creation. Digital lifestyle content is mainly associated with the social media platform Instagram, which was originally developed as a photo-sharing platform but later evolved into a multimodal application for audio-visual sharing and real-time engagement. Historically, Instagram has been associated with the presentation of well-curated visuals and the showcasing of fashion of all varieties. While there are not yet extended studies of Muslim lifestyle content creators in South Africa, close observation suggests that Muslim lifestyle content creators may or may not explicitly self-identify as Muslim or be recognized as such through their chosen dress code observances. While the majority of Muslim content creators are women, they do not present homogenously and the mainstay of the content that they produce is not defined by its religious character and covers a number of areas of interest and concern including fashion, fitness, mental health, parenting, politics, and well-ness among others. Therefore, the adjective "Muslim"[44] must be carefully considered and not conflated with the notion of Islamic, because it does not define the nature of the content but rather speaks to the religious identity of the content creator. Muslim content creators express their religious identities, beliefs, and practices patently as they see appropriate[45] and it may be implied through their lifestyle choices,[46] and this is shared via the everyday depiction of their lived realities through the capabilities that Instagram as their chosen platform allows and the conventions that content creators are expected to follow.[47] Whereas Warren, working in the UK context, claims that Muslim lifestyle media is characterized by "Muslim women producing content for other Muslim women"[48] and suggests a focus on

43. Also known as Influencers although this is a contested term that has developed derisive undertones which undermine the value of the labor in which digital content creators are involved and highlights the consumer capitalist overtones of the digital lifestyle genre.

44. See Beydoun, *American Islamophobia*, as Khaled Beydoun's discussion of the media conflation of Muslims and Islam is illuminating in this regard.

45. This kind of content increased around significant religious holidays, events or rites of passage.

46. Choices around clothing, food, endorsement, and opinions on various social and sometimes political issues.

47. Digital content creation within the context of Influencer culture represents a lucrative industry

48. Warren, "Placing faith," 1.

content that is informed by notions of Muslimness and womanhood, the ways in which Muslim women lifestyle content creators engage on their platforms contest this assertion.

Aqeelah Haron-Ally is one of the country's leading lifestyle content creators and has approximately eighty thousand followers and over three thousand posts on her feed. The amount of posts and followers is a testament to Haron-Ally's reputation as a digital content creator par excellence. Although in her early thirties she started blogging in the earlier days of social media, when MySpace was the dominant platform, since then she has managed to transfer to other platforms and remain relevant. Through these platforms she documents most facets of her life. Her followers know her as a single flight attendant, a part-time makeup artist, a bride, a wife, and a cat person. They know where she goes on holiday, why she chose to purchase a house where she did, and that she suffers from anxiety. Her followers know of her struggles to heal her body of chronic illness in order to conceive, they were informed of the ectopic pregnancy that lead to a dangerous miscarriage, and now they have witnessed her pregnancy and her journey to motherhood. Haron-Ally openly identifies as a Muslim woman and expresses this identity through the depiction of her everyday lived reality. We see her practice, what she perceives as her Islamic commitments, when she shares her baby's name-giving ceremony, or when she uses religious phrases as punctuation, or when she searches for halal restaurants for a date night. While she is not a "hijabista,[49]" while she is a Muslim content creator and she does not deliver sermons, provide religious advice, or claim religious authority, her example demonstrates that in sharing their lives within the genres, conventions, and parameters of social media platforms, Muslim women lifestyle influencers' digital content creates a space for the encounter and observation of lived religion.

Religion-and-media scholarship in Africa have favored studies of Islam and Christianity as well the study of "new religious movements," particularly those that have a Christian orientation. African indigenous religions are often mentioned.[50]

These two examples of Christian dating and Muslim lifestyle content creators demonstrate how digital media practices and affordances,

49. Kavacki and Kraeplin, "Religious Beings," 850. "A 'hijabista'—from the terms hijabi and fashionista—is a Muslim woman who dresses 'stylishly' while still adhering to the rules governing 'modest' apparel that coincides with Islamic dress code."

50. De Witte, "Media Afrikania," 207.

whether in the form of algorithms or the genre conventions of a social media platform, provide space for the expression of religious identity, beliefs, and practices that "may become authoritative voices that evoke meanings about religion without being endorsed by official voices of particular religions."[51]

Implicit Religion and Banal Religion

Implicit religion[52] along and with banal religion[53] are two generative and overlapping concepts that offer scholars of digital media frameworks way of thinking beyond religion as a community's particular set of beliefs and practices towards considering how religion and the religious may feature in more diffuse and surprising ways through digital media. While Hjarvard's theory of banal religion was developing specifically in relation to mass mediatization, it remains relevant for thinking of how to study religion and digital religion since it locates the religious "as a broader field of representations and practices disseminating across culture and society with no particular organizational foundation or demarcated set of followers."[54] Banal religion advances an acknowledgement and understanding of the "authority of the popular" that resonates with the kinds of meanings and motivations that sustain the continued growth and growing salience of digital media content creation and consumption.

Evolvi and Campbell suggest implicit religion may offer a framework for understanding a spectrum of behavior and practices that explores "how technology or technological practices may themselves be judged to have religious-like qualities or behavior associated with them."[55] One example of a technologically mediated practice that resembles religiously inspired activities and opinions is revealed in the practices of regulating and enforcing social norms and values through calling out unacceptable behavior, practices, and opinions, spotlighting, and sharing them, and

51. Following Edward Bailey in 1969, in this chapter "implicit religion" is used more broadly as the foundation for a framework for understanding the religious-like salience that commitments held outside of religious institutions may have for individuals and communities.

52. Hjarvard, "Mediatization," 13.

53. Hjarvard, "Mediatization," 13.

54. Hjarvard, "Mediatization," 13.

55. Campbell and Evolvi, "Contextualizing Current Digital Religion," 13.

demanding explanations and restitution.[56] This practice is described as "online shaming"[57] and is synonymous with practices known popularly as "cancel culture."[58] Varying motivations, including a collective sense of justice and accountability, may have resurrected a version of public shaming that aligns with the affordances that digital media provides. Online shaming in its many guises is a generally accepted and to some extent expected part of life in the digital age. It represents a sphere of social activity firmly located and produced within digital culture but that often has offline consequences.

Ethical Considerations

The real-life consequences that any online activity may inspire are for better or worse a part of the ethical responsibilities that the researcher may attend when designing and executing their project. According to Johns,[59] "scholars of religion have employed the full range of methods used in the social sciences and the humanities to better understand religions and the practices of their adherences." As such, scholars have had to navigate issues related to ethics as it applies to a variety of religious contexts. While we may draw from these resources, as this essay has shown, religiosity in a variety of forms finds expression in and through digital media and, while there is certainly continuity between the online/offline, the religion does not feature online in exactly the same ways that it does offline. The Internet as a tool, a field, and location of research raises a number of questions related to the meaning and practice of ethical research. Internet research ethics constitutes another field of study and practice that digital religion researchers increasingly rely on for guidance on how to navigate the complexities of researching digital worlds. Internet research ethics do not exist in isolation from other ethical frameworks that inform research ethics. In fact, approaches to Internet research ethics should be deliberately formed by these existing frameworks (including utilitarianism, feminist ethics, deontological ethics, and virtue ethics) and in light of the various ways in which Internet research is conceived and deployed within the enterprise of academic knowledge production, should favor

56. Ronson, *So You've Been Publicly*.

57. Muir et al., "Portrayal of Online," 1.

58. Vogels et al., "Americans and 'Cancel Culture.'"

59. Johns, "Ethical Issues," 250.

being specific and discursive in orientation as opposed to overly general or specific. Furthermore, ethical decision-making in research should always be underwritten by the primary ethical principles, which are established as "respect for persons, beneficence, and justice."[60] The Association of Internet Researchers (AoIR) has emphasized Internet research ethics as an ongoing concern in scholarly conversations from a variety of disciplinary backgrounds. The association publishes and regularly updates a set of guidelines that are intended for researchers to consult. These guidelines are rooted in the principle of "ethical pluralism"[61] and emphasize the importance of cross-cultural awareness and consideration. This challenges African researchers to begin developing ethical guidelines and frames that reflect the unique conditions of the communities in which the research is located.

This chapter has mapped some of the theoretical, conceptual, methodological, empirical, and ethical potentials and possibilities for the study of religion and digital media in the African context. Through the empirical examples referred to, I have hoped to show just a small sample of the kinds of research possibilities that exist, and to inspire enthusiasm for this burgeoning area of inquiry on the continent. Although focused on the South African context, I hope that colleagues will add their voices to this conversation and consider the prospects that a focus on digitality and religiosity might yield within various social locations. While many other questions, trends, and foci could be considered important in the study of digital culture and religion, this chapter has sought to provide an introductory map to a few possibilities through expanding existing research and honoring the possibilities that are yet to be explored.

Bibliography

Africa, Keshia. "Top 5 TikTok Creators to Look Out for in 2022." January 2022. https://www.iol.co.za/weekend-argus/lifestyle/top-5-tiktok-creators-to-look-out-for-in-2022–48281 8fa-32c9–4bd8–8418-c745fa6c34ff.

Atton, Chris, and Hayes Mabweazara. "New Media and Journalism Practice in Africa: An Agenda for Research." *Journalism* 12 (2011) 667–73. https://doi.org/10.1177%2F1464884911405467

Becker, Felicitas, and Joel Cabrita. "Introduction: Religion, Media, and Marginality in Modern Africa." In *Religion, Media and marginality in Modern Africa*, edited by Felicitas Becker, Joel Cabrita, and Marie Rodet, 1–37. Ohio: Ohio University, 2018.

60. Franzke et al., "Internet Research," 2.

61. Franzke et al., "Internet Research,"5.

Beydoun, Khaled A. *American Islamophobia: Understanding the Roots and Rise of Fear.* Berkeley: University of California Press, 2018.

Campbell, Heidi A. "Surveying Theoretical Approaches within Digital Religion Studies." *New Media & Society* 19 (2017) 15–24. https://journals-sagepub-com.ezproxy.uct.ac.za/doi/pdf/10.1177/1461444816649912.

Campbell, Heidi A., and Guilia Evolvi. "Contextualizing Current Digital Religion Research on Emerging Technologies." *Human Behavior and Emerging Technologies* 2 (2020) 5–17.

Campbell, Heidi A., and Ruth Tsuria. *Digital Religion: Understanding Religious Practice in Digital* Media. New York: Routledge, 2022.

Chidester, David. *Religion: Material Dynamics.* Berkeley: University of California Press, 2018.

Darwin Holmes, Andrew G. "Researcher Positionality—A Consideration of Its Influence and Place in Qualitative Research—A New Researcher Guide." *International Journal of Education* 9 (2020) 1–10. https://doi.org/10.34293/education.v8i4.3232

De Witte, Marleen. "Media Afrikania: Styles and Strategies of Representing 'Afrikan Traditional Religion' in Ghana", in *New Religious Transformations in Africa*, edited by Rosalind I.J. Hackett and B. Soares, 207–26. Bloomington: Indiana University Press, 2015.

Dramat, Sakeenah. "Representations of Islam and Muslims on a Public Broadcast Television Programme in South Africa: A Case Study of An Nur The Light." Masters diss., University of the Western Cape, 2021. http://etd.uwc.ac.za/xmlui/handle/11394/8727.

Faimau, Gabriel, and William O. Lesitaokana, eds. *New Media and the Mediatisation of Religion: An African Perspective.* Newcastle, UK: Cambridge Scholars, 2018. https://www.cambridgescholars.com/product/978-71-5275-902-3.

Frahm-Arp, Maria. "Pentacostalism, Politics, and Prosperity in South Africa." *Religions* 9 (2018) 1–16. https://doi.org/10.3390/rel9100298.

Franzke Aline S. "Internet Research: Ethical Guidelines 3.0 Association of Internet Researchers." 2019. https://aoir.org/reports/ethics3.pdf.

Hjavard, Stig. "Mediatization and the Changing Authority of Religion." *Media, Culture & Society* 38 (2016) 8–17. https://journals.sagepub.com/doi/10.1177/0163443715615412.

Houtman, Dick, and Birgit Meyer, eds. *Things: Religion and the Question of Materiality.* New York: Fordham University Press, 2012.

Kavakci, Elif, and Camille R. Kraeplin. "Religious Beings in Fashionable Bodies: The Online Identity Construction of *Hijabi* Social Media Personalities." *Media, Culture & Society* 39 (2016) 850–68. https://doi.org/10.1177%2F0163443716679031.

Meyer, Birgit, ed. *Aesthetic Formations: Media, Religion, and the Senses.* London: Palgrave Macmillan, 2009. https://link.springer.com/book/10.1057/9780230623248.

Meyer, Birgit, and Annelies Moors, eds. "Religion, Media, and the Public Sphere." *Visual Anthropology* 21 (2008) 460–62. https://www.tandfonline.com/doi/abs/10.1080/08949460802342025?journalCode=gvan20.

Miller, Daniel, and Don Slater. *The Internet: An Ethnographic Approach.* New York: Berg, 2000.

Morgan, David. "Mediation or Mediatisation: The History of Media in the Study of Religion." *Culture and Religion* 12 (2011) 137–52. https://doi.org/10.1080/14755610.2011.579716.

Muir, Shannon R., et al. "The Portrayal of Online Shaming in Contemporary Online News Media: A Media Framing Analysis." *Computers in Human Behavior Reports* 3 (2021) 1–12. https://doi.org/10.1016/j.chbr.2020.100051.

Petersen, Ashleigh. "'He Asked Me to Pray Afterward': Exploring Cheryl Zondi's Mediated Court Testimony as a Narrative of Clergy Sexual Abuse. Master's diss., University of the Western Cape, 2021. http://etd.uwc.ac.za/xmlui/handle/11394/8747.

Ronson, Jon. *So You've Been Publicly Shamed.* New York: Riverhead, 2015.

Scharnick-Udemans, Lee. "Gender Perspectives and African Scholarship: Blind Spots in the Field of Religion, Media, and Culture." *Journal of Gender and Religion in Africa* 23 (2017) 145–63. https://journals.uj.ac.za/index.php/ajgr/article/view/866/504.

———. "Biographies and the Mediatization of Religion." *Religion & Education* 45 (2018) 11–124. https://doi.org/10.1080/15507394.2017.1407623.

Scharnick-Udemans, Lee-Shae S., and Rosalind Hackett. "Introduction: Religion and Gender in the Media Marketplace." *African Journal of Gender and Religion* 25 (2019) 1–13. https://journals.uj.ac.za/index.php/ajgr/article/view/874/512.

Schoon, Alette, et al. "Decolonising Digital Media Research Methods: Positioning African Digital Experiences as Epistemic Sites of Knowledge Production." *African Journalism Studies* 41 (2020) 1–15. https://doi.org/10.1080/23743670.2020.1865645.

Stokel-Walker, Chris. *TikTok Boom: China's Dynamite App and the Superpower Race for Social Media.* Surrey, UK: Canbury, 2021.

Strijdom, Johan. "The Material Turn in Religious Studies and the Possibility of Critique: Assessing Chidester's Analysis of 'the Fetish.'" *HTS Theological Studies* 70 (2014) 1–7.

Tsuria, Ruth, et al., "Approaches to Digital Methods in Studies of Digital Religion." *The Communication Review* 20 (2017) 73–97. http://dx.doi.org/10.1080/10714421.2017.1304137.

Tsuria, Ruth., and Heidi A. Campbell. "Introduction to the Study of Digital Religion." In *Digital Religion: Understanding Religious Practice in Digital Media*, edited by Heidi A. Campbell, and Ruth Tsuria, 1–21. New York: Routledge, 2022.

Vogels, Emily A. et al. "Americans and 'Cancel Culture': Where Some See Calls for Accountability, Others See Censorship, Punishment." May 2021. https://www.pewresearch.org/internet/2021/05/19/americans-and-cancel-culture-where-some-see-calls-for-accountability-others-see-censorship-punishment/.

Waisbord, Silvio. "My Vision for the Journal of Communication." *Journal of Communication* 65 (2015) 585–88.

Warren, Saskia. "Placing Faith in Creative Labour: Muslim Women and Digital Media Work in Britain." *Geoforum* 97 (2018) 1–9. https://doi.org/10.1016/j.geoforum.2018.10.003.

Part II

Interreligious Relations

Chapter 4

Dialogue in Interreligious Relations

Possible and Necessary?

Pieter Verster

Introduction

The relation among religions in the present hugely challenging world is extremely important. Dialogue helps enhance relations among religions. The viewpoints for approaching religions should be stated clearly. One should also explain the implications of dialogue for interreligious relations. A great deal can be inferred from the issues one mentions in dialogue, but it is necessary to understand that there are some shortcomings in dialogue. If the approach is not open and trustworthy, it can easily derail. To achieve this, one must lay down the principles that are important for structuring the dialogue in the best way possible. The most important issue it addresses is the issue of peace. Africa is radically in need of peace, and interreligious dialogue is needed to bring about peace. There are enormous challenges for Africa. Nihinlola[1] writes:

> Contemporary African life is characterized by poverty in almost every sphere of life—economic, social, political and religious. Many Africans cannot afford the basic human needs—good food, decent clothing and shelter. There is absence of peaceful

1. Nihinlola, "Human Development in Africa," 161.

> co-existence in many African societies due to political, religious and ethnic hostilities. Political leadership in many nations is marked by disorientation and perfidy. Quite unfortunately, the religious scene is full of deceit and bigotry.

Oyeshile[2] refers to the fact that poverty in Africa also deprives one of the fullness of life and that "there is visible misery, persistent destitution, endemic hunger or starvation and visible malnutrition, and World Bank gave the figure of 800 million as destitute in third world countries of which Africa is a part."

Oludahunsi[3] explains that the challenge now is to introduce peace in Africa, also among religions that are often in conflict with one another. Shocking statistics are still relevant: "An in-depth study of the condition of Africa shows that out of the world's 40 poorest nations, 32 are in Africa and out of these, about 13 are in abject poverty and almost in a stage of complete collapse."

Banglis[4] refers to massive challenges in Africa. Not only is there radical poverty in Africa, but there is also illness that leads to many deaths. Healthcare south of the Sahara is still a huge challenge and many are still living with and dying from HIV/AIDS, measles, and diseases such as malaria, diarrhea, and pneumonia. Some of these diseases can be cured, but access to healthcare is limited.

In such environments, religions ought to play a role of caring and helping. Often, conflict among religions leads to a worse situation. Wars and hate erupt, and even religions reject peace. One must find ways and means for religions to become instruments of peace and care. Dialogue is one way of holding discussions for peace, help, and the alleviation of poverty. It remains extremely important to empower people in Africa, and religions can play an important role. It is, however, necessary to enter into dialogue in order to achieve the best outcome. Religions must not be part of the problem, but part of the solution. One can only achieve this by respect for human beings and one another's religion, without disregarding one's commitment to one's own religion.

2. Oyeshile, "Democratic Governance in Africa," 39.
3. Oludahunsi, "Challenge to the Church," 90.
4. Banglis, "Concept of Work," 89.

Methodology and Aim

I will approach the literature study from the perspective of engaging scholars who pay attention to the rational evaluation of the differences between religions and the way in which religions can discuss these differences.[5] Melnik refers to the complexities and challenges of interreligious dialogue, which are regarded as very challenging. It asks much of the adherents of religions to enter into dialogue in order to seek peace. The most essential question is, is dialogue possible and how should it be accomplished? Is it possible to enter into dialogue when violence is present among religions? One must understand dialogue as the deep encounter and discussion between different entities to reach a better understanding of the other so as to obtain peace and new relations. It may also lead to acceptance of the other and their position. A deep encounter of the other is needed. It is also necessary to explain that people of faith enter into dialogue from the perspective of their own religions. Therefore, it is not the religions entering into dialogue with one another but the people of faith. I will discuss and evaluate the views and discuss my own perspective on dialogue. It refers to an understanding of the way in which modernity and postmodernity relate to dialogue, and how dialogue is viewed as important in the present world. It also refers to the ways in which dialogue should be established and how it could be understood. In the past, from a missiological perspective, dialogue was also extremely important. Very often, it was only the explanation of one's own religion to the other one, as the first way to convert the adherents of other religions. Migliore[6] explains that it is difficult to find common ground regarding the definition of religion. There are different views on the relations of human beings and a Supreme Being, and even the notion of a Supreme Being is sometimes challenged. The idea of the sacred is also explained as an essential concept in religions. Accepting all the differences, religions can be regarded as the concept of human beings seeking understanding beyond themselves.

The question is whether it is possible to have dialogue without preconditions. It must be established that dialogue is very difficult, because all of us discuss any topic from a certain perspective, and that perspective is established to guide us in our dialogue.

5. Melnik, "Interreligious Dialogue," 49.

6. Migliore, *Faith Seeking Understanding*, 301.

Melnik[7] writes:

> On the basis of the intention criterion, I distinguish four major types of interreligious dialogue: polemical, cognitive, peacemaking and partnership. Using such criteria as goal (what tasks do participants in interreligious dialogue set themselves?), principles (what principles lie behind the interaction?), and form (who participates in the dialogue and in what form is it expressed?) different kinds of each of the dialogue types can be identified and described.

Very often, dialogue is understood from these perspectives and when entering into dialogue with other people, one's own perspective is regarded as essential. Is it then possible to have genuine dialogue? Migliore[8] explains that one must realize that there are essential differences between religions and that dialogue should be regarded from the perspective of a specific religion, in order to avoid generalizations. Although it is not possible to be totally neutral in religion, because one cannot be totally acceptable to others in the sense that one does not have one's own position, one should enter into dialogue to establish a way in which to address the big questions of life and how other religions understand them, and to establish peace. One must be open and truthful without rejecting one's own position and one's own religion. From a Christian perspective, Migloire[9] writes:

> Dialogue between Christianity and the other religions is right and necessary because a proper understanding of the biblical message demands it and the search for peace and reconciliation in the world requires it.

Melnik[10] also explains the need for seeking peace:

> At the 'grass-root' level, especially among young people, the important goal of peacemaking dialogue is the prevention of extremist sentiments and strengthening of accord, mutual respect and friendship between representatives of various nationalities and religions. To achieve this goal, the following principles can be applied: learning more about one another's religions and cultural traditions; fostering mutual understanding by means of

7. Melnik, "Interreligious Dialogue," 54.
8. Migliore, *Faith Seeking Understanding*, 304–5.
9. Migliore, *Faith Seeking Understanding*, 328.
10. Melnik, "Interreligious Dialogue," 67.

> joint participation in socially beneficial activities; focusing on tolerance-promoting religious values; texts and stories about the life of various figures of spiritual authority; highlighting common historical and cultural background, and so on.

This kind of dialogue can also infer religious dialogue.

In Africa, it remains essential to have respect for all. Often in the past Africa was regarded as backward and African traditional religion as extremely primitive. In Africa, genuine dialogue will take all religions very seriously. Engagement will, however, always consider all aspects of the religions in the dialogue. It should never be simply accepting all aspects without also establishing in truth dangerous elements in all religions. From a Christian perspective, respect should be the influence of interreligious dialogue. There should always be a new call to new relations, but always with regard for one's own position. One of the most challenging aspects is whether it is possible to enter into dialogue when violence, abduction and war is present, such as in Nigeria. One should regard the challenges in this regard as extremely difficult. Again people of faith should seek to enter into dialogue to seek peace.

The Background to Dialogue

Swidler[11] refers to dialogue. He describes how modernity laid the foundation of rationalism, along with freedom and dynamism. These three aspects of modernity are important to view the way in which one enters into dialogue. Dialogue is necessary because rationality is important. Therefore, different views emerge and one understands that one does not know everything. Views of modernity are characterized by reason, freedom, awareness, dynamism, and dialogue. Swidler understands that one does not simply accept dialogue; it should be practiced. Swidler[12] understood it in the following way:

> I have only adumbrated the depth and breadth of the dialogues that are constant and pervasive both in our humanness and in the whole of the universe, on both the macro and micro levels. It should thus be clear that all of reality, the whole of the cosmos, and its Source, however understood, is foundationally dialogic.

11. Swidler, "Modernity," 458.

12. Swidler, "Modernity," 460.

> In brief, the whole of the universe is fundamentally a 'cosmic dance of dialogue' in which we humans are the lead dancers!

Dialogue is also important for understanding religion in Africa, as explained by Nkuiu-N'Sengha.[13] Interreligious dialogue is at the heart of Africa. Religious dialogue is essential in the landscape of Sub-Saharan Africa. There is a high need for dialogue with the Muslims, of whom Christians have a negative perspective. They should enter into dialogue with them for a better perspective and relations with one another. Although dialogue is important, it is sometimes hindered by the fact that some Africans view identity as being challenged by interreligious dialogue.

Why is dialogue so important in Africa? Because the other option is hate and strife. This is necessary in light of the deep rejection of many people's humanity. One does not reject one's own position, but one enters into dialogue to accept the other person's humanity before God. A new commitment to humility in religions is needed in Africa. This will lead to understanding the other without rejecting the essential elements of one's own religion. Mission remains possible in a new way, by regarding the other highly.

Kärkkäinen[14] writes in this regard:

> No doubt the existence of and communication among world religions is the most significant challenge to and opportunity for the Christian church in the new millennium. With regard to theology, it is no longer possible to limit the consideration of theological topics to the Christian sphere; we must take into account the questions and answers posed by other religions. This state of affairs naturally raises a host of questions that are not totally new (for Christianity emerged in a polytheistic, multireligious environment and continued to flourish side by side with other confessions), but that have gained a new urgency because of globalization.

The Principles of Dialogue

Swidler[15] explains that humankind should understand life and work in the sense of dialogue. There should be a cosmic dance of dialogue:

13. Nkuiu-N'Sengha, "Hearth of Africa," 175.
14. Kärkkäinen, *Theology of Religions*, 17.
15. Swidler, "Modernity," 465.

> Dialogue—understood in the broadest manner as the mutually beneficial interaction of differing components—is at the very heart of the cosmos, of which we humans are the highest expression: from the basic interaction of matter and energy (in Einstein's unforgettable formula, E=MC2; energy equals mass times the square of the speed of light), to the creative interaction of protons and electrons in every atom, to the vital symbiosis of body and spirit in every human, through the creative dialogue between woman and man, to the dynamic relationship between individual and society. Thus, the very essence of our humanity is dialogical, and a fulfilled human life is the highest expression of the "cosmic dance of dialogue.

Swindler[16] continues:

> If our actions are to be compatible with critical-thinking and deep-dialogue, they must strive toward being competitive-cooperative . . . If we have begun to engage the world in a deeply dialogical manner and have critically analyzed/synthesized our perceptions and thoughts, we will want to make decisions on their bases and carry out our actions in the world in an analogously dialogic/critical manner. I am suggesting that the most appropriate way to describe such action is "competitive-cooperation.

Therefore, it is very important to be committed to the following aspects, namely openness to the other, learning from the other, not making caricatures of the other, understanding the other in his or her situation, listening to the other's viewpoint, and establishing a way of relating to one another in this dialogue.

Engaging the other one should take the situation into account. Analysis is necessary. In this regard, Kritzinger[17] refers to the tools used for dialogue:

> A crucial question in this enterprise concerns the 'tools' used to analyze a context, since every analysis is a social 'construct'. There is no such thing as objective reality 'in itself', which one can discover with absolute certainty provided one uses the 'correct' analytical tools. Every context analysis is constructed in terms of the ideological framework adopted by the person making the analysis.

16. Swidler, "Global Dialogue," 471–72.

17. Kritzinger, "Contextual Christian Theology," 219–20.

It is, therefore, always necessary to explain one's own position. In Africa, with the massive challenges of political and social strife, it is necessary to show how one would regard one's own analysis. Only when one's own presuppositions are totally clear can there be genuine dialogue with reference to true humanity. Returning to the most essential question in the beginning, the answer is that dialogue is necessary because the alternative is rejection and hate of the other.

Openness to the Other

It is crucial to enter into dialogue without preconceived ideas about the other. One should always be in a relation of trust. This is, however, very difficult and one must understand that dialogue is not so easy, especially to establish it in the way in which one enters into dialogue with others. No one enters into dialogue with a clean sheet. It is, however, necessary to try to obtain a position of trust. This is extremely difficult when challenged by violence and war. Only by seeking radical peace will it be possible to enter into dialogue. One must always be clear that dialogue is an establishment of relations, and relations of human beings are always very difficult and intricate to establish. Therefore, one should always enter into dialogue from a position of humbleness, where one accepts that, from one's own position, one does not have all the aspects of life ready, but that one enters into dialogue to learn from the others openly and to listen to others.

Swidler[18] explains that these aspects of dialogue are extremely important. Secularization of communities, also in Africa, leads to new relations with religions and one should understand that dialogue must always be approached in truth. The danger is that "dialogue" becomes a faddish term. One should be aware that one does not know all the truth but that one enters into dialogue from the point of view that one understands and relates to the other person, so that one should regard one's own knowledge as limited. A paradigm shift to "de-absolutize" the understanding of truth emerged. Swidler states that "understanding of truth and reality has been undergoing a radical shift." This "new paradigm understands all statements of reality," be they historical, intentional, perceptible, "partial interpretive and dialogic." A notion of rationality is emerging which is that "all expressions" of understanding "reality are in some fundamental way related to the speaker."

18. Swidler, "Dialogosphere," 6.

> In sum, our understanding of truth and reality has been undergoing a radical shift. This new paradigm understands all statements about reality to be historical, intentional, perspectival, partial, interpretive, and dialogic. What is common is the notion of relationality, that is, all expressions or understandings of reality are in some fundamental way related to the speaker, the knower. Thus, if everything I learn about reality is necessarily shaped by my perception, that reality, then neither I nor anyone else can ever know every aspect of anything. Then how can anyone come ever closer to fully perceiving reality as it is "out there," the *Ding an sich*, the "thing in Itself," as Immanuel Kant named it? The answer is: by dialogue with those who perceive aspects of reality that I cannot perceive from my perspective, which is an endless task.[19]

It is necessary in Africa to be open to the other. Respect is possible if one regards the other highly and enters into dialogue with the other. A non-judgmental position is essential. Sometimes this is hard to obtain. Judgment of the other is part of humanity. When war and violence are present, it is sometimes nearly impossible to obtain. One should, however, reject the other possibility of hatred and more violence. Religions can help one perceive one's own shortcomings and start to live for others. Being open to the other enables one to achieve new ways of living. To achieve this, it is necessary to be open to the other's needs and to the challenges of poverty, illnesses, rejection, and want. Genuine dialogue can start once the other person is regarded as fully human. One must, however, engage fully with the other in order to understand the other's predicament. When this is achieved, new relations can become a reality.

To Learn from the Other

It is very difficult to be totally open to and understand other persons in a most positive way. Therefore, it is always necessary to look at oneself, one's own position, one's own beliefs, before entering into dialogue with openness to learn from others. A crucial aspect of dialogue is not to reject one's own position, but to seek peace with others, because one has to seek and obtain peace in the world at present. This is only possible if there is openness to learn from others. If one understands one's own position, it is also possible to learn from the other person.

19. Swidler, "Dialogosphere," 11.

The possibility to sit around a table to discuss and learn from the other must always be a reality. In these discussions, serious issues such as xenophobia must be on the agenda. There is always the danger of xenophobia in Africa, with a strong emphasis on tribe and group. Unemployment and poverty intensify the problem. Religion also plays a role. Dialogue is necessary in order to learn more about the position of the other. By learning from the other, new relations are possible and respect for the other can be enhanced. This can lead to a new position regarding the other and the rejection of xenophobic attacks. Dialogue may help address the issue in an appropriate way. The danger is that the issue is not addressed in a way that is beneficial to all. Discussions in this regard should also include immigrants and their religions, in order to address the issue of xenophobia.

Not to Make Caricatures of the Other

Varner[20] shows that in the wake of Jewish-Christian dialogue in the third to the sixth centuries, it was important not to make caricatures of one another. He refers to the fact that in the early days Christians and Jews held many dialogues such as, for example, those of Athanasius and Zacchaeus, Simon and Theophilus, as well as Timothy and Aquila. The Jewish-Christian dialogues refer to the absolute importance of biblical witness in these dialogues. They examined contradictory statements and how they entered into dialogue from Old Testament scripture. Isaiah and the Psalms are very important. Varner writes:[21]

> Even with acknowledging these valid observations, it is still probable that these dialogues represent an authentic discussion that was being carried on between the faiths. For example, the very existence of these dialogues plus the abundance of them should argue for their basic authenticity.

Christian-Hindu dialogue should also be held in truth. Klostermaier[22] refers to the issue of exclusive truth. Absolute truth should, according to him, be laid to rest. He also refers to the different influences in dialogues. The issue of what is truth is very important. This should receive attention in dialogue. The issue of absolute objective truth must

20. Varner, "Jewish-Christian," 232.

21. Varner, "Jewish Christian," 234.

22. Klostermaier, *Hindu-Christian*, 160–70.

be discussed. The value of the living traditions is important, but to provide information becomes real truth and self-realization. Liberation and religion must provide one with wisdom. Klostermaier[23] writes:

> Both agree also in maintaining that there is in humanity an urge toward Truth and Reality which keeps it going despite all untruth and unreality, an urge that 'opens' up the human world into the infinite. This urge in humanity cannot be fully rationalized; it partakes already of the nature of Truth, points to a Reality that is not simply the sum total of all experiential finite realities, but different in quality.

Dialogue with Islam has serious challenges. Oh[24] mentions that the issue of freedom of conscience emerges as one enters into dialogue with Muslims concerning the issue of human rights. He refers to the capabilities approach regarding possibilities and limitations and to the duty of human rights, woman in dialogue. He opines that, due to its importance, human rights can form a basis for entering into dialogue.

Wani, Abdullah, and Chang[25] refer to the question of diversity in the Quran, that it is a law of nature, and that it cannot be changed, while identity is a contested issue. Communalities must be sought. Civilizational dialogue is, therefore, needed. According to Wani, Abdullah, and Chang, diversity is mentioned in the Quran. The so-called clash-of-civilizations dialogue does not lead to acceptable conclusions. It is essential to seek reconciliation and transformation. Wani, Abdullah, and Chang[26] refer to two conditions for successful dialogue. It should be conducted in a way that one accepts the other person as well as the other person's religious books and background, and that we accept diversity as the divine plan. Intolerance and extremism are a reality and various mechanisms should be used to defeat this menace, for instance, "peace, education centerization, civilization, dialogue, civilizational dialogue, tolerance, conferences, joint sports and exchange of ideas made the ways forward to present unity in diversity."[27] This is one of the most challenging aspects of dialogue for people of faith. Sometimes one can regard dialogue between

23. Klostermaier, *Hindu-Christian*, 170.

24. Oh, "Ethics," 410.

25. Wani et al., "Islamic Perspective," 645–47.

26. Wani et al., "Islamic Perspective," 651.

27. Wani et al., "Islamic Perspective," 659.

Christians and Muslims as totally impossible. The only possible way forward is to seek peace with all their hearts.

This does not mean that the uniqueness of one's own religion is rejected. Kärkkäinen[28] refers in this regard to an Asian Anglican and writes:

> Ramachandra's theology of religions is inclusivist in the sense that it refuses to limit the saving grace of God to the members of the Christian church, but it rejects the inclusivism that regards the non-Christian religions as vehicles of salvation. It is pluralist in the sense that it acknowledges the gracious work of God in the lives of all human beings, but it rejects a pluralism that denies the uniqueness and decisiveness of what God has done in Jesus Christ.

In Africa, it is extremely important to accept the other person and not to make caricatures of the other person's position. One must regard all as human beings, also in their religions. Many xenophobic attacks are the result of caricatures of the other. Dialogue can help bring about true humanity. Dialogue should address the question of how one regards the other, even though the other may differ totally from one. Many caricatures of people in Africa are used to downgrade the other person. Dialogue is necessary to end these views.

To Understand the Other in His or Her Situation

Johnson's[29] article on dialogue in a school in Belgium pays attention to the issue of dialogue with Muslims in that country. How this should be established and realized in that country, where there are many Catholics and Muslims, should receive attention on how to enter into dialogue with one another. It is established that many schools in Belgium enter into dialogue with Muslim people. This leads to a better understanding of the other.

Turnau[30] addresses the question of Christian engagement in a post-Christian context. He refers to the fact that we are now living in a post-Christian world, but that a roundtable must be established. He explains that one should be committed to cultural change, to spiritual formation in the community, and to a practical faithful presence of the common good. Turnau explains that the post-Christian world in which we live and

28. Kärkkäinen, *Theology of Religions*, 340.

29. Johnson, "Belgium," 84–91.

30. Turnau, "Cultural Engagement Part 2," 25.

its challenges call for dialogue from a kind of roundtable where people should discuss with one another the issue of the roundtable. He mentions that there should be critical engagement of the Christian story in these dialogues.[31] Therefore, even in a secular community dialogue leads to a better understanding of the other. Love for God and love for others should be essential in dialogue; contextualization is not a threat, but helpful in this situation.

Johansson[32] refers to the fact that, although many aspects of religion are emerging in Iceland, the claims of absolute truth are problematic. How should that be understood? He refers to the Christians' feeling of superiority. One must seek a solution. According to him, a new paradigm is needed. Compassion, a very important issue in all religions, should be emphasized and is crucial.

Without minimizing Christianity's claim of truth, one needs to listen to the other in order to engage in the other's life. This is extremely important in an Africa of poverty and want. One can address this only when one has regard for the other. Dialogue is necessary to realize how broken the world is. Being broken also means that one will accept that the other also has many challenges and that it is necessary to reach out to the other. In Africa one must be very careful to try entering into dialogue from a clean slate. In this broken continent one must enter into dialogue from the perspective of brokenness.

To Listen to the Other's Viewpoint

Freeman[33] explains that one should listen to other viewpoints:

> here is a difference between being knowledgeable about religions other than your own and having been exposed to different religions. The problem for interreligious relations and dialogue arises when one is exposed to various religions without having any knowledge of the histories, traditions, and principles of these religions. It is possible that this exposure without knowledge can create a problem when people from different religions are forced to live and work together. This problem can possibly be cleared up, or at the very least be unravelled, by an openness to dialogue.

31. Turnau, "Cultural Engagement Part 1," 69.
32. Jóhannsson, "Religion," 37–39.
33. Freeman, "Models for Interreligious Dialogue," 214.

Does this mean that one rejects one's own religion and that one does not perceive how one's religion should be established and explained to others? No, this is not true. One always enters into dialogue from one's own position. One regards one's own position as very important. One establishes and explains one's own position to the other person in a very intricate way. One must understand and work with one's own religion in a very important way. One does not even leave behind the claim of truth of one's own religion, but one listens attentively to the other.

Clifford[34] refers to the Second Vatican Council in 1962–1965 and how dialogue became important at the Council and how that should be understood in a new way. Vatican 2 regarded as relevant dialogue with society and culture, other religions, and other Christian churches. Within the Catholic Church, community itself became an important aspect of dialogue. The Council taught that dialogue with humanity is highly important. Clifford[35] mentions that it is important for the missionary task of the church to enter into dialogue with other religions. Dialogue within the church and with others led to the fact that there are so many Catholics in the world that the figure has doubled since 1962. This was viewed as positive for the pastoral life of the church.

Paul's[36] article on the role of interreligious dialogue in religious studies programs at Indonesian state Islamic universities emphasizes how an academic study of religion can be used to enter into dialogue with different religious groups. It explains how Islam is taught at universities and how religious studies should be approached in that sense. The current trends differ from the previous ones. One should enter into dialogue to understand the interfaith relation of people and how that should be established. It is, however, different from the Western approach and should be established in a different way. Although it is different, it should also be in a relation with a growing body of scholars in the Western world.

Moyaert[37] asks whether we are examining the form of exclusivism and the end of dialogue. Therefore, a postliberal theology of religions is emphasized. Dialogue remains a fundamental theological principle. She challenges postliberalism and refers to a "Theological Trajectory namely a) creation, b) ecclesiology, c) anthropology." Dialogue is the basic

34. Clifford, "Vatican II," 40.

35. Clifford, "Vatican II," 41–42.

36. Paul, "Islamic," 163–66.

37. Moyaert, "Interreligious Dialogue," 70.

principle of theology in creation and postliberalism and the Trinity. She warns against the fact that, in understanding some of the views, religious dialogue becomes absolute, and that people do not want to learn from other religions. Religious dialogue becomes the expression of a group interest and ends in a form of exclusion.

Interreligious relations should be established and therefore dialogue is even more necessary in the present world, with the dangerous situation in which we live. There are many different worldviews in Africa. Often, these worldviews are exclusive. There must be a definite and radical attempt to reach out to the other in this regard. Listening to the other's worldview enables one to reach out to the other about dialogue concerning religions.

To Establish a Way of Relating to One Another in This Dialogue

Joas[38] refers to the fact that the most important aspect of dialogue can be the personhood of God.

> What we find in the contemporary intellectual landscape of dialogical thinking, therefore, is a rich variety of sources that can be compared or contrasted with one another. This also makes us aware that it is a myth if the Western intellectual tradition is presented as being completely dominated by a nondialogical understanding: a possessive individualism, a monological understanding of subjectivity, epistemological solipsism. This "Western" tradition has never been so uniform. What is true for the British tradition often is not true for the French or the German or the Russian traditions; what is true for Protestantism often does not apply to Catholicism or Judaism. I think it still makes sense to defend and propagate the superiority of a dialogical or intersubjectivist approach, but one has to do that without proclaiming an epochal rupture with all previous thinking.

Illman[39] refers to the power relations in dialogue. He requests a new face for interreligious dialogue. An attack on a Buddhist temple in Finland shows the problems of reciprocity in dialogue. Is reciprocity in dialogue a necessary condition for dialogue?[40] He writes:[41]

38. Joas, "Problem of Dialogue," 107.

39. Illman, "Reciprocity and Power," 49.

40. Illman, "Reciprocity and Power," 59.

41. Illman, "Reciprocity and Power," 60.

> The intricate balance between distance and unity, alterity and proximity, trust and vulnerability described in this article—and the responsibility connected to such balancing act can be regarded as the central axis around which this argument revolves. Therefore, I claim, there is a continuous need to explore the creative ruptures in the traditional dialogue canopy created by nonbinary ways of approaching the subject.

Relations among people can be enhanced if one can understand the other person's own position. This can be achieved by means of dialogue and by engaging the others in new relations. Communities are important in Africa. Relations between communities are also important for the larger groups. Dialogue must seek to bring communities together.

Conclusion

From a Christian perspective, Kärkkäinen[42] explains the way in which dialogue between religions can develop:

> While Christian theology of religions is not the only form of theology of religions, it is by far the most developed currently. Yet to be seen are the results and implications when theologies of religions from various world religions begin to talk with each other. Until now, we have only had representatives of various religions speak to each other in interfaith dialogues; a next step will be taken when Buddhist, Hindu, Taoist, and other theologians of religions begin to dialogue and perhaps carry out common research projects. Whether that will lead to the kind of 'neutral' search for the truth that Wolfhart Pannenberg predicts nobody can say. Whatever the form of that kind of dialogue, it will probably raise interfaith dialogue to a new level.

There are clearly enormous challenges to dialogue. It is crucial that one should always enter totally humbly into such discussions. The moment one enters conceitedly into dialogue, it leads nowhere. This does not mean that one must not regard one's own religion highly. Nor does it mean that one wants to explain all aspects of one's religion for the benefit of the other. The key is to obtain peace. Religions are often the vehicle of conflict, hate, and war. It is necessary to do one's utmost to bring about peace. To enter into dialogue with other religions is an important way of achieving this. Some religions would be more hesitant to enter into

42. Kärkkäinen, *Theology of Religions*, 354.

dialogue than others, but one must find a way to seek peace. In Africa, this means that all efforts must be made to seek relations between people. Africa is beset with massive challenges, even on religious grounds, and the way to solve this is by seeking peace.

Returning to the essential question in the beginning, namely whether dialogue is possible and how it should be accomplished, the answer is that it is possible even under extreme circumstances of war and violence if it is achieved by being humble and broken. Both parties should ascribe to this position. If it is not achieved, one should try again and again. Peace must be achieved. The other possibility is too ghastly to contemplate.

In Africa, the call for dialogue is crucial. It is radically necessary:

- to seek respect for humanity,
- to enhance new relations,
- to deal with the extreme challenges,
- to look beyond the present to the future,
- to seek common ground in dealing with poverty,
- to help one another seek peace,
- to be instruments of peace in both Africa and the world,
- to help communities stop xenophobia,
- to have full respect for the truth of one's own religion but also to reach out to others,
- to engage all communities in the area to help them make new relations with others.

In Africa, political challenges presently prevail. Peace is needed. Religions are also sometimes instruments of hate, conflict, and war. With respect to the position of the other, one can seek ways and means to honor the other, to establish new hope. In this regard, dialogue is one instrument among others to establish new relations.

Bibliography

Banglis, Webuin Rudolf. "The Concept of Work in Proverbs 6:6–11 and Its Relevance to Poverty Eradication in Africa." *Ogbomoso Journal of Theology* 14/2 (2009) 87–103.

Clifford, Catherine, E. "Learning from the Council: A Church in Dialogue." *Theoforum* 44 (2013) 27–46.

Freeman, Tessa. "Theology of Religions: Models for Interreligious Dialogue in South Africa." In *Perspectives on Theology of Religions*, edited by Jaco Beyers, 148–223. HTS Theological Studies / Teologiese Studies Supplement 12. https://doi.org/10.4102/hts.v73i6.4885.

Illman, Ruth. "Reciprocity and Power in Philosophies of Dialogue: The Burning of a Buddhist Temple in Finland." *Studies in Interreligious Dialogue* 21/1 (2011) 47–63.

Jackelén, Antje, and Philip J. Hefner. "Concluding Dialogue: Challenging the Past, Grasping the Future." *Zygon* 39/2 (2004) 401–12.

Joas, Hans. "Martin Buber and the Problem of Dialogue in Contemporary Thought." *Journal of Jewish Thought and Philosophy* 25/1 (2017) 105–9.

Johnston, Laurie. "The Dialogue School in Belgium." *Concilium* 2020 4 (2020) 84–91.

Jóhannsson, Hjörtur Magni. "Religion, the Problem or the Solution?" *Dialogue & Alliance* 28/1 (2014) 36–41.

Kärkkäinen, Veli-Matti. *An Introduction to the Theology of Religions: Biblical, Historical and Contemporary Perspectives*. Downers Grove, IL: IVP Academic, 2003.

Klostermaier, Klaus K. "Hindu-Christian Dialogue on Truth." *Journal of Ecumenical Studies* 12/2 (1975) 157–71.

Kritzinger, Johannes Nicolaas Jacobus. "A Contextual Christian Theology of Religions." *Missionalia* 19/3 November (1991) 215–31.

Melnik, Sergey. "Types of Interreligious Dialogue." *Journal of Interreligious Studies* 31 (November 2020) 48–72.

Migliore, Daniel L. *Faith Seeking Understanding: An Introduction to Christian Theology*. Grand Rapids: Eerdmans 2004.

Moyaert, Marianne. "Postliberalism, Religious Diversity, and Interreligious Dialogue: A Critical Analysis of George Lindbeck's Fiduciary Interests." *Journal of Ecumenical Studies* 47/1 (2012) 64–86.

Nihinlola, Emiola. "Poverty and a Theology of Human Development in Africa." *Ogbomoso Journal of Theology* 14/1 (2009) 161–75.

Nkulu-N'Sengha, Mutombo. "From Philadelphia to Kamina: Bumuntu Interreligious Dialogue in the Heart of Africa." *Journal of Ecumenical Studies* 50/1 (2015) 174–81.

Oh, Irene. "Approaching Islam: Comparative Ethics Through Human Rights." *Journal of Religious Ethics* 36/3 (2008) 405–23.

Oludahunsi, Joshua K. "Poverty in Africa: A Challenge to the Church." *Ogbomoso Journal of Theology* 10 (2005) 90–99.

Oyeshile, Olatunji A. "Poverty and Democratic Governance in Africa." *Ogbomoso Journal of Theology* 14/1 (2009) 37–48.

Pohl, Florian. "On the Role of Interreligious Dialogue in Religious Studies Programs at Indonesian State Islamic Universities." *Journal of Ecumenical Studies* 50/1 (2015) 159–66.

Ristau, Harold. "'Lest We Forget'": Forgetting and Remembering in the Art of Hermeneutics and Dialogue." *Dialogue & Alliance* 29/1 (2015) 60–69.

Swidler, Leonard. "Dialogue: The Latest Mark of Modernity." *Journal of Ecumenical Studies* 53/4 (2018) 453–60.

———. "The 'Dialogue of Civilizations' at the Tipping Point: The 'Dialogosphere.'" *Journal of Ecumenical Studies* 50/1 (2015) 3–17.

———. "Humankind from the Age of Monologue to the Age of Global Dialogue." *Journal of Ecumenical Studies* 47/3 (2012) 463–77.

Turnau, Ted. "Dialogues Concerning Cultural Engagement: Part One." *Foundations (Affinity)* 70 (2016) 31–78.

———. "Dialogues Concerning Cultural Engagement: Part Two." *Foundations (Affinity)* 71 (2016) 5–25.

Varner, William. "In the Wake of Trypho: Jewish-Christian Dialogues in the Third to the Sixth Centuries." *Evangelical Quarterly* 80/3 (2008) 219–36.

Wani, Hilal, Raihanah Abdullah, and Lee Wei Chang. "An Islamic Perspective in Managing Religious Diversity." *Religions* 6/2 (2015) 642–56.

Chapter 5

Christian-Muslim Relations in Africa

Chances and Challenges of Dialogue, Relations, and Cooperation

Margaret Makafui Tayviah

Introduction

Religion plays an important role in many contemporary societies in the world. According to Leonard Swidler, at the heart of dialogue is interreligious dialogue, because religion is the most comprehensive of all the human "disciplines," since religion is "an explanation of the ultimate meaning of life, and how to live accordingly."[1] Therefore, religious people should have the chance to dialogue, interact and relate with each other. Basically, dialogue in any form creates the opprotunity of, "I can learn from you, and you can learn from me." In the same way, religious people may also have challenges in the way they dialogue or relate with each other. This article is limited to Christian-Muslim relations and since Christian-Muslim relations are studied contextually, this paper focuses on the chances and challenges of dialogue, relations, and cooperation between Christians and Muslims in West Africa, and Ghana in particular. This paper seeks to suggest that although there may be challenges to the way Christians and Muslims dialogue, relate, and cooperate in many West African countries, the chances and opportunities for these two religious

1. Swidler, "History of Inter-Religious Dialogue," 3.

adherents are greater and can be used to promote good-neighborliness in the subregion.

Dialogue

Dialogue is when two or more people have a conversation or discussion. In other words, dialogue is an exchange of opinions by two or more people. Dialogue, in its ideal form, involves a conversation or exchange in which participants are willing to listen to and learn from one another.[2] According to Catherine Cornille, dialogue has become increasingly common in describing or prescribing the proper relationship between religions. Religions have also adopted dialogue as a more conciliatory and constructive attitude toward one another, by collaborating in social projects and exchanging views on common religious questions rather than competing with one another over territories, converts, or claims.[3]

Thus, through dialogue, people appreciate each other while they seek cooperation for the pursuit of common goals and coexist peacefully. Although dialogue is often used as a peaceful way of interacting and exchanging views, it can also lead to debates and arguments. In today's pluralistic world, dialogue is positively used and has become much more important and necessary because it enables religious traditions to interact and cooperate peacefully. Dialogue also helps religious people to understand each other in order to curb or prevent misunderstandings, which tend to be a source of religious conflict in many societies. "Dialogue" as a term is "used to cover a wide range of engagements between religious traditions, from daily interaction between believers living in the same neighborhoods to organized discussions and debates between expert scholars, and from formal or casual exchanges between spiritual or institutional leaders to inter-religious activism around social issues."[4]

Although the aims or goals of dialogues may differ, the common denominator in all these forms of interreligious engagement is mutual respect and openness to the possibility of learning from the other.[5]

2. Cornille, "Conditions for Inter-Religious Dialogue," 20.

3. Cornille, "Introduction," xii.

4. Cornille, "Introduction," xii.

5. Cornille, "Introduction," xii.

Interfaith or Interreligious Dialogue

"Interfaith dialogue" and "interreligious dialogue" are often used interchangeably to mean a conversation, discussion, or interaction between two or more adherents of different faiths or religions. Sergey Melnik states that the establishment of positive relationships between followers of different religions is usually called "interreligious dialogue."[6] On the hand, Catherine Cornille also defines "interreligious dialogue" as a term used to refer to any form or degree of constructive engagement between religious traditions.[7]

Terrence Merrigan posits that everyone uses the term "interreligious dialogue" but no one is able to explain it because even the term "dialogue" is probably the most ambiguous term that has developed around the challenge to religions posed by globalization and pluralization.[8] According to Merrigan, if one scratches the surface of the term "dialogue," a whole range of interrelated issues arises, including questions about the precise aims of dialogue, the appropriate (or necessary) conditions for dialogue, the topics to be discussed (or avoided) during dialogue, and the criteria for evaluating the success (or meaningfulness) of dialogue.[9] Therefore, it appears that interreligious dialogue is a complex and many-faceted phenomenon.[10]

Interfaith or interreligious dialogue allows people of different religions or faiths to mutually appreciate, tolerate, respect, and understand each other's way of doing things. Interfaith or interreligious dialogue can be done at both individual and institutional levels with the intention that each party remains true to their own beliefs while they respect the rights and practices of the other.[11] It can take place between individuals and communities and on many levels. In Ghana, for instance, dialogue takes place in the everyday lives of citizens as well as in both formal and informal settings: in schools, places of work, and in the community. Christians and Muslims in Ghana belong to the same family, tribe or clan, ethnic group, and community; live with each other as neighbors; use the same markets, shops, and transport services; attend the same schools; and share the same

6. Melnik, "Types of Interreligious Dialogue", 48.
7. Cornille, "Introduction," xii.
8. Merrigan, "Introduction," 2.
9. Merrigan, "Introduction," 2.
10. Moyaert, "Interreligious Dialogue," 201–12.
11. The "other" here means a person of a different faith or religious background.

social amenities. This kind of dialogue is what has been termed as "dialogue of life"[12] because it involves daily contact or the way people live their normal lives with each other in the community. In other words, the dialogue of life creates an atmosphere of good-neighborliness and peaceful coexistence. Interfaith or interreligious dialogue does not deal with mere talks or conversations but also involves interaction and relationships. This is to say that the goal or objective of interfaith or interreligious dialogue is peace, and therefore the process of dialogue must be peaceful.

Types or Levels of Interfaith or Interreligious Dialogue

Since interfaith or interreligious dialogue is a multifaceted phenomenon, classifying its types or levels calls for more research. In this paper, the various types or levels of interfaith or interreligious dialogue will be discussed.

The Roman Catholic Church classified interfaith or interreligious dialogue into four types: dialogue of theological exchange (theological dialogue, dialogue of study), dialogue of religious experience (dialogue of spirituality, spiritual dialogue), dialogue of action, and dialogue of life.[13]

Thomas Thangaraj similarly discusses four levels of interfaith or interreligious dialogue[14] as follows:

1. **Dialogue of life:** People live together in an open and neighborly spirit, sharing their joy and sorrows, their human problems and preoccupations.
2. **Dialogue of action**: People of all religions collaborate for integral development.
3. **Dialogue of theological exchange**: Religious leaders seek to deepen their understanding of their respective religious heritages and to appreciate each other's spiritual values.
4. **Dialogue of religious experience**: Persons with much knowledge of their religious traditions share their spiritual riches about prayer and contemplation, faith, and ways of searching for God or the Absolute.

12. Samwini, "Dialogue of Life."

13. Pontifical Council for Interreligious Dialogue, "Dialogue and Proclamation."

14. Thangaraj, *Common Task*, 95–96. See also, Pontifical Council for Interreligious Dialogue, "Dialogue and Proclamation," no. 42.

Consequently, the aforementioned types of interfaith or interreligious dialogue gave rise to another form of classification: "head" (where religious people use their intellectual abilities for exploring another religion), "heart" (where religious people gain insight into the perspective of the religious experience of the other), "hands" (undertaking practical activities), and "daily life." Hence, the theological, spiritual, and practical kinds of interreligious dialogue are sometimes respectively called "dialogue of head," "dialogue of heart," and "dialogue of hands."[15] Leonard Swidler further theorizes interreligious dialogue in three primary modes: reaching out to learn from other religions/ideologies more fully the meaning of life (dialogue of the head), joining with the other to make the world a better place in which to live (dialogue of hands), and an awe-filled embrace of the inner spirit and aesthetic expressions of the other (dialogue of heart).[16]

Irrespective of the type of interfaith or interreligious dialogue, dialogue, conversation, and relations consequently seek to explore the differences and deepen the understanding of the other's faith. Through interfaith or interreligious dialogue, religious people learn about their prejudices and blind spots about the other as well as discover new insights about their own faith and religious tradition. Interfaith or interreligious dialogue helps religious people to work together for peace and peaceful coexistence. Catherine Cornille sets some conditions for interfaith or interreligious dialogue. According to her, humility, commitment, interconnection, empathy, and hospitality are the conditions for interfaith or interreligious dialogue. However, she suggests that mutual learning should be the goal of all interfaith or interreligious dialogue, since religious people learn from each other.[17]

Christian-Muslim Relations in Africa

Islam and Christianity are both monotheistic religions with a belief in one God. Christian-Muslim relations are when Christians and Muslims live, dialogue, interact, and relate with each other. In many parts of Africa, and Ghana in particular, Christians and Muslims live in the same community and agree that their daily lives or day-to-day relations are

15. Melnik, "Types of Interreligious Dialogue", 50.

16. Swidler, "History of Inter-Religious Dialogue", 5–6.

17. Cornille, "Conditions for Inter-Religious Dialogue," 21–29.

harmonious except for some tensions, which may probably arise because of politics. Although many African constitutions are against the formation of parties based on a religion or ethnic group, some African countries have witnessed this and this can be destructive to peace and good relations among members of a community.[18] Many African countries like Ghana, Nigeria, Togo, and others may have their peace threatened by the "politicisation of religion and the religionisation of politics," as will be discussed later. Since Africa is home to both Christians and Muslims, their different views and strong missionary enthusiasm can easily lead to conflicts between adherents of the two religions, yet this atmosphere can also create the possibility for Christians and Muslims to mutually respect, understand, and live together. Thus, there is no place in Africa where one would not find Christians and Muslims. In many parts of Africa, Christians and Muslims live together and practice the "dialogue of life." That is, they attend the same schools, seek heath care in the same clinics and hospitals, work together, and belong to the same political parties.

Christian-Muslim relations in Africa date back to 615 AD, when the persecuted Muslims sought political asylum with the *negus* of Axum (Ethiopia). Martha Frederiks asserts that the understanding of Surah 19 (*Sura al-Maryam*) played an important role because it served as the basis for the hospitality that was granted to the group of Muslim refugees.[19] The first Christian-Muslim encounter on African soil was peaceful and this hospitality and interreligious acceptance are still frequently referred to as the African matrix for interfaith encounters.[20]

Since Christians and Muslims have lived together for many centuries, the history of the interaction between the two religious traditions varies and goes way back. Both religious traditions carry historical wounds that could affect relationships in contemporary times; therefore, these historical wounds need to be understood and addressed. This reflects the common perception among adherents of the two religions that historically Christians and Muslims have not found it difficult to live together, nor would there be tensions and conflicts if party politics did not interfere. Today many African countries have allowed politics to pose a threat to their peace and peaceful coexistence.

18. Tayviah, "Colonial Impact in Christian-Muslim", 237.

19. Frederiks, "Let Us Understand," 2. The *negus* of Ethiopia saw Surah 19 as similar to the story of Mary in the Bible. He saw the belief of the Muslims to be similar to his, so he accepted them and provided them with hospitality.

20. Frederiks, "Let Us Understand," 3.

Christian-Muslim relations in the world today have been characterized by imbalances in their status as one of the two claiming majority or minority, their access to power, their vulnerability, and perceptions of self-sufficiency. Ghana is known as a secular state where the statement "we are all equal citizens" is often repeated. However, questions of minority, power, and influence arise among adherents of the two religions under study as to how adherents of one religious group regard themselves and the other. Thus, in analyzing Christian-Muslim relations one cannot dismiss the questions of numbers, power, and self-perception as irrelevant.[21] All these can also pose a threat to peace and peaceful coexistence.

Chances of Dialogue and Cooperation

Dialogue between Christians and Muslims has played and will continue to play important roles because it enables adherents of both religions to understand, cooperate, and live with each other peacefully. M. M. Ali posits that for Christians and Muslims to achieve good-neighbourliness and have healthy relations with each other, adherents of both religions should understand that there must be an interpersonal relationship before any sort of dialogue or conversation across religious and cultural lines can be successful. Ali further argues that before dialogue can be successful, there must be an attempt to understand the worldviews of the participants in the dialogue.[22]

Sabra also states that it is almost impossible for Christians and Muslims to live together without engaging each other. This form of dialogue, which he terms "dialogue of life," is where Christians and Muslims come together to discuss and exchange views on issues such as social, economic, political, justice, peace, moral values, and freedoms of expression that emerge out of living together.[23] Dialogue has helped Christians and Muslims in the world to know each other, trust one another, and work together on issues of common concern, and in times and moments of tension adherents of both religions come together to search for mutually acceptable solutions. Although dialogue cannot solve all problems or bring all conflicts and tensions in the world to an end, efforts of dialogue between Christians and Muslims become alternatives to any forms of

21. Thomas, "Social and Religious Factors," 55.

22. Ali, "Muslim Interfaith Initiative," 121.

23. Sabra, "Common Word," 90.

violence and conflict. Dialogue is done with the hope that unforeseen conflicts in the future can be avoided when Christians and Muslims understand and cooperate with one another. In recent times, interfaith or interreligious marriages have been one of the major means through which dialogue and interfaith understanding have been achieved. This happens because both partners from different religious traditions live together in a shared spirit of mutual respect and tolerance. Even though there are many challenges or restrictions with interfaith marriages about Christian or Muslim teachings on marriage and interfaith marriages, there are many Christians and Muslims who marry each other and this is the first point of dialogue because it starts among the couple and then continues to affect the lives of their children and the rest of the household.

Several chances and opportunities exist to make Christians and Muslims come together in Ghana. Thus, Christians and Muslims in Ghana have, relatively, always lived together in peace in the local communities and towns. In other words, Christians and Muslims are found in every town or village in Ghana either as a minority or a majority. In Ghana, it is very common to find members of the same family belonging to different religious traditions. Muslims visit their Christian relatives and friends during Christmas and Easter to wish them well and Christians also visit their Muslim friends and relatives during their Islamic festivals; *Id-ul-Fitr* and *Id-ul-Adha*. During child-naming, wedding ceremonies, ordination of priests or pastors, and funerals, Muslims come to church and vice versa without the question of religious affiliation because the ceremony involves a friend or relative.[24] The important thing is to share in the joy or pain or loss of a relative or a loved one. The "dialogue of life"[25] is well practiced at the grassroots level in Ghana. Other chances

24. A more recent one is when the national chief imam, Sheikh Osman Nuhu Sharubutu, on Sunday, 21 April 2019, joined an Easter Mass service at the Christ the King Catholic Church in Accra to mark his one-hundredth birthday anniversary. See more: https://www.ghanaweb.com/GhanaHomePage/NewsArchive/National-Chief-Imam-attends-Catholic-mass-for-100th-birthday-thanksgiving-740200. See also: https://www.myjoyonline.com/news/2019/April-21st/ghanaians-hail-national-chief-imam-for-joining-easter-service.php. On the 9 November 2014, the entire Muslim family of Nathan Samwini traveled down south to witness his induction as the bishop of the Northern Ghana Diocese of the Methodist Church in Ghana. All the above instances show the nature of the relationship that exists between Christians and Muslims in Ghana.

25. Nathan I. Samwinin defines "dialogue of life" as coexisting peacefully with the other in spite of obvious religious differences. In the dialogue of life, people from different religious traditions live and interact in their everyday lives. See also: Samwini,

and opportunities that make Christians and Muslims meet or relate are discussed below.

Family and Ethnic Bonds

Many families in Ghana are interfaith households because members of the same family belong to different religious traditions. In such cases, bonds of family, blood ties, and ethnicity are stronger than religious affiliations, which in turn neutralize any form of religious hostility. In Ghana, people participate in the celebration of festivals irrespective of their religious background because these festivals are opportunities for people of a community to renew ties, solidarize, and contribute to developmental projects. In Ghana, therefore, it is difficult to find religious conflicts of the magnitude of what occurs in Nigeria, because of these good relations that exist between members of the same family and ethnic group.

Education

In Ghana, school is the first place where students of different religions meet to learn. Thus, the teacher or school authorities and the students belong to different religious traditions and this does not affect teaching and learning in Ghana. The Ministry of Education in Ghana has also included Religious and Moral Education (RME) in the basic education curriculum. In Basic schools, pupils are taught about the three main religions in the country, namely African traditional religion, Islam, and Christianity. This basic education forms the foundation of future interfaith relations in the mind of the Ghanaian child. Since Christianity is the dominant religion in Ghana, many schools have adopted Christian liturgical practices such as the recitation of the Lord's Prayer during morning and afternoon assembly meetings, and the pupils recite it irrespective of their religious background. In Islamic schools, which are open to any pupil irrespective of their religious background, the *Surah al-Fatiha* is recited instead of the Lord's Prayer. All pupils and students of these schools, Christians included, recite the *Surah al-Fatiha*. If a child is sent to a missionary school, whether Christian or Muslim, that child should be ready to abide by the rules and regulations of that school, which are often guided by the religion of the missionaries. Examples of such schools are St Mary's

"Need for and Importance of Dialogue."

Senior High School, Pope John Senior High School and Minor Seminary, Presbyterian Boys' Senior High School (Legon), Ghana Muslim Mission Senior High School, T.I. Ahmadiyya Senior High School (Kumasi); and Ejura Islamic Senior High School.

Political Parties

Muslims and Christians are members of the different political parties in Ghana. It is common to find Muslims and Christians campaigning together on common political platforms. Christians and Muslims are elected or appointed to high governmental positions equally based on competence and political affiliation, not on religious affiliation.[26] The Christian can be a minister of state with a Muslim as his or her deputy or vice versa. Thus, in Ghana, people are generally voted for or appointed based on their competence or political ties rather than on lines of religious affiliation.

Working Relationships

In Ghana, people work together for economic gains peacefully irrespective of different religious backgrounds. Muslims manage organizations with Christian subordinates and vice versa. Christians and Muslims buy and sell from the same market, share the same transport services, and work together in many organizations. Again, people are appointed as members of committees irrespective of their religious affiliations. The National Peace Council of Ghana, formed in 2012, is made up of Christians, Muslims, and traditional leaders. These religious leaders have worked together towards peaceful coexistence since its formation. Religious leaders in Ghana have also come together to seek and pray for peace, especially during general elections, observe and write reports about the outcome of general elections, and held meetings for peaceful coexistence and security of citizens. Religious leaders in Ghana have together helped to formulate policies on Ebola, cholera, and the fight against HIV/AIDS and advocate for those living with HIV/AIDS to be treated with compassion. Also, in many public encounters where prayers are required in Ghana,

26. The exception to this may occur where necessary. For instance, a Christian cannot head the National Hajj Council, which has the oversight responsibility for the annual Ghanaian *hajj* pilgrims to Mecca.

the opening and closing prayers are said by a Christian and a Muslim respectively, or vice versa.

Health

Health is an important factor in human life and every community makes sure that its citizens are healthy. In Ghana, Christians and Muslims are careful to live in a clean environment. When there is an outbreak of disease, it affects all members of the community irrespective of religious background. When there was an outbreak of Ebola in some West African countries, every Ghanaian was concerned and efforts were put in place to protect all Ghanaians from acquiring the virus. Health officials who work in the hospitals and clinics in Ghana belong to different religious traditions but they all save lives.

Today, Ghana has become an example or model for the world in the area of Christian-Muslim relations because of the coexistence and peace that is enjoyed in the country. This peaceful coexistence among Ghanaian citizens can be attributed to the fact that people mutually respect, tolerate, and cooperate with each other irrespective of their religious backgrounds.

Challenges of Dialogue and Cooperation

Irrespective of the many positive interactions, opportunities, and chances that occur during Christian-Muslim dialogue, some challenges are also discovered.

1. **Reaffirmation of faith:** During dialogue, people are tempted to reaffirm their respective religious beliefs, values, and teachings. It is important for religious people to hold on to their faiths and traditions during dialogue; however, the danger or challenge may arise that religious groups may push for their beliefs, values, and teachings to be accepted above others during dialogue.
2. **Nature of the community:** This depends on how religious groups are allowed to practice their religions freely. In this case, religious adherents check to see if some religious groups are favored in the practice of their religion more than others. This poses a threat

especially when one religious group feels the other is being treated better and is being favored more than the others are.

3. **Majority/minority status:** This has to do with either Christianity or Islam being the major or minor religion in a country. Thus, adherents assume the majority or minority status based on the population census of the country. Many times, structures of government and laws are influenced by this status since the adherents of religion in the majority seem to have more influence than the others. Meanwhile, in many African secular countries like Ghana, every citizen should be treated the same irrespective of their religious background.

4. **Christian evangelism and Muslim *da'wa*:** Another issue that poses a challenge to healthy Christian-Muslim relations is the way both religions seek converts as part of their evangelism or *da'wa* duties. Both religions have the religious duty to seek, invite, and make others join their respective faiths. Yet, both Christians and Muslims are tempted to aggressively or polemically win converts, which may not auger well for good and healthy Christian-Muslim relations. In many African countries, seeking converts is not the problem, but the mode of achieving this religious duty is what causes the challenge. Thus, this duty should be done in a spirit of good-neighbourliness void of polemics. This would ensure adherents of both religions respect the freedom and dignity of others and, in the end, maintain healthy relations between Christians and Muslims.

5. **Religious extremism and violence:** Another issue that poses a challenge to healthy Christian-Muslim relations in the world today is Religious extremism and violence. Many African countries such as Burkina Faso, Mali, Nigeria, and Cote D'Ivoire have witnessed many forms of religious extremism and violence. This phenomenon is the belief that one's belief is the best and only way to salvation, excluding and downplaying the rest. To the religious extremist, no other religious traditions exist and even if they exist, they are not significant. Therefore, the religious extremist believes that such insignificant religious traditions must be destroyed and eliminated for his or her own to dominate. This mindset and ideals of a religious extremist make him or her intolerant of other religions. To the religious extremist, it is anathema to cooperate with adherents of other religions because the religious views of other people are irrelevant.

This makes good and healthy Christian-Muslim relations and cooperation impossible.

6. The concept of *jihad* has been misinterpreted and misunderstood by many people and this poses a challenge to good and healthy Christian-Muslim relations. The notion that Islam is and must be spread by or through the sword is wrong. The term *jihad* has been simply translated as "holy war" and misunderstood as an aggressive war Muslims wage against non-Muslims. Surah 2:257 suggests that there are three types of wars in Islam, namely: war fought in self-defense, war undertaken as a chastisement against aggression, and finally war fought for the establishment of freedom of religion. The Koran teaches Muslims in Surah 2:256 that there should be no compulsion in religion because when people are forced and coerced to accept Islam, they only become hypocrites instead of genuine believers. The sword only puts fear in people but does not and cannot win hearts. Therefore, it is a misconception that Islam teaches Muslims to force others to convert to Islam at the point of the sword. This misconception has rather affected how many Christians treat Islam and Muslims and causes unhealthy Christian-Muslim relations.

7. Another impediment to healthy Christian-Muslim relations and cooperation is politics. Some governments and people form their political decisions based on the population of Christians and Muslims in the country. Whichever religion is in the majority is the one that is favored by politicians. Again, politicians seem to show some form of favoritism to the religions in the majority as a means to gain votes and political favor from them. A new and rising phenomenon in many parts of Africa is the "politicization of religion" and the "religionization of politics." Johnson Mbillah explains that the religionization of politics is when religious leaders take politics into religion because they use politics and politicians to advance the course of their ambitions, while the politicization of religion is when some politicians also use religion to advance their political ambitions.[27] Whichever way religion is used in any of the above circumstances can pose a threat to healthy Christian-Muslim relations.

27. "Religionization of politics" and "politicization of religion" are terms coined by Johnson Mbillah, the immediate past General Adviser, now consultant of the Programme for Christian-Muslim Relations in Africa (PROCMURA). See Mbillah, "Attitudes towards Conflict Preventions." See also: Tayviah, "Colonial Impact," 237.

Even though no true religion advocates violence, some politicians, to achieve their selfish goals, exploit the religious sentiments of citizens. Politicians promise citizens many favors and sometimes some politicians tend to favor some religious traditions over others. Religious sentiments have also played a part in power relations and the allocation of national resources in many African countries. In many African countries, people are tempted to vote for presidential or parliamentary candidates based on their religious backgrounds instead of competence. Yet, Christians and Muslims hold government positions in many African societies and Ghana in particular. In many African countries, policies are sometimes also formulated and implemented to empower the dominant religious tradition of top government officials at the expense of others. Ironically, politicians do forget the important religious teaching that they must wish for others what they wish for themselves.

8. The developments following September 11, 2001 are another issue that has caused a challenge for Christian-Muslim relations. Since September 11, 2001, Islam has been equated with terrorism and this has affected how some Christians relate to Muslims. In Africa, this has created tension between Christians and Muslims because adherents treat each other with mistrust and suspicion.

9. The religious leaders of both Christianity and Islam have the challenge to educate their respective members on the need to harmoniously cooperate and collaborate. Thus religious leaders have to emphasize the virtues common to both religions and insist on peaceful coexistence and love for the neighbor as being pleasing to God. If Christian and Muslim leaders initiate and jointly execute projects, their followers will learn from them and do the same. Then the barriers, tensions, and fears of relating together will be a thing of the past.

If Christians gain much insight and understanding of Islam, it will enable them to relate better with their Muslim neighbors. This can be achieved through dialogue, friendship, and cooperation with Muslims. The Programme for Christian-Muslim Relations in Africa (PROCMURA), for instance, is a pan-African Christian organization that encourages Christians to engage with Muslims in a renewed process of learning and discernment, to discover how Christians can live with Muslims as neighbors across the African continent.[28]

The Way Forward

Both Christianity and Islam have come to stay. Therefore, the earlier Christians and Muslims understand this and find healthy ways of living together, understanding each other, and cooperating, the better. Indeed, the future of the world depends on peace between Christians and Muslims because the foundational principles of both Christianity and Islam, "love of God and love of the neighbor,"[29] affirm the need for peaceful coexistence. Despite the challenges that Christians and Muslims face in dialogue and cooperation, there is a need to work towards an understanding of good and healthy Christian-Muslim relations. There is a need for Christians and Muslims to engage each other more on different levels. The church, through its governing bodies and agencies, should support education on good and healthy Christian-Muslim relations by developing and making available resources for study and reflection on Islam and Muslim life, including case studies of Christian-Muslim relations in some countries of the world. This will help people learn from the experiences of others.

Churches should be encouraged to hold seminars and workshops regarding Islam and Christian-Muslim relations, to equip members with knowledge of Islam and Muslims. The church must further encourage the inclusion of Islam and Christian-Muslim relations in Bible study and curricular materials in the church so that church members will know and understand their Muslim neighbors. Periodically, common programs should be held between members of both religious traditions because this will enable both Christians and Muslims to share knowledge and learn from each other's experiences.

Interfaith or interreligious dialogue is done with the intention of learning and growing together, but not to change the other. Therefore, each person has to come to the table of dialogue with an open mind to learn and do away with their prejudices, biases, attitudes, and perceptions

28. See more in Ellingwood, "Programme for Christian-Muslim Relations."

29. See "'Common Word' 10 Years On," which states: "On Oct. 13, 2007, 138 Muslim leaders signed 'A Common Word Between Us and You,' a document stating that Christians and Muslims share two great commandments—love of God and love of neighbor—and should work for peace together."

of the other. Dialogue should also be done in honesty and sincerity to build mutual trust so that the religious identity and experience of others is respected so they can also reciprocate that gesture. Interfaith or interreligious dialogue should not be done with assumptions of issues of agreement or disagreement, which may exist or not exist. During dialogue, each person should avoid presumptions and listen with empathy and sympathy about what the other will say. If there is an issue or point of disagreement, it should be respected but the commonalities should be accepted while the religious integrity of those in dialogue is maintained. During interfaith or interreligious dialogue, one must be prepared to healthily critique and reflect on his or her religious tradition while holding onto the conviction and integrity of his or her religious tradition. When a person fails to acknowledge and self-criticize his or her religious tradition, that person believes he or she already has all the correct answers and sees nothing good in the other's religion and so has nothing to learn. Such an attitude makes dialogue seem not only unnecessary but almost impossible.

Conclusion

Hans Küng, as cited by Zoran Brajovic, stated that "there can be no peace in the world without peace among the religions."[30] This implies that religious people must practice peace as their sacred teachings require them to do. Since many countries of the world are religiously pluralistic, they must learn to coexist peacefully and have mutual relations and cooperation with each other.

Bibliography

Abdul-Hamid, M. "Christian-Muslim Relations in Ghana: A Model for World Dialogue and Peace. *Ilorin Journal of Religious Studies* (*IJOURELS*) 1/1 (2011) 21–32

Ali, M. M. "A Muslim Interfaith Initiative and Its Christian Response." *Insights* 2/1 (2009)115–54.

Ariarajah, Wesley. "The Impact of Interfaith Dialogue on the Ecumenical Movement." In *Pluralism and the Religions*, edited by John D'Arcy May, 7–21. London: Cassell, 1998

Azumah, John. "Muslim-Christian Relations in Ghana: Too Much Meat Does Not Spoil the Soup." *Current Dialogue* 36 (2000) 5–9.

30. Brajovic, "Potential of Inter-Religious Dialogue," 153.

Brajovic, Zoran. "The Potential of Inter-Religious Dialogue." In *Peacebuilding and Civil Society in Bosnia-Herzegovina*, edited by Martina Fischer, 149–79. Münster: Lit-Verlag, 2007.

Brown, Stuart E. *Meeting in Faith: Twenty Years of Christian-Muslim Conversations Sponsored by the World Council of Churches*. Geneva: WCC, 1989.

Brown, Stuart, E. *The Nearest in Affection: Toward a Christian Understanding of Islam*. Geneva: WCC, 1994.

"'A Common Word' 10 Years On: Christians and Muslims Must Work Together for Peace." October 15, 2017. https://www.acommonword.com/a-common-word-10-years-on-christians-and-muslims-must-work-together-for-peace/.

———. "Conditions for Inter-Religious Dialogue." In *The Wiley-Blackwell Companion to Inter-Religious Dialogue*, edited by Catherine Cornille, 20–33. Chichester: Wiley, 2013.

Cornille, Catherine. "Introduction." In *The Wiley-Blackwell Companion to Inter-Religious Dialogue*, edited by Catherine Cornille, xii–xvii. . Chichester: Wiley, 2013.

Ellingwood, Jane. "The Programme for Christian—Muslim Relations in Africa (PROCMURA): An Evolutionary Perspective." *The Muslim World* 98 (January 2008) 72–94.

Frederiks, Martha. "Let Us Understand Our Differences: Current Trends in Christian-Muslim Relations in Sub-Sahara Africa." *Transformation: An International Journal of Holistic Mission Studies* 27/4 (2010) 261–74. http://trn.sagepub.com/content/27/4/261.

Goddard, Hugh "Christian-Muslim Relations: A Look Backwards and a Look Forwards." *Islam and Christian-Muslim Relations* 11/2 (2000) 195–212.

———. "Christian-Muslim Relations: Yesterday, Today and Tomorrow." *International Journal for the Study of the Christian Church* 3/2 (2003) 1–14.

Hock, Klaus. "Christian-Muslim Relations in the African Context." *International Journal for the Study of the Christian Church* 3/2 (2003) 36–57.

Melnik, Sergey. "Types of Interreligious Dialogue." *Journal of Interreligious Studies* 31 (November 2020) 48–72.

Merrigan, Terrence. "Introduction: Rethinking Theologies of Interreligious Dialogue." In *The Past, Present, and Future of Theologies of Interreligious Dialogue*, edited by Terrence Merrigan and John Friday, 1–14. Oxford: Oxford University Press, 2017.

Mbillah, Johnson. "Attitudes towards Conflict Prevention, Peace and Reconciliation as Illustrated by Animal Behavior." Paper presented at the West Africa Regional Consultation for Christian and Muslim Religious Leaders on Conflict Prevention and Peace Building, Lome-Togo, 24–28 August 2015.

Michel, Thomas. "Social and Religious Factors Affecting Muslim-Christian Relations." *Islam and Christian-Muslim Relations* 8/1 (1997) 53–66.

Moyaert, Marianne. "Interreligious Dialogue." In *Understanding Interreligious Relations*, edited by David Cheetham, Douglas Pratt, and David Thomas, 201–12. Oxford: Oxford University Press, 2013.

Pontifical Council for Interreligious Dialogue. "Dialogue and Proclamation: Reflection and Orientations on Interreligious Dialogue and the Proclamation of the Gospel of Jesus Christ." May 19, 1991. https://www.vatican.va/roman_curia/pontifical_councils/interelg/documents/rc_pc_interelg_doc_19051991_dialogue-and-proclamatio_en.html.

Pratt, Douglas. *Being Open, Being Faithful: The Journey of Interreligious Dialogue.* Geneva: WCC, 2014.

Sabra, G., "The 'Common Word' Letter in the Context of Christian-Muslim Dialogue." *Theological Review* 30 (2009) 89–98.

Samwini, Nathan Iddrisu. "The Need for and Importance of Dialogue of Life in Community Building: The Case of Selected West African Nations." *Journal of Inter-Religious Studies* 6 (April 2011).

Swidler, Leonard. "The History of Inter-Religious Dialogue." In *The Wiley-Blackwell Companion to Inter-religious Dialogue*, edited by Catherine Cornille, 3–19. Chichester: Wiley, 2013.

Tayviah, Margaret Makafui. *The Colonial Impact in Christian-Muslim Relations in Ghana and Togo: A Comparative Assessment.* Hamburg: Missionshilfe, 2019.

Thangaraj, M. Thomas. *The Common Task: A Theology of Christian Mission.* Nashville: Abingdon, 1999.

Thomas, David. "This Issue of Islam and Christian-Muslim Relations." *Islam and Christian Relations* 20/3 (2009) 211–13.

———. "The Past and the Future in Christian-Muslim Relations." *Islam and Christian Relations* 18/1 (2007) 33–42.

Part III

Socio-Economic Matters

Chapter 6

Socio-Economic Development, Developmental Preservation, and the Environment in Africa

Religious Reflections toward a Stewardship-Based Alternative

Ben-Willie Kwaku Golo

Introduction: Socio-Economic Development and Environmental Problems in Africa

Africa's environmental problems are diverse and many and, at the risk of oversimplification, include environmental pollution and degradation, depletion of natural habitat for aquatic and land animals, decline in biological diversity, and desertification. The view, though not undebatable, is generally held that at the root of environmental problems in Africa are poverty, inadequate infrastructure, and/or lack of technological and industrial capability, and lack of economic activity.[1] Therefore, the view is held that what Africa (in this chapter, my emphasis is on Sub-Saharan Africa) needs is the process of economic and industrial development in order to overcome its environmental concerns.[2] It is common knowledge, however, that global environmental problems, such as

1. Howard-Clinton, "Emerging Concepts," 1.
2. Howard-Clinton, "Emerging Concepts," 3.

diminishing natural resources, carbon emissions and pollution of all kinds, and climate change, have direct links with socio-economic development processes. For instance, with the industrialization of Africa as a link to its development, at minimum there has been a doubling of the trajectory of carbon emission.[3] In most African countries various types of environmental challenges have become evidence of the socio-economic development pursued.

Globally, concerns with development-related environmental degradation have led to efforts towards an alternative development thinking. This has culminated in the concept of sustainable development, suggesting that there are more sustainable routes to development. The World Commission on Environment and Development (WCED) of the United Nations in its report *Our Common Future*, also known as the Brundtland's Commission Report, has recommended sustainable development as a healthier way to proceed with development if the protection of the natural environment is a priority. The report defines sustainable development as "development that meets the needs of the present without compromising the ability of future generations to meet their own needs."[4] Sustainable development is a "process of change in which the exploitation of resources, the direction of investments, the orientation of technological development, and institutional change are made consistent with future as well as present needs."[5] It is that development which strives for a balance between human well-being and the preservation of nature's resources and systems. However, after many years, Africa still reels under development-induced environmental burdens. While space may not allow an exhaustive discussion of environmental problems that have occasioned Africa's quest for socio-economic development in recent decades, a brief survey of the trend in Ghana, as a case, will set the tone for further discussion.

Ghana has diverse natural resources pertinent to its development processes. However, "uncontrolled manner of utilization of these natural resources has resulted in reversible and irreversible changes within the environment."[6] It has also been noted that when Ghana was in economic crisis in the 1980s, just before the inception of the idea of sustainable

3. Adekunle, "On the Search," 14607.

4. United Nations, *Our Common Future*, 16.

5. United Nations, *Our Common Future*, 17.

6. Tamakloe, "Ghana's Environment," 1.

development, the timber industry had virtually collapsed and the IMF had to intervene with the Structural Adjustment Program (SAP), which promoted the expansion of Ghana's exports to enable the country acquire additional foreign exchange.[7] The timber sector was then given much attention through the World Bank's Export Rehabilitation Project of 1983–86 in which sawmills were improved, logging operations modernized, harbors rebuilt, and timber exports increased.[8] The result was the contribution of Ghana's forests to a significant increase in the country's GDP and in reversing economic decline at the time. However, this growth was achieved through the unsustainable logging of the forests as production was inefficient, wastage was very high, and wood priced below its real market value.[9]

In recent decades new forms of development-related environmental problems have emerged, such as unsustainable mining, particularly artisanal small-scale mining, which has diverse unmanageable and rippling environmental effects.[10] There are also problems such as e-waste dumping and metal scrapping, particularly in the cities.[11] One can also mention the commonly known continuous logging of Ghana's forests, pollution of land and water bodies from agribusiness, sand and soil weaning from both land and the coasts, and other problems characterizing urbanization such as the problems of waste and filth and many urban areas in Ghana. Consequently, and from the perspective of environmental sustainability, socio-economic development and/or simply development, which for the Ghanaian would be "essentially a cure for major environmental problems of poverty and inadequate infrastructure,"[12] has rather become a source of the problems of pollution.

While many African countries may have contributed to development-induced environmental degradation, many of the environmental burdens borne by the continent are due to environmental injustice.[13] This is because, in the case of emissions for instance, "those communities and social groups in Africa who suffer most from the effects of negative

7. Glastra, "Cut and Run," 59.
8. Glastra, "Cut and Run," 66.
9. Glastra, "Cut and Run," 66.
10. Hilson, "Environmental Impact," 59–61.
11. Oteng-Ababio, "E-Waste Scavenging," 3.
12. Clinton, "Emerging Concepts," 187.
13. Golo, "In Search of a Sustainable Society," 77–78.

climate change are the ones who emit only a small amount of greenhouse gases (GHGs) into the atmosphere."[14] The continent "accounts for the smallest share of global greenhouse gas emissions, at just 3.8%, in contrast to 23% in China, 19% in the US, and 13% in the European Union."[15] Thus, the Kyoto Protocol–listed forty "Annex 1" countries, which are the industrialized countries and roughly representing only 24 percent of the world's population, generate about 65 percent of global anthropogenic greenhouse gas emissions.[16] It is further suggested that these countries "will also remain the largest emitters for some time to come under business-as-usual projections."[17]

Similarly, about 80 percent of developed countries' e-waste meant for recycling ends up in developing countries, such as Ghana and Nigeria, for recycling.[18] The result is developing countries, such as those of Africa, being disproportionately burdened with environmental problems and sustainability issues that they have done less to create, and with limited or no institutional and technological capacity to deal with them.[19] It is not therefore surprising that goals 11–15 of the Millennium Development Goals (MDGs) of the UNDP, successor to the earlier Sustainable Development Goals (SDGs), focus on environmental sustainability issues related to development processes.

It is suggested that the religious traditions in Africa have sound ecological ontologies derived from their religious understanding of the natural world and the role of humankind in it, and which are capable of averting the destruction of the natural world, with the most common being their claim to environmental stewardship.[20] Considering the religious visibility in diverse forms and high claims to religiosity in the African subregion, and against the background of the environmental scenario sketched earlier, one then questions why these have not featured in the development policies and practices on the continent, thereby averting the current development-related environmental destruction in Africa. This is because if religious people and groups are to be actors and beneficiaries

14. Golo, "In Search for a Sustainable Society," 77.

15. Von Czechowski, "CDP Africa Report," 3.

16. Russel, "Burden Sharing," 67, 71–72.

17. Russel, "Burden Sharing," 72.

18. Lundgren, "Global Impact of E-Waste," 9.

19. Lundgren, "Global Impact of E-Waste," 9; Adekunle, "On the Search," 14608.

20. Golo, "Sabbath," 249.

in the development process and its outcomes, then their values and perspectives, which form their ways of looking at the world and the way they relate with it, become important in the development discourse.

In this chapter, I explore the concepts of environmental stewardship in light of lived religion in Africa, offer a reflection on some apparent faultiness between socio-economic development and environmental sustainability in Africa, analyze the potential of religion and environmental stewardship to sustainable development in Africa from the perspective of environmental stewardship and *developmental preservation*, and finally make a proposal for what a stewardship-informed sustainability would look like in Africa; and the last section concludes the chapter.

Religion and Environmental Stewardship

Environmental stewardship is defined as "a sacred duty imposed on humans with very practical dimensions for safeguarding both human wellbeing and environmental sustainability."[21] It is also seen as "the responsible management of human activity affecting the natural environment to ensure the conservation and preservation of natural resources and values for the sake of future generations of human and other life on the planet, together with the acceptance of significant answerability for one's conduct to society."[22] From a typically religious dimension, religious environmental stewardship is defined as "those typically religious beliefs, norms and values that emphasize human obligations to care for God's creation"[23] and "motivates religious communities to care for creation."[24]

The religious idea of stewardship, in relation to the natural world, "has long been prominent in modern Jewish, Christian, and Islamic environmental thought (as *khilafa* in the latter), probably because its basic form of responsibility is especially compatible with accountability to a Creator for use of creation."[25] With its roots in the old English word "steward," meaning "a servant who looks after a hall, a manor or landed estate"[26] and connoting "entrusted responsibility for something properly

21. Golo et al., "Akan Ontology," 26.
22. Welchman, "Defence," 303.
23. Golo, "Sabbath," 249.
24. Golo, "Sabbath," 250.
25. Jenkins et al., "Religion and Climate," 95.
26. Welchman, "Defence," 299.

belonging to another,"[27] "stewardship" has become used widely in relation to "caring for things or persons on another's behalf."[28] Environmental stewardship is a recurring metaphor in the global resurgence in religious environmentalism,[29] and remains a popular theme for many religious groups that have constructively engaged environmental problems such as climate change in recent decades.[30] Generally, claims to some form of interpretation of stewardship responsibility commit them to act in safeguarding the integrity of the natural world because stewardship is a duty imposed by the sacred or deity.

It is suggested that the three major religions that have extensive stakeholder connections and influences to both local communities and political corridors in Africa—Christianity, Islam, and the Indigenous African Religion—all share a common understanding of stewardship and its ethical implications.[31] While it is suggested that various religions offer different perspectives on environmental stewardship, the concept underscores that humans are to nurture and protect the natural world while benefiting from it, and they are not to destroy it.[32] The clarity in all forms of stewardship is that the natural world was purposefully created by the Ultimate Reality and humans have been given the duty and responsibility to take care of it as stewards.

To religious people, the natural world is also of a supernatural and sacred origin that requires a human response of appreciation and responsibility in ways human beings interact with it while benefiting from it, hence moral and religious limits imposed on the use of its resources.[33] This religious cosmology largely foregrounds the stewardship convictions and ecological ontologies of many religiously oriented Africans, not only those of indigenous religion.[34] The sacredness of land and its religious and moral duties and responsibilities are more pronounced and lived in the indigenous religion and culture than Christianity and Islam, although these two religious traditions have more systematic formulation

27. Jenkins et al., "Religion and Climate," 95.
28. Welchman, "Defence," 299.
29. Golo, "Sabbath," 249.
30. Jenkins et al., "Religion and Climate," 95.
31. Golo and Yaro, "Reclaiming Stewardship," 287.
32. Golo and Yaro, "Reclaiming Stewardship," 287.
33. Golo and Yaro, "Reclaiming Stewardship," 287.
34. Golo and Yaro, "Reclaiming Stewardship." 287.

of stewardship and its environmental dimension. For instance, among the indigenous Akans of Ghana, because of their religious orientation to the natural world, their indigenous African cosmology and ontology consider the natural world as not only comprising of bio-physical components for the uncontrolled harnessing of humans, but also a medium of sacred communication and interaction.[35] Hence, as part of their stewardship responsibility, the indigenous people have devised strict mechanisms of "diverse practices, usually religious prohibitions called taboos, that control human conduct in their interactions with the natural environment."[36] This accounts for indigenous religious cultures in Africa being acknowledged as "crucial for mitigating attitudes that are responsible for negative environmental change and are resourceful to the sustainability discourse."[37]

Africa's Socio-Economic Development Discourse and Environmental Problems: Identifying Some Apparent Faultlines in their Relationships

Development is rather a complex concept with diverse meanings to diverse groups of people and disciplines. It is said that "Development's buzzwords gain their purchase and power through their vague and euphemistic qualities, their capacity to embrace a multitude of possible meanings, and their normative resonance."[38] Purposively, and within the context of this chapter, however, I would proceed with the definition of development as "the process of enhancing individual and collective quality of life in a manner that satisfies basic needs (as a minimum), is environmentally, socially, and economically sustainable, and is empowering in the sense that the people concerned have a substantial degree of control over the process through access to means of accumulating social power."[39]

The goals of development are utopian and ideal, probably "a secular doctrine of salvation,"[40] and which are central to its meaning. This uto-

35. Golo et al., "Akan Ontology," 19–20.

36. Golo et al., "Akan Ontology," 21.

37. Golo et al., "Akan Ontology," 2.

38. Cornwall, "Buzzwords," 472.

39. Simon and Narman, "Development as Theory," 21.

40. Haynes, *Religion and Development*, 2.

pian dimension of development "lies in the a priori positive meaning of the word 'development', which derives both from its supposedly 'natural' existence and from its inclusion in a cluster of unquestionable shared beliefs."[41] This a priori meaning, according to Rist, holds sway to the extent that "those who are ready to recognize that 'development' has not really kept its promises are also loath to discard the notion altogether."[42] This is because, notwithstanding "the undeniable success of 'development' linked to its undeniable failures in improving the conditions of the poor,"[43] the entire notion of development must be brought into question. He therefore submits that "the essence of 'development' is the general transformation and destruction of the natural environment and of social relations in order to increase the production of commodities (goods and services) geared, by means of market exchange, to effective demand."[44] He notes that while this definition may appear scandalous when compared to the wishful thinking that usually characterizes definitions of "development," the definition is a true reflection of the actual process observable when a country or a region is "developing."[45]

The socio-economic development process, therefore, which ideally would be a process that facilitates the holistic and sustainable realisation of the basic needs and quality of life of a people, has, in various ways, had negative impacts on the natural environment. African nations, which are in a hurry to attaining these ideals, are not exceptions to this ecological deficit of socio-economic development, as earlier mentioned. This is particularly interesting when one considers the religious vitality in Africa, including the healthy and interactive relationships between religion and states, religious actors and political actors, and the eco-dimensional cosmologies and ontologies of religious traditions in Africa. A fundamental question, however, is whether the improvement of individual and collective well-being necessarily must lead to negative transformation and destruction of the natural environment. Are they not, particularly, from an African perspective on well-being, capable of existing in tandem?

In the context of this paper, I would like to look at two major related fault lines endemic in the relationship between socio-economic

41. Rist, "Development as Buzzword," 22.

42. Rist, "Development as Buzzword," 22.

43. Rist, "Development as Buzzword," 22.

44. Rist, "Development as Buzzword," 23.

45. Rist, "Development as Buzzword," 23.

development and environmental sustainability—human's stewardship of the natural environment—in a religion-pervaded Africa. The first major issue, which I consider a condition for the success of the second, is the trivialization and externalization of religious beliefs and norms in development policies in a secularizing Africa. This is regardless of the continuous socio-economic partnership role of religious institutions in many modern African states. The second, which is globally known and debated and to which Africa seems to be a latecomer in the quest to attain a "developed" status, is the dominant model and goal of the type of socio-economic development practised in Africa.

The Idea of Religion as Problematic to Development

The first major issue fault line in the development and environmental sustainability relationship is the trivialization and externalization of religious beliefs and norms in development policy. Because religion has largely been considered problematic to development, if not one of the problems itself that development must deal with,[46] it was thought that the "vocabulary and approach of spirituality seemed, often though not always, inimical to the technical, hard-nosed approach of development practice."[47] Consequently religion, thought of as anti-developmental and posing impediments to development, became "a marginal, if not a neglected topic"[48] in development thought and/or divorced from development theory, policy, and practice[49] since the modern era.

Thus, irrespective of whatever model of development was practiced, the consensus was that "religion's social, political and economic standing needed to be reduced or even eliminated in order to usher in both development and modernity."[50] This has become the challenge for religions in the modern secular world, especially following the separation between state and institutionalized religion, courtesy of modernist thought and secularization of the state[51] and its suspicions and apprehensions of re-

46. Haynes, "Religion and Development," 1.

47. Marshall, "Development and Religion," 343.

48. Marshall, "Development and Religion," 339.

49. Ter Haar and Ellis, "Role of Religion," 352; Golo and Novieto, "Neo-Pentecostal Economies," 74.

50. Haynes, "Religion and Development," 6.

51. Marshall, "Development and Religion," 343.

ligion. What is evident is that in Africa, with the turn of most countries into liberal secular societies, religious beliefs and norms no longer serve as the crucible for policy-making concerning the direction of states. It is, however, asserted that the idea of development has its roots in the Western Christian religion and would be "seen as the secular translation of the belief that the kingdom of God, where all things will be perfect, will eventually arrive."[52]

This developmental thinking, and the model of development structured on it, is particularly unhelpful to Africa, where many individuals and communities hardly make a distinction between physical and spiritual realities. Thus, there is practically no separation between religious life and socio-political life in the lived realities of many Africans. This is irrespective of the formal separation between state and religion. It is for this reason that in many African states institutional religion and religious functionaries are still visible in the social and political sphere and arrangements of states, thereby making many of African nations liberal secular. The supernatural theistic worldview with which many Africans still operate means that religious and cultural worldviews and frameworks feature in their developmental thinking and choices.

This supernatural dimension and worldview, which largely forms the context for the indigenous understanding of human well-being and the role of humans in the natural world, does not place human well-being totally in the possibilities offered by human agency, but "recognises human imperfection and therefore generally accepts that life will not be perfect either.[53] What Gerrie ter Haar calls the "secular utopia," which has become characteristic of not only development theory but also the goal of modern society and the aspirations of many people, with the goal to "eliminate evil in all its forms from the earth,"[54] sees human well-being from a different perspective from that of indigenous Africans. This secular utopian goal, which drives current global models of development, sees progress and human well-being in terms of economic and material security.

Thus, the modernist approach paved the way for development and its practitioners to assume freedom from religious normative frameworks and criticisms for their choices and actions. This allowed them to pursue

52. Ter Haar, "Religion in Development Debate," 5.

53. Ter Haar, "Religion in Development Debate," 5.

54. Ter Haar, "Religion in Development Debate," 5.

an economic growth model of development as if social, environmental, and religious dimensions to the quest for social and economic well-being do not centrally matter. The obvious is that religious perspectives and ontologies regarding the natural world, and modalities in practicing them, have found no place in the modern development agenda until recently being acknowledged in sustainable development approaches. However, it is important to underscore that "religion is such a pervasive and vital force at the individual and community level that the tendency to ignore it has had important, even grave, consequences in some situations."[55] One such consequence would be the negative environmental situation in Africa. Yet, religious views and contributions towards development provide qualitatively sustainable alternatives to the dominant model of socio-economic development currently pursued in Africa.[56] It is therefore suggested that the underlying factors of environmental challenges in Africa "are not unconnected to collapsed and faded indigenous and local knowledge system."[57]

The Dominance of Economic Growth Preferences—Growth Obsession

It came to light in the socio-economic development debate, since the second half of the twentieth century, that the dominance and privileging of economic growth preferences in development theory and practice has been at the expense of the social and ecological consciousness.[58] This approach to development policy has an emphasis on economic growth with its logic being the rule of commodities, money, and capital.[59] As suggested by an earlier definition of development, for many decades most secular development experts thought that development had to do with "finding ways to generate economic growth and then to distribute the resulting wealth among a country's population according to varying ideas of what is just and equitable,"[60] thereby reducing development largely to its economic dimensions.

55. Marshall, "Development and Religion," 343.
56. Golo and Novieto "Neo-Pentecostal Economies," 80, 82.
57. Adekunle, "On the Search," 14608.
58. Alvater, "Growth Obsession," 74.
59. Alvater, "Growth Obsession," 76.
60. Haynes, "Religion and Development," 4.

The assumption is that wealth creation is the foundation for economic stability and that economic stability promotes human well-being, with developing countries achieving parity in economic status with the developed world.[61] Thus, the belief was that economic growth would lead to the improvement in the lives of many, especially among the poor majority. This utopian doctrine of economic growth has gained the position of undisputable truth within modern society and development thinking, such that even those who are convinced of its weakness and consequences seldom dare to question it publicly.[62] Rist summarises the power of development thus:

> Whatever their ideological creed, no politician would dare to run on an election platform that ignores economic growth or 'development', which is supposed to reduce unemployment and create new jobs and well-being for all. Small investors and ordinary people expect an increase in profits or wages that is supposed to follow a 'secular trend'. 'Development' has become a modern shibboleth, an essential password for anyone who wishes to improve their standard of living.[63]

An explanation of how economic growth preferences and processes impact the environment has to do with the dynamic development and expansion of productive forces, which has increased productivity.[64] The expansion of productive forces and technological capacity, with its attendant expanded necessity of using this capacity to provide economic support for populations, has been thought to be that which propels economic growth.[65] This largely implies that population is a push factor for technological expansion in socio-economic development and growth processes. With increased productivity being the main aim, the idea was to expand the industrial sector to supply the needs of the domestic market as well as to generate surplus goods for trade on export markets, and to increase crop yields through technological and scientific advancement for the agricultural markets.[66] Therefore, these forms of development

61. Peters, *Ethics of Globalization*, 73.
62. Rist, "Development as Buzzword", 22.
63. Rist, "Development as Buzzword," 22.
64. Alvater, "Growth Obsession," 73.
65. Alvater, "Growth Obsession," 73.
66. Peters, *Ethics of Globalisation*, 73.

have deep economic origins, namely rising productivity, accumulation, and technological innovation."[67]

However, the question whether sustained and unlimited economic growth on a finite planet is feasible remains.[68] Technology in the service of economic growth, whilst being very helpful to humanity in many respects, is a potential devourer of ecosystems because, in most circumstances, "classical technology is energy-hungry, dirty and ecologically destabilizing"[69] as far as its toll on the environment is concerned. Science and technology may not be inherently dangerous to the environment per se, because it has helped humanity greatly in our contemporary world. However, the unregulated use of technological advancement and industrialization is disconnected from humankind's stewardship of the natural world. Gecaga expounds this view:

> Understood thus positively, technology can be regarded as the stewardship of our extensive and expanding habitat. Nevertheless, in its operation there are major ambiguities. The forces of greed, incarnate pride, profiteering and the service of partisan interests have all played their part. All too often, the underlying rationale of the technological enterprise is that nature is a 'thing' to be used up, controlled and dominated. Technological reasoning degrades nature to mere quantity or extension, at the mercy of scientists and technologists. Nature is then treated as a raw material for production.[70]

Another explanation is urbanization and the growth of urban areas and cities as evidence of socio-economic development in Africa.[71] The provision of the necessary infrastructure for urban areas, such as road networks, water supply, residential facilities and corporate edifices, and sanitation and drainage systems, has its environmental impacts. From the physical space utilized in such structural growth processes (which in the ordinary language is referred as "development") to energy use in their provision, the physical resources used in building and maintaining urban areas, as well as the production of waste and pollutants, impact negatively on the natural environment. For instance, urbanization in Ghana has brought about atmospheric pollution with carbon dioxide and other

67. Boff, *Cry of the Earth*, 66.

68. Conradie, *Critique of Consumerism*, 21.

69. Boff, *Cry of the Earth*, 64.

70. Gecaga, "Creative Stewardship," 30.

71. Adekunle, "On the Search," 14608.

harmful substances in the cities, such as the constant burning of scraps and electronic waste from scrap yards.[72] There is also the improper management and disposal of waste, particularly electronic waste in the urban areas such as Accra, the capital city's Agbogbloshie enclave.[73]

It is important to mention that not all scholars are unanimous on the opinion that economic growth preferences in the development process are detrimental to the natural environment. These scholars recognize that there exists no strong correlation between economic growth and environmental degradation. They are convinced that there exist "forms of economic growth with very limited impact and that wealthy countries seem to be able to address immediate environmental problems more successfully."[74] For instance, with reference to deforestation, Mather and Needle suggest that environmental improvement can go hand in hand with high levels of development, arguing that the developed and developing worlds have contrasting trends in forest area over recent years. However, they admit that on the outset of development, especially with market integration for the first time, there is the tendency for ecological disorganization during the early stages of development, but only when development is attained and stable ecological gains are possible.[75] The reasoning here suggests that development is a goal to be attained and not a process providing continuous opportunities towards improvement in the lives of people and the natural environment.

However, this optimistic view has been contested. It is agreed that it "may not be entirely false with respect to 'dirty', i.e. visible and perceptible, pollution"[76] that high development, particularly economic growth, does not harm the environment, but that economic stagnation does. The contention, however, is that "'clean' lifestyle-pollution, e.g. the emission of greenhouse gases or the 'externalization' of ecologically destructive effects into remote areas or into the far future (nuclear waste), is without doubt also a side-effect of growth and welfare creation."[77] In this regard, one may contend that economic growth has become a necessary evil. It does seem that ecosystem disorganization is a bitter pill nations

72. Darko, "Stewardship and African Philosophy," 28.

73. Oteng-Ababio, "E-Waste Scavenging," 3, 7.

74. Conradie, *A Critique of Consumerism*, 21.

75. Mather and Needle, "Development, Democracy," 105–18.

76. Alvater, "Growth Obsession," 75.

77. Alvater, "Growth Obsession," 75.

and communities have to swallow when embarking on socio-economic development and where economic growth looms large; and that achieving environmental protection requires an enduring conflict with the treadmill of production.[78] Alvater argued that the outcomes/outputs of economic growth are so alluring that even when many decision-makers are aware that ecosystem disorganization is the likely outcome, they will still pursue economic growth for some obvious reasons. One of these reasons is that growth increases employment, incomes, and taxes. It also provides resources for the alleviation of social conflicts, the eradication of poverty, and even the implementation of environmental standards—all which stand to be true of growth.[79]

While not without critiques, such as its labelling as oxymoronic, for "it still remains captive of the development-and-growth paradigm,"[80] the idea of sustainable development "serves as an important corrective against the expansionist notions of economic growth that disregard the environmental impact of such economic activities."[81] Thus, Vischer concludes that the term "sustainable development" has "turned the compatibility of the two discourses into a kind of axiom. What is required to achieve sustainable development are only corrections of the growth-grounded economic system. Sustainability can be reached through efficiency, international agreements and increased international solidarity."[82]

As it were, the two discussed fault lines in the relationship between socio-economic development and the sustainability of the natural environment reveal the underlying assumptions and models of the dominant socio-economic development processes. These, which have been seeded and replicated in Africa, have not been compatible with humankind's stewardship of the natural environment because, "While Africa's search for inclusive growth and poverty eradication continues, little attention has been paid to the consequences of these environment-degrading growth strategies."[83]

With no religious outlook on the natural world within development policy and practice, the natural world, understood by religious people

78. Schnaiberg and Gould, "Environment and Society," 70.

79. Alvater, "Growth Obsession," 75.

80. Boff, *Cry of the Earth*, 66. See this critique on 66–67 and in Conradie, *Critique of Consumerism*, 24–26.

81. Conradie, *Critique of Consumerism*, 24.

82. Vischer, "How Sustainable?," 39.

83. Adekunle, "On the Search," 14607.

as creation and created by the Creator, the Ultimate Reality, simply becomes the bio-physical world of natural resources to be used for economic growth. This is because economic growth is believed to lead to the improvement of social, economic, and environmental well-being of human populations. The safeguarding of the integrity and intrinsic worth of the natural world, and the acknowledgement of its Creator as religious communities in Africa do, particularly the indigenous religious community, do not factor in the analysis. While it may be argued that the world is at the third global stage of economic development, the postmodern phase, characterized by modest levels of economic growth,[84] the positive environmental effects on Africa are yet to be seen.

Religion, Developmental Preservation, and Environmental Sustainability in Africa

It would be unjustified to imagine that the natural world will ever be left unaltered. Neither would it be justified to suggest that the disruption of the ecosystem started with the technological revolution and its deployment in economic growth in recent years. Human history reveals a longstanding but changing pattern of anthropogenic environmental degradation, such as neolithic, ancient, medieval, and modern agricultural practices that cause soil erosion, siltration of surface waters, deforestation, and other forms of vegetation cover removal.[85] That even "prehistoric Homo Sapiens profoundly altered the character of biotic communities"[86] is undeniable. Inasmuch as human beings depend on the natural world for their needs, some level of ecological disorganization is inescapable. However, the extent of environmental destruction caused since the inception of economic development certainly surpasses all the destruction caused since the tenancy of humankind on this planet.[87]

In the context of environmental decline in Africa, amidst religious communities and people who lay claims to environmental stewardship, African nations and leaders cannot continue to pursue developmental policies that cause imbalance in the natural world as if there were no religious responsibilities and obligations towards the earth and future

84. De Jong, "Religious Values," 5.

85. Tucker and Grim, *Worldviews and Ecology*, 32.

86. Tucker and Grim, *Worldviews and Ecology*, 32.

87. Goldsmith, "Global Trade," 81.

stewards (generations). Therefore, while not being unaware that "stewardship frameworks are liable to the criticism that they entrench anthropocentric arrogance and legitimate an exploitative ideal of global ecological control,"[88] I engage in the discussion below with the conviction that environmental stewardship has the potential of contributing to sustainable development in Africa. This is particularly so where environmental stewardship analogues with the secular discourse of developmental preservation. I submit that considering the core thesis of developmental preservation, any development option informed by the secular concept of developmental preservation is indirectly stewardship informed and vice versa.

Developmental preservation, developed by Wardekker et al., is a religious discourse within the stewardship framework on sustainability issues in terms of core values on preserving creation, using Christian groups and voices in the US public debate on climate change. They identified three discourses, namely conservational stewardship, developmental stewardship, and developmental preservation. They describe these three as: "Religiously inspired opponents of strict climate-policy express views that could be described as 'developmental stewardship'. Proponents of strict climate-policy express views of 'conservational stewardship' and 'developmental preservation'."[89] Developmental preservation discourse is identified as similar to conservation stewardship discourse, except that it holds a more positive view of humankind as compared to conservational stewardship, which holds a negative view of humankind. Developmental preservation "presents a belief in (God-granted) human ingenuity and technological and entrepreneurial capacity to prevent conflicts between development and preservation. Climate policy should not hamper developing countries: the developed countries have the responsibility to take action."[90] This suggested discourse, which takes a stewardship approach similar to the concept of "ecosystem services,"[91] "seems much more appealing to political conservatives (while both discourses find support among political progressives). The recent evangelical initiatives mainly display this type of discourse."[92]

88. Jenkins et al., "Religion and Climate," 95.
89. Wardekker et al., "Public Perception," 515.
90. Wardekker et al., "Public Perception," 517.
91. Wardekker et al., "Public Perception," 517.
92. Wardekker,et al., "Public Perception," 517.

With focus on human ingenuity as a display of God-given talent and progress, the ideological view of development preservation is generally described as: "Creation is 'good' and changing; progress and preservation should be combined. God has granted us the creativity to find solutions. Technology and development can present challenges as well as help us in this task."[93] Suggesting that climate change is evidence of improper stewardship, the discourse proposes immediate and urgent action to mitigate climate change, which is doable if humans make the effort.[94] It is in this light that *developmental preservation* lends itself as an environmental stewardship concept that connects religion to sustainable development. Already, stewardship claims of religious people, in Ghana for instance, have been defined as consistent with developmental preservation. This is because it resonates the theological presuppositions of the believers of the three major African religions researched—Christianity, Islam, and Indigenous African Religion,[95] which coincidentally are the dominant religions in perspective in this chapter.

As with the Judeo-Christian understanding of stewardship, "the steward makes decisions and benefit directly from the resources pooled and actions exercised but, in simultaneity, fighting for the right for future generations (heirs) to also benefit from the proceeds."[96] It is against these central tenets of environmental stewardship that sustainable development is considered as the secular rendition of the stewardship ideal and owing a lot to this old environmental ideal embedded in religious traditions, if not a precursor to it.[97] Chirisa therefore suggests that "stewardship goes hand-in-glove with the concept of sustainable development,"[98] as the idea of sustainable development resonates with human stewardship of the earth and could be grounded on it.

However, the related predicaments of the non-privileging and trivialization of religious norms and values and modern society's privileging of economic growth are the syndromes that have robbed Africa of the rich and deep ecological ontologies found in African communities. This is because, drawn into the modernist culture with all its structural and

93. Wardekker et al., "Public Perception," 517.

94. Wardekker et al., "Public Perception," 517.

95. Golo and Yaro, "Reclaiming Stewardship," 298.

96. Chirisa, "Analysis," 41.

97. Golo, "Sabbath," 247; Golo and Yaro, "Reclaiming Stewardship," 297.

98. Chirisa, "Analysis," 41.

material embellishments driven by economic growth, African societies have turned their back on the indigenous and the religious on their march to an end called "development." The theistic views held about the natural world as creation and its inherent sacredness, with restrictive norms and ontologies, guide human intrusions into it. Therefore, what remains are physical entities and resources to be plundered by humans without reference to any transcendent power and authority. It is for this reason that some religious people, particularly those of indigenous religion, get upbeat with the modern state and express their frustration at how religious modalities of social control are being eroded. In the case of religious environmental control and the exercise of stewardship, it is unsurprising that consensus among the religious people in Ghana suggests that current environmental problems are caused by "the absence of human stewardship or the poor show of it,"[99]just as the development preservation discourse suggests.

Towards a Stewardship-Based Sustainable Development in Africa

I do not intend to assert that religious beliefs, systems, and communities in Africa have the solutions to the continent's environmental problems. However, if one agrees that development does not take place in a vacuum and that "sustainable development cannot marginalize the religious ontologies of the religiously vibrant context of Africa."[100] the role of religion contributing to sustainable development in Africa becomes obvious. I argue that a constructive reflection on the cosmologies and environmental ontologies of the religious communities in Africa, such as environmental stewardship, can engender transformative reflection and action towards attaining sustainable development in Africa. Haynes avers that the emerging consensus that religion's developmental potential has long been underutilized "reflects a widespread agreement that development is a complex process, difficult to attain, and a realization that it is necessary to look to various non-state, including faith-based, entities to maximize chances of achieving it."[101]

99. Golo and Yaro, "Reclaiming Stewardship," 298.

100. Golo, "Sabbath," 250.

101. Haynes, "Religion and Development," 7.

Therefore, the development community and the secular state need to move away from labeling religion "anti-developmental," to working out the eco-dimensional aspects in religious cosmologies and ecological ontologies. This would also enable the development community to partner with faith communities in Africa as stakeholders to engender environmental sustainability in the development process—sustainable development. The question is: what alternate option and vision of development can religious communities proffer that will be imposing on even the secular as a workable and better option to conceiving and proceeding with development in Africa? In the following paragraphs I propose two of such closely related options.

Affirmation of the Religious Ontology on the Intrinsic Values and Integrity of the Natural World

From the perspective of environmental stewardship, particularly developmental preservation, and as required from the steward, humans are permitted to use the earth's resources for their well-being and improve on it as much as they are capable. Thus, humans may improve on its resources as much as their ingenuity and innovation allows. It is an acknowledgement that humans will seek progress and make use of the resources entrusted to them by a benevolent creator God who created the world with value and divine purpose. In doing these, they are guided against undermining the integrity of the natural world and its ability to provide for the needs of other trustees (future generations) who have equal right to access these resources—environmental stewardship.

From the Christian perspective, and with reference to Genesis 2:15, Asante writes: "The other expression *tilling* implies that humanity, is to serve the created order by applying itself to improving or developing its productive capacity. The other expression . . . *keeping*, which implies that humanity preserve, maintain and ensure the safe-keeping of the created order."[102] Similarly, the indigenous Akan of Ghana aver that "God created the natural world for the benefit of humans; so that human beings would find life and meaning within the natural world, while safeguarding and preserving it."[103] Thus, working to maintain the intrinsic value of the natural world, maintaining its integrity, and not overruling and reducing

102. Asante, "Ecological Crisis," 14.

103. Golo et al., "Akan Ontology," 13.

it to the whims of human desires, as is endemic in the contemporary form of socio-economic development, are required of the steward.

In the context of environmental problems in Africa, a development policy and practice that emphasizes the intrinsic worth of the natural world, even its religious value, and what this means practically for environmental sustainability would be opting for a development that is stewardship based. This would mean acknowledging and affirming the values, cosmologies, and ontologies in the various religious traditions and developing contextually shared values and norms towards a transformative affirmation of the intrinsic value of nature. This would be necessary in working out a subversive religious ethic that frustrates any unsustainable growth-oriented approach to development that denigrates the value of the world and degrades it.

The values and norms required to maintain the intrinsic worth of creation abound in the religious traditions and cultures of Africa. Christianity and Islam do not lack these either. For instance, using the discourse of the Sabbath (the period of rest away from the land and other productive elements of the natural world so that they also have a period of reprieve and regenerate), it is underscored how affirming and respecting the intrinsic value of creation, through the Sabbath, is compatible with the contemporary current world of productivity and consumption. This is particularly so regarding the Sabbath's requirement of restraint and limits.[104] Similarly, research among indigenous communities has also underscored how compatible economic activities are with maintaining and respecting the integrity of the natural world.[105] They devise mechanisms that place limits on the extent to which humans can go in attaining human well-being and livelihood—development. It is reiterated that it would be wrong to think indigenous people preserve the resources of the natural world through prohibitions and restrictions because they are unaware of their economic value and tradability, instead of acknowledging that their religious ontology supports sustainable use of them.[106] While indigenous people benefit from the resources in their various vocations and trades, respecting the integrity and the value of the natural world means they are conscious of their limits as required of their stewardship. This brings clarity to the discourse of development preservation in lived experience.

104. Golo, "Sabbath," 261.

105. Golo et al., "Akan Ontology," 23.

106. Golo et al., "Akan Ontology," 23.

Bringing this to the development discourse in Africa would require partnership between the development community and the religious community, which has the capacity to motivate people. The purpose of this partnership would be to harness religious resources, such as beliefs and teachings, in developing environmentally sensitive and conscious attitudes and lifestyles that do not fuel economic growth choices by the secular state. This would also entail using same resources in building resilience and the agency to act as stewards of the natural world when confronted with earth-devouring secular growth choices. It is on this score that the enduring culture of materialism and consumerism, which has gripped some of the religious stakeholders instead of working to safeguard the intrinsic worth and value of the natural world, is worrying. This is rather morally perplexing because it undermines and brings into question the stewardship of religious communities.

A Development Option Conscious of the Interrelatedness of Life, Human Limitations, and Placing Limits on Human Interferences in the Natural World

The stewardship of humankind is grounded in the fact that human beings take care of the natural environment so that the natural environment caters for their needs and progress, in return. This is the natural interrelationship and community within creation where the well-being of the one engenders that of the other. Human well-being and environmental well-being are two sides of the same coin.[107] This is the basic understanding of ecological relationships. As stewards with limitations (humans are not God), human beings can benefit from the resources entrusted to them, and they can make innovations thereby "fulfilling a key role in the working out of God's plan for the whole creation."[108] This opportunity extended to humanity must be considered as "far from the warrant for 'domination' and 'exploitation that it has so often be taken to be."[109]

Therefore, related to affirming the intrinsic value of the natural world, a development option that fulfills human stewardship obligations would also consider the limits of human beings and their technological capabilities in the interventions in the natural world. Scientific and

107. Golo et al., "Akan Ontology," 26.

108. Gecaga, "Creative Stewardship," 37.

109. Gecaga, "Creative Stewardship," 37.

technological arrogance cannot be the attitude of the steward, but rather the acknowledgement and affirmation of human dependence on an Ultimate Being, the Creator. Basically, what the religious view of the natural world does is that it "recognises human imperfection and therefore generally accepts that life will not be perfect either,"[110] as the economic growth supporters would like us to believe.

Much more apparently than the other religious traditions, the indigenous religious traditions of Africa have lessons to offer in restraining humanity from unsustainable benefits from the natural world. These may be adapted for resource use control in the socio-economic development process. In indigenous African anthropology, human well-being and social improvement, which is the core of development, is measured in terms of the health and/or well-being of the natural world. This is because Africans believe there is "an uninterrupted interaction between human persons and the cosmos, that is, the human persons and the cosmos complement each other to the extent that they cannot exist without this interdependence."[111] It is emphasized in African anthropology that the well-being of the community is defined to include the ecological community—the natural world—which in turn enhances the well-being of human individuals.

Thus, all species and parts of the natural world—humans and nonhumans—are interrelated and depend on each other organically, and the bio-physical world is also in relationship with the spiritual world. It is for this reason that activities of humans in meeting their material needs among indigenous people are regulated using ritual prohibitions, such as taboos, to protect the well-being of the community.[112] The improvement of life and efficient functioning of the social and economic system, which is the focus of socio-economic development, is tied to that of the natural world. This requires that development policies and practices must operate within ecological limits. This sensitive interrelatedness underscored by indigenous local knowledge must direct development policy and practice in Africa, even if they are religiously derived. This is because indigenous people claim it has been and continues to be effective in environmental sustainability, when practiced.[113] It is against this background

110. Ter Haar, "Religion in Development Debate," 5.

111. Bujo, "Ethical Dimension," 209.

112. Golo et al., "Akan Ontology," 21–22.

113. Golo et al., "Akan Ontology," 20, 24.

that one appreciates the concerns of religious and faith leaders in their communiqué to COP-15:

> We must realise that well-being cannot be equated with material wealth. The quality of life is not dependent on the quantity of material things or growth measured by GDP. Instead, our standard of living depends on our standard of loving and sharing. We cannot sustain a world dominated by profit-seeking, rampant consumerism and gross inequalities, and an atmosphere of competition where the powerful take advantage of the weak without caring for the wellbeing of every form of life. Development cannot be sustained if the affluent project themselves as examples to be copied by everyone else, and if the poor model their lifestyles on such examples. These insights draw from the rich moral and spiritual traditions on our continent and elsewhere in the world. Despite the historical violence and disorganisation that Africa has suffered and inflicted on itself, these insights have been transmitted to us by our ancestors who believed in the harmony of vital forces, between human beings and the rest of creation. In our African spiritual heritage and our diverse faith traditions, trees, flowers, water, soil and animals have always been essential companions of human beings, without which life and being are inconceivable. We express this in different ways through our understanding of the world as God's own beloved creation, and our sense of place and vocation within it.[114]

As it were, human stewardship imposes practical demands and widespread responsibilities on individuals, policy-makers, communities, and societies toward the earth.[115] What this would mean for a stewardship-based approach to socio-economic development is a consciousness of the relationships that exist between the approaches adopted by policy-makers and development practitioners and the sustainability of the natural world. Similarly, the development of alertness to mitigate any potential negative impact of such relationships through policies and systems, as would be required of a good steward, would be crucial. For instance, the indiscriminate clearing of forests and vegetation to pave way for development projects and/or logging for trade, the pollution and toxification of land and water bodies in agribusiness, and the emission of all forms of pollutants into the atmosphere would be considered irresponsible stewardship.

114. Rautenbach et al., "Religions for Climate Justice," 28.

115. Golo and Yaro, "Reclaiming Stewardship," 297.

Conclusion

The natural world has a Creator and values that impose on the human community stewardship responsibilities. Consequently, pursuing unrestrained socio-economic development in Africa in ways that undermine and degrade the natural world is a fundamental affront to the religious sensibilities of many Africans and their stewardship obligations to the natural world, as typified by the Ghanaian context explored in this chapter. Therefore, for development policies to reflect and meet the socio-economic, cultural, and environmental needs of many Africans, there will be the need to strive for a development that does not only focus on their genuine economic and material needs but also emphasizes their religious ontologies of the natural world. These would include their stewardship responsibilities and what is required of them in attaining these. These would also require acknowledging and affirming the intrinsic worth of the natural world and its resources, as well as the interrelatedness of the created order, as affirmed by the stewardship of religious communities in Africa.

Bibliography

Adekunle, Ibrahim Ayoade. "On the Search for Environmental Sustainability in Africa: The Role of Governance." *Environmental Science and Pollution Research* 28 (2021) 14607–20.

Alvater, Elmar. "The Growth Obsession." *Socialist Register* 38 (2002) 73–92. https://socialistregister.com/index.php/srv/issue/view/439 on 11/07/2019.

Asante, Emmanuel. "Ecological Crisis: A Christian Answer" *Trinity Journal of Church and Theology* 9/2 (1994) 8–25.

Boff, Leonardo. *Cry of the Earth, Cry of the Poor*. New York: Orbis, 1997.

Bujo, Benezet. *The Ethical Dimension of Community: The African Model and the Dialogue between North and South*. Nairobi: Paulines, 1998.

Chirisa, Innocent. "An Analysis of the Environmental Stewardship Concept and Its Applicability in Peri-Urban Towns: Lessons from Epworth in Zimbabwe." *Journal of Sustainable Development in Africa* 12/4 (2010) 41–57.

Conradie, Ernst M. *Christianity and a Critique of Consumerism: A Survey of Six Points of Entry*. Wellington, South Africa: Bible Media, 2010.

Cornwall, Andrea. "Buzzwords and Fuzzwords: Deconstructing Development Discourse." *Development in Practice* 17/4–5 (2007) 471–84.

Darko, Isaac Nortey. "Environmental Stewardship and Indigenous African Philosophies: Implications for Schooling, and Health Education in Africa: A Case of Ghana." PhD thesis, University of Toronto, 2014. https://tspace.library.utoronto.ca/bitstream/1807/94543/3/Darko_Isaac_N_201406_PhD_thesis.pdf.

De-Jong, Eelke. "Religious Values and Economic Growth: A Review and Assessment of Recent Studies." NiCE Working Paper 08–111. Nijmegen: Nijmegen Center for Economics (NiCE), 2008.

Gecaga, Margaret, "Creative Stewardship for a New Earth." In *Theology of Reconstruction: Exploratory Essays*, edited by Mary Getui and Emmanuel A. Obeng, 28–49. Nairobi: Acton, 1999.

Glastra, Rob, ed. *Cut and Run: Illegal Logging and Timber Trade in the Tropics*. Ottawa: International Development Research Centre, 1999.

Goldsmith, Edward. "Global Trade and the Environment." In *The Case Against the Global Economy*, edited by Jerry Mander and Edward Goldsmith, 78–91. San Francisco: Sierra, 1996.

Golo, Ben-Willie Kwaku. "In Search of a Sustainable Society in Africa: Christianity, Justice and Sustainable Peace in a Changing Climate." *Philosophia Reformata: An International Philosophical Journal of Christianity, Science and Society* 83/1 (2018) 68–89.

———. "Religious Environmental Stewardship, the Sabbath and Sustainable Futures in Africa: Implications for Sustainability Discourse." In *Religion, Sustainability and Education: Pedagogy, Perspectives, and Praxis Towards Ecological Sustainability*, edited by Mary Philip et al., 242–65. Steinkjer, Norway: Embla Akademisk, 2021.

Golo, Ben-Willie Kwaku, and Ernestina E. Novieto. "Religion and Sustainable Development in Africa: Neo-Pentecostal Economies in Perspective." *Journal of Religion and Development* 1/1 (2022) 73–95.

Golo, Ben-Willie Kwaku, and Joseph A. Yaro. "Reclaiming Stewardship in Ghana: Religion and Climate Change." *Nature and Culture* 8 (2013) 282–300.

Golo, Ben-Willie Kwaku, et al. "Akan Religious Ontology and Environmental Sustainability in Ghana." *Worldviews* (2022) 1–29. doi:10.1163/15685357-20221001

Haynes, Jeff. *Religion and Development: Conflict or Cooperation*? Basingstoke: Palgrave Macmillan, 2007.

Hilson, Gavin. "The Environmental Impact of Small-Scale Gold Mining in Ghana: Identifying Problems and Possible Solutions." *The Geographical Journal* 168/1 (2002) 57–72.

Howard-Clinton, Edward G. "The Emerging Concepts of Environmental Issues in Africa." *Environmental Management* 83/3 (1984) 187–90.

Jenkins, Willie, Evan Berry, and Luke Beck Kreider. "Religion and Climate Change" *Annual Review of Environment and Resources* 43 (2018) 85–108. https://doi.org/10.1146/annurev-environ-102017-25855.

Lundgren, Karin. *The Global Impact of E-Waste: Addressing the Challenge*. Geneva: International Labour Organization, 2012.

Marshall, Katherine. "Development and Religion: A Different Lens on Development Debates." *Peabody Journal of Education* 76/3–4 (2011) 339–75.

Mather, A. S., and C. L. Needle. "Development, Democracy and Forest Trends." *Global Environmental Change* 9/2 (1999) 105–18.

Oteng-Ababio, Martin. "When Necessity Begets Ingenuity: E-Waste Scavenging as Livelihood Strategy in Accra, Ghana." *African Studies Quarterly* 13/1–2 (2012) 1–21.

Rautenbach, Ignatius, et al. *Religions for Climate Justice. International Interfaith Statements 2008–2014*. Globethics.net Text 3. 2014. http://hdl.handle.net/20.500.12424/222249.

Rist, Gilbert. "Development as Buzzword" In *Deconstructing Development Discourse: Buzzwords and Fuzzwords*, edited by Andrea Cornwall and Deborah Eade, 19–27. Bourton on Dunsmore, Rugby: Practical Action, 2010.

Russell, Cathriona. "Burden-Sharing in a Changing Climate: Which Principles and Practices Can Theologians Endorse?" *Studies in Christian Ethics* 24/1 (2011) 67–76.

Schnaiberg, Allan, and Kenneth Alan Gould. *Environment and Society: The Enduring Conflict*. New York: St. Martin's, 1994.

Simon, David, and Anders Narman. *Development as Theory and Practice*. Harlow: Longmann and Todd, 1999.

Tamakloe, W. *State of Ghana's Environment—Challenges of Compliance and Enforcement*. 2000. https://aquadocs.org/bitstream/handle/1834/409/04h_ghana.pdf?sequence=1&isAllowed=y.

Ter Haar, Gerrie, and Stephen Ellis. "The Role of Religion in Development: Towards a New Relationship between the European Union and Africa." *European Journal of Development Research* 18/3 (2006) 351–67.

Ter Haar, Gerrie. "Religion in the Development Debate" *Ghana Bulletin of Theology* 3 (2008) 1–8.

Todd-Peters, Rebecca. *In Search of the Good Life: The Ethics of Globalisation*. New York: Continuum, 2002.

Tucker, Evelyn M., and John A. Grim, eds. *Worldviews and Ecology: Philosophy and the Environment*. New York. Orbis, 1994.

United Nations. *Our Common Future*. Report of the World Commission on Environment and Development. Oxford: Oxford University Press, 1987. https://sustainabledevelopment.un.org/content/documents/5987our-common-future.pdf.

Vischer, Lukas. "How Sustainable Is the Present Project of World Trade?" In *Sustainability and Globalisation*, edited by Julio de Santa Anan . Geneva: WCC, 1998.

Von Czechowski, Aditi Surie. *CDP Africa Report: Benchmarking Progress towards Climate Safe Cities, States, and Regions*. Charlottenburg: CDP Worldwide, 2020. https://cdn.cdp.net/cdp-production/cms/reports/documents/000/005/023/original/CDP_Africa_Report_2020.pdf?1583855467.

Wardekker, Arjan J. et al. "Ethics and Public Perception of Climate Change: Exploring the Christian Voices in the US public debate." *Global Environmental Change* 19/4 (2009) 512–21.

Welchman, Jennifer. "A Defence of Environmental Stewardship." *Environmental Values* 21/3 (2012) 297–316.

Part IV

Methodology

Chapter 7

Rituals of Gender and Race

Assessing Chidester's Material Analysis of Their Intersection in African Indigenous Religion

Johan Strijdom

Taking up the leading question of this book, "What has religion studies been up to in Africa?," this contribution intends to assess the analysis of rituals of gender and race in African indigenous religion by David Chidester, one of the most important scholars of religion from South Africa.[1] Foregrounded will be a clarification of the theoretical depth given by Chidester to the key concepts of ritual as material mediation of religion, gender, and race, and an assessment of the extent to which he has applied these theorized concepts to two pertinent case studies from indigenous religion in South Africa.[2] The first example concerns the ritual of marriage between African men at mining compounds in Johannesburg at the beginning of the twentieth century, whereas the second

1. For an appreciation of Chidester's award-winning work, see the introduction and collection of essays in Strijdom and Scharnick-Udemans, *Materializing Religion*. This *Festschrift* also includes a bibliography of Chidester's publications.

2. In "Postgraduates Producing Knowledge," Chidester himself argued that our best hope to produce innovative insights in the study of religion depends on giving theoretical depth to key concepts, and applying such theorized concepts to case studies. This contribution tests to what extent Chidester has been successful in implementing this thesis.

example deals with the ritual of virginity testing and sexual purity at the Reed Dance festival in KwaZulu-Natal at the end of the twentieth century and beginning of the twenty-first century. In these case studies the intersection between gender and race will become apparent.

Ritual as Material Mediation of Religion

The term "ritual," like "religion,"[3] is not necessarily an emic or insider category, but a concept invented and filled with content by scholars for analytical purposes. According to Jonathan Z. Smith, this is a necessary strategy to provide interpretive maps for scholars, whose task should not be limited to parroting and paraphrase.[4]

The modern meaning of "ritual" *as fixed, repetitive action* can, according to the classicist Jan Bremmer, be traced to the end of the nineteenth and beginning of the twentieth century.[5] Reacting to the Protestant prioritization of *beliefs* in defining religion, British scholars such as Robertson Smith and Jane Harrison inaugurated an innovative shift in the academic study of religion by focusing on *rituals*—an innovation that was taken up and developed in France by Durkheim, Mauss, and Hubert in their social theories of religion.

If the French social theories emphasized that the function of beliefs and ritual practices is to *unify* adherents into a group,[6] the anthropologist Arnold van Gennep instead argued that rites of passage serve to *transform* or *change* the role of individuals within their societies—a perspective that

3. Smith insists on the analytical importance of distinguishing between "religion" as generic category (e.g., as defined by Durkheim in sociological terms) and "religions" as species or examples of the genus "religion." He captures the point in the conclusion to his well-known essay, "Religion, Religions, Religious": "Religion is not a native term; it is a term created by scholars for their intellectual purposes and therefore is theirs to define. It is a second-order, generic concept that plays the same role in establishing a disciplinary horizon that a concept such as 'language' plays in linguistics or 'culture' plays in anthropology. There can be no disciplined study of religion without such a horizon'" (Smith, *Relating Religion*, 193–94).

4. Smith, *Relating Religion*, 30–31, 134, 175, 201, 204, 206–9, 219, 221–22, 368, 372. For a discussion of this foundational point in Smith's approach to the study of religion, see Strijdom, "Uses of Social Theory," 19–21.

5. Bremmer,"Ritual," 32. For his more detailed tracking of the genealogy of the term "ritual," see Bremmer, "'Religion,' 'Ritual,'" 14–24.

6. This is the main point of Durkheim's concept of "religion," elaborated in Durkheim, *Elementary Forms*.

was revived in the 1960s and 1970s' second turn to ritual, with Victor Turner as prominent exponent.[7]

The more recent *material* turn in the study of religion takes this trajectory further with its foregrounding of bodily rituals that involve objects and the senses as necessary mediations of religion.[8]

David Chidester, as one of the pioneers in the study of the material dynamics of religion, has argued not only for a rectification of the Protestant bias, but has also contrasted phenomenological "snapshots" of phenomena and its search for recurrent stable patterns with historical approaches that focus on discontinuities and surprises within changing social, political, economic, and cultural contexts.[9] Applied to ritual, Chidester thus holds that a ritual "is not the reenactment of an authenticating original. Rather, as a dynamic, embodied practice, every ritual act is a new performance . . . Not a repetition of an original, every ritual act is a new act."[10] Moreover, Chidester holds that the traditional phenomenological claim to offer neutral descriptions hides the unequal power relations that are at work in religious negotiations, which deserve our attention now.[11]

Following on my title *Rituals of Gender and Race*, I need to briefly indicate the content that Chidester gives to the concepts of gender and race, before I turn to a close reading of two case studies from his oeuvre to establish to what extent he has applied these theoretical perspectives.

7. For a helpful survey of classical theories of ritual, in addition to Bremmer, see Brunotte, "Classic Ritual Theories," 351–65. Chidester too underlines the role of Robertson Smith in the turn from a focus on beliefs to rituals: "Although imperial comparative religion was primarily focused on beliefs, concentrating on distilling a primitive psychology, mentality or 'belief in spiritual beings,' theorists also had to pay attention to religious practices. William Robertson Smith (1846–1894) was at the forefront of directing attention to ritual in the study of religion" (Chidester, *Empire of Religion*, 164).

8. For a discussion of this shift towards material mediations in the academic study of religion, with further references, see Strijdom, "Material Turn," 1–2.

9. For his discussion of Bleeker and Capps as exponents of these contrasting approaches, see Chidester, *Religion: Material Dynamics*, 152–65.

10. Chidester, *Savage Systems*, 261–62.

11. Although foregrounded in Chidester's oeuvre, the point is explicitly argued in Chidester, "Poetics and Politics of Sacred Space," 211–31. For an assessment of Chidester's application of this point, see Strijdom, "Gerardus van der Leeuw," 243–51.

Gender

How does Chidester conceptualize gender? In his first book, *Patterns of Action* (1987), which offered a phenomenological description of recurrent ethical patterns in religious traditions, Chidester devoted a section to gender.[12]

Focusing on "traditional" religions, from ancient Greece through Abrahamic and Eastern religions, he observed that these traditions generally tend to classify human beings by subjugating women to men, assuming that there are "different social roles . . . appropriate for men and women," and "different ethical rights and responsibilities that correspond to these social roles."[13]

To this ethics of obedience he noted two responses, recent at the time of writing his book. One was from feminists—with Mary Daley as prominent representative—who "attacked sexism in religious language" or more radically "urge(d) women to separate themselves from men to refuse to work with them, to refuse sexual relations with them, to refuse to associate with them," thus creating an ethics for women of "self-sufficient life styles independent of men."[14]

Another response, however, by Ivan Illich, with a clear "nostalgia" for preindustrial gender arrangements, contrasted traditional "gendered" with modern "sexed" societies, in which the former differentiates between male and female roles as separate, but equal and complementary, while the latter "transformed" men and women into "unisex, interchangeable economic units in the industrial machinery of production."[15]

As part of his discussion of "ethical rules in the human life cycle," Chidester showed how initiation and marriage rituals symbolize and incorporate, transform, and enact gender roles.[16] Marriage rituals[17] are considered to "incorporate a community's primary classification of male and female genders" and to "reinforce" expressions of sexuality and desire, which are "socially acknowledged and often religiously sanctioned."[18] Importantly, with reference to Van Gennep, marriage as "a rite of passage in

12. Chidester, *Patterns of Action*, 155–59.
13. Chidester, *Patterns of Action*, 155.
14. Chidester, *Patterns of Action*, 157–58.
15. Chidester, *Patterns of Action*, 158.
16. Chidester, *Patterns of Action*, 130–72.
17. See also Chidester, *Religions of South Africa*, 22–23.
18. Chidester, *Patterns of Action*, 148.

the human life cycle" marks the *transition* or *change* or *passing* "from one social category to another" by *separating* individuals "from their previous social category, within one family unit," and *incorporating* them "into a new family pattern."[19] Although patterns of marriage between men and women vary from monogamous to polygamous and from exogamous to endogamous across cultures, they are considered normative and obligatory by the respective communities, with culturally specific ethical rules to *govern* tensions within marriage, extramarital sex and divorce, and with exceptions occurring for ascetic practices and homosexual relations in some communities.

During initiation rituals,[20] which play a crucial role in the "transition from childhood to adulthood" in indigenous[21] cultures, adolescent boys and girls are traditionally *segregated* from their families, and taught about their respective roles as adult men and women, before they are *reintegrated* into their communities as adults with particular normative gender obligations. This transition or transformation from child to adult, Chidester observed, is often marked on the body of the boy or girl by circumcision or scarring that serves to bind the age group together, and to focus the new adult roles and responsibilities by means of a painful ritual ordeal.[22]

Race

How does Chidester theorize the concept of race? If gender in traditional religions is about the *subclassification* of women, the concept of race can be traced to "the classification and ranking of people into quasi-scientific racial categories" in nineteenth-century European theories, which—mixed with romantic ideals of a pure nation—constituted the sources of racist ideology. Thus emerged the Nazi ideal of a pure German *Volk* from which those of Jewish blood were to be purged,[23] as well

19. Chidester, *Patterns of Action*, 148.

20. See also Chidester, *Religions of South Africa*, 24.

21. In *Patterns of Action*, Chidester still uses the term "tribal," but in his later work he uses the more acceptable term "indigenous." This change in use of terminology reveals an increasing awareness by Chidester, when he started to engage with imperial theories of religion, of the use of terminology in the study African religions.

22. Chidester, *Patterns of Action*, 134–38.

23. Chidester, *Christianity*, 495–501 and 507–8.

as British colonial and Afrikaner racist nationalist identities in South Africa.[24]

In his academic work spanning more than thirty years, race and racism have been of continuous concern as he has examined the construct of evolutionary theories of religion in Western imperial centers, and the interaction between white and black people in his analysis of changing myths, religious practices, and institutions under systemically dehumanizing colonial and apartheid conditions.[25]

The term "racism" was already central in Chidester's analysis of Jim Jones's movement, understood as the *subclassification* of human beings within the racist American system.[26] It was then further elaborated in *Shots in the Street: Violence and Religion in South Africa*, where he argued that the term "apartheid" had become "an international, generic term for racism."[27] Giving content to the term, he emphasized that the term "does not merely define *personal* prejudice or bigotry," but that it "designates a racism that is enforced by legalized coercion and maintained by military power," being "a generic term for *institutionalized* racism" (my emphasis), of *systemic* discrimination, political exclusion and domination, and economic exploitation, based on racial subclassifications of human beings.[28]

Central to Chidester's analysis from a South African location is that evolutionary theories of religion that were constructed in British imperial centers in the latter part of the nineteenth century were complicit in the racist dehumanization of indigenous black South Africans. Simultaneously, however, Chidester has been at pains to emphasize the agency of indigenous people under those oppressive conditions. Not only did nineteenth-century Zulu speakers reinterpret their creation myths within the context of land dispossession by white Europeans and invented rituals to deal with dreams in which ancestors demanded sacrifices of cattle and the return to their homesteads,[29] but South African black intellectuals of the emerging ANC in the first half of the twentieth century also reacted

24. Chidester, *Religions of South Africa*, 91.

25. Notably in Chidester, *Savage Systems* and *Empire of Religion*.

26. Chidester, *Salvation and Suicide*, 52.

27. Chidester, *Shots in the Streets*, 3.

28. Chidester, *Shots in the Streets*, 3 and 68.

29. For a discussion of this analysis, see Strijdom, "Senses," 173–75.

by reinterpreting the concept of race within an ideal of a non-racial, inclusive nationalism in contrast to opposing exclusionary views.[30]

Taking this bare outline as framework, we may now turn to the selected case studies, both taken from Chidester's more recent work, to assess to what extent Chidester's analysis is informed by and applies these theoretical perspectives.

First Case Study: Same-Sex Marriages between African Men

In *Empire of Religion: Imperialism and Comparative Religion*, in which Chidester shows how imperial theories of religion were constructed by means of a triple mediation, from indigenous informants through colonial middlemen to European theorists, he discusses the interaction between the missionary to the rural Thonga[31] in Mozambique, Henri-Alexandre Junod, and his evangelist and informant, Elias "Spoon" Libombo, on the marriage rituals that they witnessed between African men at the mining compounds and hostels of Johannesburg at the beginning of the twentieth century. Chidester sketches the event as follows:

> At one of the compounds, men were dancing in celebration but also in anticipation, awaiting the arrival of a procession that, as the European missionary observed, included many women. Knowing that very few women lived around the mines, the European missionary asked his African colleague why so many women were participating in this ceremonial procession. The African evangelist explained: "They are not women! They are *tinkhontshana*, boys who placed on their chests the breasts of women carved in wood, and who are going to the dance in order to play the part of women."[32]

How did Junod and Elias Libombo understand this marriage ritual? For the indigenous evangelist, the ritual was according to Chidester "effective in *marking* and *making*—juniors and seniors, males and females, wives and husbands—in the life of the mining compound" (my emphasis).[33]

30. See, e.g., Chidester, *Religions of South Africa*, 223, 238, 248; and *Shots in the Street*, 140.

31. For Junod's construct of a homogenous Thonga identity, based on a presumed common language, culture, and religion, see Chidester, *Empire of Religion*, 169.

32. Chidester, *Empire of Religion*, 159.

33. Chidester, *Empire of Religion*, 160.

Husbands were to give money to their wives or even pay *lobola* to the families of the "brides"[34] and sacrifice a goat to the ancestral spirits.

For the white missionary, however, the ritual was shocking, an immoral and "unnatural vice" in the mining compounds that he did not observe amongst the rural Thonga, whose sexual practices he described in his ethnography.[35] Although he considered the "sex life" of Bantu speakers as "primitive" and "shocking" to "our moral feelings," i.e., to Western Victorians, who as "white masters" had the duty to keep their African subjects under their "supervision" and civilize them (particularly by eradicating *lobola* and polygamy),[36] he held that the "terrible evil" of sex between men was imported by white people from Europe with a destructive impact on indigenous culture, and made practical proposals on how it might be stopped by "prohibit(ing) curtains, prevent(ing) beds from touching each other, introduc(ing) guards, and install(ing) electric lights" in the mining compounds.[37] Instead of accepting imperial evolutionary theories of religion from his mentor James Frazer uncritically, Chidester observes, Junod was "entangled in the colonial contradictions of civilization," with his concerns here reflecting "a certain ambivalence about the beneficial effects of European civilization."[38]

Chidester, furthermore, importantly points out Junod's use of his personal friend Van Gennep's threefold structure of rites of passage to analyze not simply the process of transformation that indigenous individuals *traditionally* underwent as they passed from one life stage to another in their villages, but also the changes that the *modern*, industrialized conditions on the mines brought about: *separation* from their villages was followed by a *liminal* stage at the mines, which transformed them profoundly, before they returned and were again *reincorporated* with a new status at home. In this process money came to play an important role, with promises when they left home that they would compensate the diviner for his services on their return from the mines.

34. *Lobola* here refers to "the ritualized payment of bridewealth," which was "conventionally paid in cattle to the father of the bride" to serve "a number of interlocking interests in sealing a marriage arrangement, not merely between two individuals, but between two extended family groups" (Chidester, *Religions of South Africa*, 24).

35. Chidester, *Empire of Religion*, 160.

36. Chidester, *Empire of Religion*, 170.

37. Chidester, *Empire of Religion*, 177.

38. Chidester, *Empire of Religion*, 177.

How does Chidester analyze this marriage ritual between African men at the mines? Although Chidester's stance is not always clear, it does seem that he would agree with Elias Libombo that the rituals *enacted* gender relations by *making* husbands and wives. He would also agree with Junod's use of Van Gennep's tripartite structure of rites of passage, and would stress that the *liminal* phase of same-sex marriage rituals of "processions, marriage payments, and sacrificial offerings" were "new," "marginal," "even counter-rituals" within an alien, industrial context, which *made* or *remade* "'brides' and 'husbands' in the mining compounds," with particular economic duties.[39] Although Chidester would note the gender *hierarchies* that were created by the rituals, he does not in his analysis of this case study—as he would do for the dehumanizing colonial political and economic context—*problematize* the power relations at work in the indigenous same-sex relations at the mines, for which Foucault's assessment of Greek pederasty might have served as model.[40]

Second Case Study: The Reed Dance, Virginity Testing, and Sexual Purity

In *Wild Religion: Tracking the Sacred in South Africa*, in which he offers an analysis of indigenous and unconventional forms of religion in post-apartheid South Africa from 1994 to the World Cup in 2010, Chidester briefly analyzes the annual Reed Dance festival and virginity testing under the category of "sexual purity."[41] Citing from a tourist website, Chidester describes the festival as follows:

> Convened once a year, in September, at the palace of the Zulu king, the festival draws thousands of Zulu participants, "more than 10 000 invited virgin girls," and, of course, tourists, who can witness the ceremony as part of a package that includes touring sugarcane fields, wildlife reserves, magnificent coastlines, and

39. Chidester, *Empire of Religion*, 177–79.

40. As part of his *History of Sexuality* project, Foucault analyzed pederasty as an institutionalized form of sexuality in ancient Athens. His purpose was not to argue that we should return to such as system of institutionalized asymmetrical power relations, but to show by means of alternative constructs of sexuality that the dominant construct of sexuality need not be accepted as normal sexuality and can be changed.

41. Chidester, *Wild Religion*, 132–51. This analysis opens the chapter as an introduction to his more extensive use of "sexual purity" to analyze the sexual controversies around the then president, Jacob Zuma.

> "undulating hills and valleys, silently speaking to your soul with its natural beauty."[42]

Interestingly, the same website includes an analytical comment whose point Chidester summarizes before continuing with the quotation from the website:

> Performed over four days, the Reed Dance *enacts* the ritual unity of a Zulu nation that is *embodied* in the ritual purity of young women. As the tourist site explains: "The royal reed dance festival in Zululand illustrates the proud heritage of the Zulu nation and plays a huge part in the unification of the nation's people and the king. To ensure ritual purity, only virgin girls are permitted to partake in the ceremony. There are many myths surrounding the festival, one is that if a girl is not pure her reed will break when presenting it to the King, publicly disgracing her and her community." (my emphasis)[43]

What does Chidester make of this festival? How does he analyze this collective ritual? Taking ritual as the focusing lens to analyze this dance, Chidester foregrounds the concept of purity.[44] What strikes him is that the purity is here "specifically cast as female virginity that is performatively demonstrated in a public display" and that the purity "is underwritten by a myth that national identity depends upon sexual purity."[45] He concludes that "the intersection between the most intimate personal subjectivity of young women and a broader social, political and even national collectivity . . . (in) this ritual display of the purity of ten thousand virgins is clearly overdetermined."[46] A crucial function of the dance by sexually pure virgins for the king is, in other words, political: it serves to unite adherents. Up to this point, we may observe, Chidester's analysis is Durkheimian, but with the additional lens that focuses on the sexual purity of virgins.

42. Chidester, *Wild Religion*, 132.

43. Chidester, *Wild Religion*, 132.

44. Although one might expect Chidester to invoke in this case study Mary Douglas's theory of purity as order, and impurity as matter out of place (Douglas, *Purity and Danger*), as he does elsewhere in the book (Chidester, *Wild Religion*, 62), he does not do so. The focus of his analysis here is instead on the political function of these gendered rituals.

45. Chidester, *Wild Religion*, 133.

46. Chidester, *Wild Religion*, 133.

Although Chidester notes that cultural theorists have attended to inventions and manufacturing of heritage in the Reed Dance in ethno-tourism, it is in his analysis of "virginity testing" that he shifts our attention more specifically to historical change. Although claims were made that virginity testing had revived ancient Zulu tradition, Chidester argues that the ritual was a *new* ritual of sexual purity that was introduced as a response to the AIDS epidemic.[47] In this *new* ritual, Chidester summarizes, "elder women inspect younger women to determine their purity, designating them in three classes—A, B, C—as those who have never had sex, those who have had sex but are still virginal, and those who are no longer virgins," and would also in one project invoke Nomkhubulwane as goddess of virginity.[48]

To what extent does Chidester foreground the *power relations* that are at work in this case study? Here again he is brief, noting the "political ramifications" of the ritual of virginity testing in one sentence only: "not only in its sexual politics of community healing, social mobilization, and collective purity, but also in the opposition it has provoked among human rights advocates, who have invoked constitutional principles of individual freedom, equality, and dignity to propose legislation outlawing it."[49] As in the previous case study, no further ethical argument is here provided by Chidester—a crucial point to which I will return in my conclusion.

Conclusion

What have we learned? What remains to be done? I highlight three interlinking points.

First, *theorized concepts*. If Chidester is correct that our best hope to produce innovative insights in the study of religion lies in giving key concepts theoretical depth,[50] and using these as lenses to analyze selected case studies, to what extent has he succeeded in the project under discussion here?

47. Chidester, *Wild Religion*, 134 and 204.

48. Chidester, *Wild Religion*, 134. In an earlier work, Chidester remarked that as "a nature goddess—Nomkhubulwana, 'Princess of Heaven' – . . . was honored by young, unmarried women through seasonal rituals" (Chidester, *Religions of South Africa*, 8).

49. Chidester, *Wild Religion*, 134.

50. Chidester, "Postgraduates Producing Knowledge," 5–8.

Taking "ritual" as a primary term, we have not only seen Chidester's conscious appreciation of the turn from the Protestant focus on beliefs to a focus on practices, which anticipates the recent material turn in the study of religion, but also an application of Durkheim and Van Gennep's theories to the case studies. In the case of marriages between African men, the ritual processions, marriage payment, and goat sacrifices served not only to *unite* the participating group, but the performance also enacted *new, transformed* gender roles by creating husbands and wives during what can be understood as a liminal phase in the lives of those participants. Conceptualizing "gender" not simply as biological fact, but as a social construct that is ritually enacted in same-sex marriage and in dances by virgins, has assisted him in analyzing rather than merely paraphrasing the observed phenomena.

A consciousness of the genealogy of the concepts of race and racism has furthermore contributed to this end by letting us see the ambiguous relationship of the colonial middleman, the missionary Junod, to imperial evolutionary theories of indigenous religion, with specific reference to his Victorian values on same-sex relations applied to the marriages between African men at the mines. In the case of the Reed Dance too, Chidester's historical review of the concept of sexual purity shows us how the impact of white missionaries and AIDS transformed the construct of virginity among Zulu speakers in rural Kwazulu-Natal. In both case studies, it is indeed a focus on the *intersection* of the categories of race and gender performed in the selected rituals within changing contexts that may help us see the observed phenomena in a new light.

Secondly, *historical approach.* If Chidester is correct in arguing that "snapshots" are not sufficient to understand observed phenomena, but that a historical analysis of these as moving images or an understanding of their "material dynamics" within changing political and economic contexts is more productive in generating insight, to what extent has Chidester succeeded in doing just this in his analysis of the selected case studies? In his earliest work, we have seen him employing a phenomenological approach with the explicit aim of identifying and describing diverse patterns of life cycle rituals like marriage and initiation across religious traditions. In his later work, however, his approach is more historical as he focused on the *changes* that rituals undergo within new contexts, illustrated by his analysis of the selected case studies of marriages between African men under conditions of migration and urban industrialization, and the ethno-tourism of the Reed Dance and virginity testing.

Lastly, *ethical stance.* If Chidester is correct that a phenomenological approach often hides power relations at work in describing myths, rituals, and institutions, and that we now need a *critical* phenomenology that foregrounds precisely the uneven power relations at work, to what extent has he succeeded in doing so in his analysis of the selected case studies and how might his work be taken further by elaborating ethical arguments?

In his earliest phenomenological work, his aim was to describe ethical patterns in religious traditions, including a description of critical stances against dominant systems, but without arguing for or taking a normative position himself. In his subsequent works in the 1990s he indeed foregrounded hierarchical gender, racial, and political relations, in colonial and apartheid churches in South Africa and imperial religious studies, but also in Indigenous African Religion. At this stage of his research, he not only described such power relations, but also at crucial moments took an ethical stance in designing new education policies based on human rights.[51]

In his work since 2000, however, he has become more reticent in emphasizing and taking a normative stance on gender and racial relations in indigenous African religion. We have seen in his analysis of the selected case studies, that although gender and race are important in his analysis, he did not problematize the asymmetrical gender relations at work in the marriages between African men at the mines, and only in passing noted the critique of human rights activists in the case of virginity testing.

It is at this point, I submit, that Chidester's work may be taken further, by making our ethical arguments and stances explicit and applying them transparently and consistently, as is done for example in Martha Nussbaum's application of her capabilities approach to gender problems[52] in order to aim—in the words of the Mozambican social anthropologist and activist Alcinda Honwana, reflecting on her responsibility as an academic—"to better the lives of the people in the places we study"[53] by

51. For Chidester's publications on human rights and education policy in teaching about religions in schools, see Chidester, "Chidester Publications," 280–93.

52. For development of this argument drawing on Nussbaum's capabilities approach, see Strijdom, "Towards a Critique of Indigenous African Religion," 1–4.

53. Chidester does conclude *Patterns of Power* by taking a general ethical stance, arguing that learning about others as fellow human beings will help to "affirm the reciprocal recognition of human beings in patterns of power that allow them to be fully human" (Chidester, *Patterns of Power*, 307). However, in his analysis of indigenous religions, as seen in the selected case studies here, Chidester has refrained from criticizing the legitimation and practices of gender inequality.

combining "rigorous academic work and effective policy development to help shape our tomorrow."[54]

Bibliography

Bremmer, Jan. "'Religion,' 'Ritual' and the Opposition 'Sacred vs. Profane': Notes Towardsa Terminological 'Genealogy.'" In *Ansichten griechischer Rituale: Festschrift für Walter Burkert*, edited by F. Graf, 9–32. Stuttgart: Teubner, 1998.

———. "Ritual." In *Religions of the Ancient World: A Guide*, edited by S.I. Johnston, 32–44. Cambridge: Belknap, 2004.

Brunotte, Ulrike. "Classic Ritual Theories." In *Religion, Theory, Critique: Classic and Contemporary Approaches and Methodologies*, edited by R. King, 351–65. New York: Columbia University Press, 2017.

Chidester, David. "Chidester Publications (1982–2018)." *Journal for the Study of Religion* 31 (2018) 280–93.

———. *Christianity: A Global History*. San Francisco: HarperCollins, 2000.

———. *Empire of Religion: Imperialism and Comparative Religion*. Chicago: University of Chicago Press, 2014.

———. *Patterns of Action: Religion and Ethics in a Comparative Perspective*. Belmont, CA: Wadsworth, 1987.

———. *Patterns of Power: Religion and Politics in American Culture*. Englewood Cliffs, NJ: Prentice Hall, 1988.

———. "The Poetics and Politics of Sacred Space: Towards a Critical Phenomenology of Religion." In *From the Sacred to the Divine: A New Phenomenological Approach*, edited by A.T. Tymieniecka, 211–31. Analecta Husserliana: The Yearbook of Phenomenological Research 43. Dordrecht: Kluwer 1994.

———. "Postgraduates Producing Knowledge." *Journal for the Study of Religion* 26 (2013) 5–8.

———. *Religion: Material Dynamics*. Berkeley: University of California Press, 2018.

———. *Religions of South Africa*. London: Routledge, 1992.

———. *Salvation and Suicide: An Interpretation of Jim Jones, the Peoples Temple, and Jonestown*. Bloomington: Indiana University Press, 1988.

———. *Savage Systems: Colonialism and Comparative Religion in Southern Africa*. Charlottesville: University Press of Virginia, 1996.

———. *Shots in the Streets: Violence and Religion in South Africa*. Cape Town: Oxford University Press, 1992.

———. *Wild Religion: Tracking the Sacred in South Africa*. Berkeley: University of California Press, 2012.

Douglas, Mary. *Purity and Danger: An Analysis of the Concepts of Pollution and Taboo*. London: Routledge and Keegan Paul, 1966.

Durkheim, Emile. *The Elementary Forms of the Religious Life*. Translated by Joseph W. Swain. New York: Free Press, 1965.

Foucault, Michel. *The History of Sexuality*, vol. 2, *The Use of Pleasure*. London: Penguin, 1984.

54. Honwana, "Honorary Doctorate," 1.

Honwana, Alcinda. "Honorary Doctorate Conferred by Utrecht University: Acceptance Speech by Alcinda Honwana." 2021. https://www.uu.nl/sites/default/files/OAJ-2021-Eredoctoraat-Alcinda-Honwana-Word-of-Thanks.pdf.

Smith, Jonathan Z. *Relating Religion: Essays in the Study of Religion*. Chicago: University of Chicago Press, 2004.

Strijdom, Johan. "Gerardus van der Leeuw at the Voortrekker Monument: A Postcolonial Critique of his Concept of Sacred Place." *NTT Journal for Theology and the Study of Religion* 72 (2018) 243–51.

———. "The Material Turn in Religious Studies and the Possibility of Critique: Assessing Chidester's Analysis of 'the Fetish.'" *HTS Theological Studies* 70 (2014) 1–7.

———. "'Senses': Assessing a Key Term in David Chidester's Analysis of Religion." *Journal for the Study of Religion* 31 (2018) 161–79.

———. "Towards a Critique of Indigenous African Religion." *HTS Theological Studies* 67 (2011) 1–4.

———. "Uses of Social Theory in Comparative Religious Studies: Assessing Chidester's Sociological Analysis of 'Wild Religion' in Post-apartheid South Africa." *Journal for the Study of Religion* 27 (2014) 10–24.

Strijdom, Johan, and Lee-Shae Scharnick-Udemans. "Materializing Religion: Essays in Honor of David Chidester." Editorial introduction. *Journal for the Study of Religion* 31 (2018) 1–6.

Part V

Cultural Studies

Chapter 8

Religion, Culture and Health in Zimbabwe

Exploring the Significance of African Indigenous Knowledge Systems in a COVID-19 Context

Molly Manyonganise *and* Lillian Mhuru

Introduction

In this section, we examine the contestations around the intersection among religion, culture, and health as presented in literature. The intention is to locate the relevance of the arguments arising from existing literature to the Zimbabwe in a COVID-19 context. Proceeding from the foregoing, scholarship on religion, culture, and health are generally agreed that there is a close connection among these three concepts. Religion has been acknowledged as a great influence in shaping the health discourses of many social contexts.[1] Eckersley[2] opines that human health has multiple sources that are material, social, cultural, and spiritual. Hordern[3] is of the view that religion, belief, and culture should be recognized in healthcare as potential sources of moral purpose and personal

1. Chatters, "Religion and Health," 335–67; Eckersley, "Culture, Spirituality, Religion and Health," 54–56; Bhui, "Culture, Religion and Health Care," 57–59; Hordern "Religion and Culture," 589–91.

2. Eckersley, "Culture, Spirituality, Religion and Health," 54.

3. Hordern, "Religion and Culture," 589.

strength in the middle of the experience of ill health, healing, and dying. Focusing on culture, Eckersley[4] argues that "cultures are about how we think the world works: the language, knowledge, beliefs, assumptions and values that shape how we see the world and our place in it; give meaning to our experience; and are passed between individuals, groups and generations." Helman, cited in Bhui,[5] concurs with the above view on culture and states that culture is a "set of guidelines which individuals inherit as members of a particular society which tells them how to view the world, experience it emotionally and how to behave in relation to other people, supernatural forces or gods and to the environment." This culture is transmitted through symbols, language art, and ritual.[6] While the definition of religion continues to trouble scholars, most of them are agreed that religion is a part of culture.[7] Bensonn, Thistlethwaite, and Moore[8] are of the view that religious beliefs form a part of a person's culture. Eckersley[9] has cautioned us not to treat culture and religion as two distinct elements because religion is and should be treated as an element of culture. Beyers[10] argues at length how religion can be conceived as part of culture as well as how it can function as a cultural identity marker.

While some scholars have acceded to the notion that there exists a strong connection among religion, culture, and health, they have also noted the challenges that emanate from this intersection. For example, Chatters[11] cautions us from overstating the extent to which research and practice communities endorse the proposition of the significance of religious involvement to individual and population health. She notes the prevalence of skeptical resistance in this area and then lists a number of challenges encountered thereof. She argues that there are three main challenges: (i) It is particularly challenging to understand the complex multi-factorial processes through which religion affects individual and population health. This is because the study of religion and health involves multiple disciplines, which makes it difficult to appreciate

4. Eckersley, "Culture, Spirituality, Religion and Health," 54.
5. Bhui, "Culture, Religion and Health Care," 57.
6. Bhui, "Culture, Religion and Health Care," 57.
7. Defining religion is beyond the scope of this chapter.
8. Bensonn, Thistlethwaite, and Moore, *Mental Health across Culture*, 56.
9. Eckersley, "Culture, Spirituality, Religion and Health," 54.
10. Beyers, "Religion and Culture."
11. Chatters, "Religion and Health," 336.

disciplinary differences in conceptual frameworks, methodological and analytical approaches, relevant contextual issues, and levels of inquiry (e.g., individuals versus populations).(ii) Long-standing scientific and professional perspectives have fostered stereotypes and misconceptions about issues of religion and/or openly antagonistic attitudes that preclude a consideration of these questions. The other challenge she notes is that researchers and practitioners in the behavioral, social, and health sciences may themselves be less religiously active than the general population and therefore may dismiss or deprecate the relevance of religion for human affairs. (iii) The third challenge is the absence of thoughtful and comprehensive discussions of the ethical considerations, practice and policy implications, and professional ramifications of the integration of religion and health, which has made researchers and practitioners wary of addressing those questions in their work. These three challenges that exist at the intersection of religion and health are critical for this study because they have to a large extent shaped discourses of health and religion in Zimbabwe in a COVID-19 context. As shall be shown later, the advent of COVID-19 has called us to rethink the relationship among religion, culture, and health. From Eckersley's perspective,[12] the continuing debate among researchers about religion's effect on health complicates the relationship between religion and health. He notes the two schools of thought regarding this relationship. First, there are those who argue that the connection between religion and health is not so robust and depends on unknown confounders[13] and covariates.[14] Second, others dismiss the existence of a connection between religion and health. For Eckersley[15] the nature of religion is mysterious and elusive, making it extremely difficult for science to define and measure.

Regardless of the doubts shrouding the perceptions of some scholars, it has further been argued in scholarship that religion influences the type of treatment a patient chooses. For example, the Advent Health University blog[16] opines that individuals may go about addressing medical is-

12. Eckersley, "Culture, Spirituality, Religion and Health," 54.

13. A confounder is a variable that is associated or has a relationship with both the exposure and the outcome of interest.

14. A covariate is an independent variable that can influence the outcome of a given statistical trial, but which is not of direct interest.

15. Eckersley, "Culture, Spirituality, Religion and Health," 54.

16. "The Importance of Spiritual Care in Health Care," August 15, 2018, https://www.adventhealth.com/blog/importance-spiritual-care-health-care.

sues in completely different ways depending on their religion's teachings and traditions. From Foege's perspective,[17] religion, culture, and tradition may provide both positive and negative influences on public health. Making reference to AIDS, Foege[18] notes that the religious prohibition on condom use resulted in many people getting HIV. Within the African continent, Foege[19] argues that both religion and culture have contributed to the disempowerment of women, which led to the significant spread of AIDS. These negative aspects of religion and culture have led to contestations around the nature of their relationship with health.[20] Despite the negative influence of religion and culture on health, some scholars are of the view that their positive role outweighs the negatives. Hence, they have called for approaches to public health that do not trivialize religion and culture. Yehya and Dutta[21] propose a culture-centered approach to health, which for them allows for a co-construction of meanings through direct engagement with cultural communities. The Advent Health University blog[22] calls for cultural competence on the part of health practitioners. A cultural competent health practitioner is described as one who is aware of the cultural, social, and linguistic backgrounds of people. Yehya and Dutta[23] argue that it is important to consider the cultural constructions of health in religious contexts as this enables the opening up of the discursive spaces of health communication in relation to alternative cosmologies of health, illness, healing, and curing. We argue in this chapter that COVID-19 has opened new avenues of conceptualizing illness as well as treating it. In the next section, we undertake to give the historical context of COVID-19 within Zimbabwe.

Theoretical Framework

This chapter foregrounds Afrocentricity as the theory that informs it. The basic premise of an Afrocentric approach is that culture matters—in

17. Foege, "Positive and Negative Influences," 378.

18. Eckersley, "Culture, Spirituality, Religion and Health," 54.

19. Foege, "Positive and Negative Influences of Religion," 378.

20. Eckersley, "Culture, Spirituality, Religion and Health," 554.

21. .Yehya and Dutta, "Health, Religion and Meaning," 845–58.

22 "The Importance of Spiritual Care in Health Care," August 15, 2018, https://www.adventhealth.com/blog/importance-spiritual-care-health-care.

23. Yehya and Dutta, "Health, Religion and Meaning," 845.

the past, present, and future. The proponent of the theory, Molife Kete Asante,[24] defined it as a "paradigmatic intellectual perspective that privileges African agency within the context of African history and culture trans continentally and trans-generationally." Asante further privileges location as critical to any analysis that involves African culture and behavior whether literary, economic, political, or cultural. Afrocentricity traces its theoretical heritage to African ideas and African authors.[25] In this case, we write this chapter on COVID-19 and indigenous knowledge systems from an insider position, which gives us the edge to explain the Afro-centered response to the pandemic because we do so not only as Africans but also ones who deployed African healing practices to avert the pandemic.

There is a tendency in global health systems to distort Africa's contributions or to look down upon African healing practices and beliefs. Asante[26] bemoans the way in which the West has either outrightly distorted or deliberately negated African people or their ideas. Such perceptions ignore the contribution of Africa to world development. The major arguments proffered for sidelining African healing practices have been that they have not been tried and tested according to Western modes. Chirimuuta and Chirimuuta[27] opine that in most cases medicinal interventions from the African continent have hit a brickwall as they are expected to pass the tests set by Western scientists. However, Afrocentricity as a theory allows for conclusions to be arrived at "based on arguments in literature and orature."[28] It is common knowledge that most African indigenous knowledge systems, particularly on health and healing, are not codified. Hence, the response to COVID-19 using indigenous knowledge systems in Africa largely depends on unwritten codes. The global dependence on written codes has resulted in the decentering of Africa from global health discourses. However, the decentring of Africa from global health discourses has resulted in the marginalization of African health narratives. Yet the narratives are useful in constructing African lived experiences, which, if taken onboard, can offer new pathways to pandemic

24. Asante, *Afrocentric Manifesto*, 2.

25. Asante, *Afrocentric Manifesto*, 3.

26. Asante, *Afrocentric Manifesto*, 3.

27. Chirimuuta and Chirimuuta, "Preparedness of Africans," 19–43.

28. Asante, *Afrocentric Manifesto*, 3.

responses. Chawane[29] through the utilization of the Afrocentric theory argues that it is imperative to examine all data from the viewpoint of Africans as subjects and human agents rather than as objects in a European frame of reference. In this case, the reverting of Africans to indigenous knowledge systems as a response to COVID-19 needs to be considered as African agency in the face of a calamitous pandemic. While it is true that Africa suffered in the same way as other continents, it somehow survived the dire effects of the pandemic to the surprise of many. Maeda and Nkengasong[30] posit that many public health experts had been puzzled by the COVID-19 pandemic because Africa has reported far fewer cases and deaths from COVID-19 than predicted. In this case, questions have been raised as to why Africa did not suffer the most despite its perceived dilapidated formal health care as well as the vaccine apartheid that ensued. Most explanations to these questions have not considered the way Africans resorted to indigenous knowledge systems as a response to the pandemic. It seems there is a continued desire to marginalize African epistemological processes in response to viral diseases and there is a deliberate effort to make them invisible in health discourses of COVID-19. However, this chapter's use of Afrocentricity allows for the relocation and centering of the African person as an agent in the history of the response to the pandemic. This is done as a way of doing away with illusions that try to locate Africa at the margins of human history and development. This chapter argues that in a COVID-19 context, African indigenous knowledge systems provided an alternative response to the pandemic regardless of the fact that this has not been formally acknowledged in "modern" or conventional health spaces. In the next section we provide the historical context of COVID-19.

The Historical Context of COVID-19

According to the World Health Organisation (WHO), the coronavirus disease (COVID-19) is an infectious disease caused by the SARS-CoV-2 virus. It was first detected in the Chinese city of Wuhan in December 2019. It then spread to other countries in 2020. The WHO declared it a global pandemic in March 2020. Up to now in 2022, no cure has been found for the virus. Instead, the COVID-19 pandemic has largely destabilized the

29. Chawane, "Development of Afrocentricity," 78–99.

30. Maeda and Nkengasong, "Puzzle of the COVID-19," 27–28.

formal health systems of the global world in general and, for purposes of this paper, Zimbabwe in particular. Currently, most countries have experienced a fourth wave of the pandemic. It is now estimated that globally millions of people have died from this respiratory disease. A WHO report indicates that as of 4 March 2022, records show that 440,807,756 people had been infected with the coronavirus. Of these, 5,978,096 people had died due to the virus. On the African continent, it has been reported that 11,478,000 people were infected and 249,000 deaths were recorded at the time of writing this chapter. Of these, Zimbabwe accounts for 239,000 infections and 5,399 deaths. In Zimbabwe, health experts are predicting that in the coming winter season a fifth wave is possible to occur. What this implies is that the effects of the pandemic around the world are far from over. Judging by the numbers coming out of Africa, it is clear that the continent has confounded pessimists who had predicted that dead bodies would litter the streets of African cities. The media is awash with questions pertaining to why Africa has been the least affected by the pandemic. Those that lean toward the supremacy of Western health systems have pointed to underreporting and lack of vigorous testing as the key factors at hand. For example, in trying to explain what could have influenced the trajectory of COVID-19 in Africa, Maeda and Nkengasong[31] point to all other possible scenarios, like limited testing; which could have limited detection and isolation, a much younger population, which could have resulted in fewer severe cases and deaths; climatic differences, which could affect transmission; pre-existing immunity; genetic factors; early implementation of public health measures; and timely leadership. This list excludes the use of indigenous knowledge systems as possible contributing factors to the low infection and death rates in Africa. In fact, none of the explanations proffered by health experts have tried to put into account the contribution of African indigenous knowledge systems in response to the pandemic as leading to the low case numbers in Africa.

The Significance of Indigenous Knowledge Systems in a COVID-19 Context: The Zimbabwean Case

According to Nlooto and Kaya,[32] "indigenous knowledge" refers to community-based systems that are used synonymously with traditional and

31. Maeda and Nkengasong, "Puzzle of the COVID-19," 28.

32. Nlooto and Kaya, "Editorial: African Indigenous Knowledge," 1.

local language. Noyoo, cited in Mokhutso, defines "African Indigenous Knowledge Systems" as a complex set of knowledge skills and technologies existing and developed around specific conditions of populations and communities indigenous to a particular geographical area. Haya[33] lists the various aspects of indigenous knowledge. He explains that indigenous knowledge (i) is generated within communities; (ii) is location and culture specific; (iii) is the basis for decision-making and survival strategies; (iv) is not systematically documented; (v) concerns critical issues of human and animal life; (vi) is dynamic and based on innovation, adaptation, and experimentation; and (vii) is oral and rural in nature. In healthcare, indigenous knowledge systems make use of African traditional/indigenous medicine (ATM/AIM). In this case, both medication and non-medication therapies are used. ATMs/AIM includes the use of herbal medicines, animal products, stones, and water among other things. From Nlooto and Kaya's perspective,[34] indigenous-knowledge-system–based healthcare uses a holistic approach in the diagnosis and treatment of diseases as it considers the physiological, psychological, spiritual, economic, environmental, and social aspects of health. In other words, when it comes to healthcare, indigenous knowledge systems do not focus on physical healing only, but on other aspects that are affected by ailments.

The struggle for the recognition of traditional medicine has a long history. When Europe colonized Africa, it condemned the traditional ways of healing while promoting theirs. The demonization of African health practitioners and ATM/AIM meant that neither could be officially recognized. It is worth noting, however, that the lack of recognition did not deter Africans from consulting indigenous health practitioners as well as using ATM/AIM. This implies that Africans did and continue to use two parallel health systems. In 1977, the thirtieth World Health Assembly of the World Health Organisation adopted a resolution promoting development, training, and research into traditional health systems.[35] In addition, the Ama Ata Declaration of 1978, which was adopted by the International Conference on Primary Health Care, was significant in that it recognized the role of traditional medicine and traditional health practitioners in primary health care.[36] In 2000, the WHO Re-

33. Haya, "Promotion of Public Health Care," 1.

34. Asante, *Afrocentric Manifesto*, 2.

35. Le Roux-Kemp, "Legal Perspective," 275.

36. Abrams, et al., "Legislative Landscape."

gional Committee for Africa adopted a resolution recognizing the value and potential of ATM for the achievement of health in the region.[37] In May 2001, the WHO Regional Director for Africa established a twelve-member committee in response to a resolution promoting the role of traditional medicine in health systems, which was adopted by health ministers at the fiftieth session of the Regional Committee for Africa in Quagadougou, Burkina Faso. In its first five years, the committee had approved twelve documents that were guidelines to help countries improve the use of traditional medicine. This was premised on the belief that both traditional and modern medicine could contribute to meeting the targets of the "Health for All" policy for the twenty-first century in the African region. Commenting on the guidelines, the WHO Regional Director, then Dr. Luis Gomes Sambo, opined that the guidelines would support countries to institutionalize traditional medicine in health systems and to harmonize their policies and regulation. He also encouraged the committee together with the WHO secretariat to support countries to produce evidence on the safety, efficacy, and quality of traditional medicine.[38] In 2001, in Lusaka, the WHO declared 2001–2010 the decade of African traditional medicine. The period was later expanded by another decade covering 2011–2020 and it was reiterated that African governments needed to ensure that knowledge systems are complementary and not competitive.[39]

In Zimbabwe, the regulation of traditional medicine had started before independence in 1980. Traditional health practitioners had been singled out by missionaries as impediments to their evangelization process. As a result, in 1899 the Witchcraft Suppression Act was passed. According to Cavender,[40] the act made it unlawful for anyone to practice as a witch doctor or witch finder. He also opines that the legislation had an adverse effect on the practice of traditional healing. The Medical Council of Rhodesia[41] considered it a violation of ethics for a physician to consult with or refer a patient to a traditional healer. Such moves removed the reputation and believability of traditional healers, which resulted in the restriction of the open practice of traditional medicine. The formation

37. Le Roux-Kemp, "Legal Perspective," 275.

38. World Health Organisation, "Promoting the Role of Traditional."

39. Nlooto and Kaya, "Editorial: African Indigenous Knowledge," 2.

40. Cavender, "Professionalization of Traditional Medicine," 251.

41. Cavender, "Professionalization of Traditional Medicine," 251.

of the African Ngangas Association in 1957 resulted in the formation of the Zimbabwe Ngangas Association, followed by the Mabweadziva Association. A plethora of other associations followed thereafter. From Cavender's analysis, the associations were formed out of a desire to foster unity among traditional healers for the purpose of promoting the value of traditional medicine.[42]Such desire found expression after independence through the government. In 1980, the new Minister of Health, Herbert Ushewokunze, made consultations with a huge number of traditional healers in Zimbabwe. The consultation gave birth to the Zimbabwe National Traditional Healers Association (ZINATHA). Cavender[43] posits that the creation of ZINATHA was an indigenous culture-restoration movement. The objectives of ZINATHA were (i) to promote traditional medicine and methods of healing, (ii) to promote research into traditional medicine and methods of healing, (iii) to promote training in the art of herbal and spiritual healing, (iv) to supervise the practice of traditional medicine and prevent abuse and quackery, (v) and to cooperate with the Ministry of Health and establish better working relations between traditional and conventional medical practitioners.[44] These were noble objectives. However, some traditional healers engaged in acts contrary to these objectives. When this was brought to the attention of government, the Traditional Medical Practitioners Act of 1981 was enacted. The act mandated the Ministry of Health to oversee the constitution of a Traditional Medical Practitioners Council (TMPC), which had to among other things register all traditional healers. However, most of the goals of both ZINATHA and the TMPC were difficult to implement owing to lack of funding among other issues. Through the enactment of health strategies, Zimbabwe has continued to emphasize the importance of traditional medicine.

Despite the above-mentioned progress, the place of indigenous knowledge systems in health care continues to be contested. Nlooto and Kaya[45] argue that indigenous knowledge has been marginalized for a long time by Western knowledge systems in the search for sustainable solutions to developmental challenges of health equity and public health.

42. Cavender, "Professionalization of Traditional Medicine," 252.

43. Cavender, "Professionalization of Traditional Medicine," 252.

44. Cavender, "Professionalization of Traditional Medicine," 252.

45. Nlooto and Kaya, "Editorial: African Indigenous Knowledge".

Haya[46] notes that despite the marginalization of ATM/AIM, a large number of African people rely on indigenous knowledge systems in their daily lives. The uncertainty that surrounded/surrounds the effectiveness of modern medicine against the coronavirus has seen innovations taking place, particularly pertaining to indigenous modes of both prevention and treatment and protection against the virus. Within the Zimbabwean context, it is notable how people have resorted to traditional forms of healing. As the virus continues to wreak havoc across the globe, Zimbabweans continue to deploy their indigenous knowledge systems in response to the pandemic.

At the onset of the pandemic in Africa, the government of Madagascar announced that it had found an indigenous herb that could be processed into a herbal drink and taken to cure COVID-19. However, this sparked "widespread criticism, cynicism and outright outrage from some quarters."[47] This was deemed irresponsible and misleading. However, in a show of pan-Africanism, some African governments came out in support of Madagascar. For example, some African countries such as Senegal and Tanzania even ordered this "cure" for COVID-19 from Madagascar. Eric Gbodossou, a doctor and president of Senegal-based Prometra International, an organization focusing on the preservation of African traditional medicine, praised the Madagascar president, Rajoelina, for his courage to test an indigenous herb in his bid to try and help his people through what he termed "COVID-Organics." Gbodossou was convinced like most Africans that a remedy for COVID-19 was going to be found on the African continent in African traditional medicine (ATM). While the WHO voiced its respect for traditional medicine, it insisted that the Madagascar "cure" be subjected to rigorous trial and it warned against self-medication. Despite the WHO skepticism, Sibanda, Muyamco, and Chitando[48] view the Madagascar announcement as an African ideology that had challenged the WHO of sustaining a colonial agenda by refusing to accept solutions from Africa. From their analysis, what this brought to the fore were the politics of "the centre versus the periphery."[49] Chirimuuta and Chirimuuta[50] have bemoaned the suspicions that were cast on the

46. Haya, "Promotion of Public Health Care."

47. Rwodzi, "COVID-19 and Southern Africa," 82.

48. Sibanda et al., "Religion and the COVID-19," 14.

49. Sibanda et al., "Religion and the COVID-19," 14.

50. Chirimuuta, "Preparedness of Africans," 34.

Madagascar remedy as proof of the various ways in which "the [Western] capitalist system would keep Africans out of the critical domains of life." Yet this is another way in which Africa would have regained its pride with a COVID-19 medicine labelled "Made in Africa." This could largely explain why Madagascar, Cameroon, and Tanzania among other African countries announced that traditional medicines would play a significant role in their response to the pandemic.[51] While the Madagascar debacle rumbled on, Zimbabweans compared the plant that was being peddled as a COVID-19 "cure" in Madagascar and found its equivalent in Zimbabwe. Most Zimbabweans became convinced that the plant was found in Zimbabwe and called *zumbani* (Lippia javanica). Traditionally, the *zumbani* herb was used to treat stomach ailments, colds, and mental illness among other conditions. Its strength lies in its perceived ability to open the respiratory tract for people with flu symptoms. In this case, the herb was quickly embraced and people started to consume it as tea. While the leaves could be used in their fresh form, others started to dry them in preparation for its out-of-season period as well as sending it to relatives in the diaspora. It was also ground into powder so that it could be mixed with other food stuffs. *Zumbani* became very popular to the extent that in no time it began to be commercialized, particularly in urban areas. Both informal as well as formal traders began selling it together with other herbs. Others created herbal gardens in which they domesticated and planted most of the herbs that are traditionally wild. Supermarkets like OK created a section for herbs that were deemed crucial for COVID-19 cure and mitigation. The *zumbani* herb was believed to be able to treat COVID-19 with some patients claiming to have been healed after inhaling the plant's steam. Yet others claimed that the herb possesses anti-inflammatory and anti-bacterial properties. The media was awash with stories of how *zumbani* was selling like hot cakes in certain cities in Zimbabwe. This was aided by some health professionals who came out in support of the use of traditional medicine in the fight against COVID-19. For example, Portia Manangazira, Director of Epidemiology and Disease Control in the Ministry of Health and Child Care in Zimbabwe, urged Zimbabweans to embrace traditional medicine and emphasized the need for the unification of traditional and conventional medicine in the fight against the COVID-19 pandemic. For her, it was crucial that Zimbabweans made maximum use of locally available medicines and herbs in

51. Sibanda et al., "Religion and the COVID-19," 14.

the supportive care and management of COVID-19 patients. What this entailed, therefore, was the necessity of a dual intervention to mitigate the effects of COVID-19. It was, therefore, not surprising that in most government hospitals where COVID-19 patients were admitted, relatives were allowed to bring *zumbani* tea each morning.

Apart from *zumbani*, other herbs were utilized as well during the COVID-19 pandemic. For example, some Zimbabweans mixed lemon, guava, and mint leaves and boiled them. They would then drink the mixture. Other herbs that became popular are *mufandichimuka* (resurrecting bush or Myrothamnus flabellifolius) and *moringa* (horseradish or drumstick tree). Others claimed that boiling leaves from a *mutsvanzva* (Ximenia caffra) tree was very effective in warding off the virus. It was interesting noticing urbanites traveling to their rural homes to get hold of these leaves. Barks of trees were also claimed to have positive healing and protection effects against viral infection from COVID-19. Barks from *mubvamaropa* (Pterocarpus angolensis) and *mumve* (Kigelia) trees were taken, pounded into powder, and either added to porridge or drunk as hot drink. In addition to these medicines, other non-medication practices were also practiced. For example, the practice of *kunatira* (steaming or steam inhaling) became popular in the fight against COVID-19. Messages circulating on WhatsApp groups showed that the practice was regarded as the most effective in preventing infection. In this case, it was encouraged that for those going to work, they needed to do this steam inhaling first thing when they got home in order to kill the virus if by any chance they would have gotten into contact with an infected person. It was also believed that the practice was effective in killing the virus if done in the first five days of one getting infected. Despite conventional medicine disapproving of the practice, most Zimbabweans went on doing this practice, the reason being that it has always been a traditional way of curing diseases. The Shona, for example, are of the view that the sweat that comes out during steaming symbolizes the coming out of the infection. From Haya's perspective, the knowledge of and uses of specific plants and animals for medicinal purposes is an important component of African indigenous knowledge systems. The usage of these herbs, barks, as well as steaming, coupled with the observance of the WHO regulations of masking up, washing of hands, and social distancing (where possible) went a long way in mitigating the transmission of coronavirus. The urgency with which indigenous knowledge systems were deployed in

Zimbabwe is commendable in this regard. Chitando[52] posits that whenever life-threatening forces besiege individuals, families, or the community, African traditional religion is quick to swing into action.

Reasons have been proffered as to why Africans in general and for purposes of this chapter Zimbabweans in particular resorted to traditional medicine during COVID-19. First, from Chirimuuta and Chirimuuta's perspective,[53] the major reason is that these are locally available and accessible either at no cost or at low cost. Added to this, it becomes important to note that in Africa everyone is a herbalist in their own right. Hence, getting the herbs or the barks did not require any protocol. Anyone from the young to the old can simply go into the forest and get the medication either for themselves or for relatives needing it for healing or prevention. Second, from informal discussions, we gathered that people were frustrated by the failure of the formal health care system to accommodate all the people that were infected. A number of times health care workers were on strike demanding better working conditions during the COVID-19 pandemic in Zimbabwe. This led most people to shun hospitals for fear of being neglected. Health care workers themselves were ill equipped at times with no personal protective equipment (PPE). Hence, in most cases they left the sick unattended for fear of being infected themselves. Private health care providers were so expensive that the poor could not even dare try them. In such a scenario, African traditional/indigenous medicine provided the much needed and sought after alternative. This was aided by the death rate that was being reported from hospitals. The general feeling among Zimbabweans was that in a COVID-19 context, hospitals had become death dungeons where once someone had been admitted, they would never come out alive. Such perceptions invigorated the desire to utilize the available indigenous knowledge systems for both prevention and healing. Joyce Guhwa, the registrar of the Traditional Medical Practitioner's Council, observed that the COVID-19 pandemic had highlighted the importance of traditional herbs, which had been downplayed due to the rise of conventional medicine.[54] This renewed interest in ATM/AIM led the Zimbabwean government to authorize herbalists to treat COVID-19. Third, vaccine apartheid left Africans in general and Zimbabweans in particular with no choice

52. Chitando, *Living with Hope*, 50.

53. Chirimuuta, "Preparedness of Africans", 36.

54. "Traditional Healers Mourn Underfunding."

save to turn to traditional medicine. It is true that when vaccination started, developed nations hoarded vaccines at the expense of developing ones. Regardless of the fact that some Africans were skeptical about the vaccines, those that needed the vaccine did not find it readily available. Sibanda, Muyambo, and Chitando[55] note how vaccine nationalism prioritized citizens of the Global North while those in the Global South had to depend on fate. It is also such experiences that have propelled African academics to rise to the challenge of trying to provide African solutions to the COVID-19 pandemic. In the next section, we examine ways in which Zimbabwean research institutions are playing a part in coming up with mitigatory solutions against COVID-19 that are embedded within the African indigenous knowledge systems.

COVID-19, Indigenous Knowledge Systems, and the Academy: The Zimbabwean Experience

The COVID-19 pandemic has provided ways in which the academy in Zimbabwe has responded. Motsi[56] observes that as the effects of coronavirus became clear, Zimbabwean universities had no option but to repurpose their resources to help fight the pandemic. The pandemic started at a time when the country`s higher education institutions were being encouraged to embrace the Education 5.0 paradigm. Within this paradigm, institutions of higher learning were expected to embrace among other things scientific innovation. Hence, when the whole world was at a race to find the cure for COVID-19, Zimbabwean universities were challenged to make meaningful contributions in this regard. Their first responses were in the area of manufacturing sanitisers and face masks among other things. The Harare Institute of Technology was touted to have come up with oxygen ventilators that could be used in hospitals. However, the rate at which Zimbabweans were utilising ATM/AIM nudged some of them to engage in research in order to establish the efficacy of these medicines. In April 2020, it was announced that renowned herbalist Kenneth Chivizhe had been authorized by the government to administer his purported medicine to COVID-19 patients. He termed his medicine *Bhanan'ana*, literally translated "thunderstorm."[57] The medicine was an

55. Sibanda et al., "Religion and the COVID-19," 15.

56. Motsi, "Covid-19 Pandemic," 221.

57. Chivizhe claimed that he had termed his COVID-19 medicine *Bhanan'ana*

herb that had been pounded into powder. In September of the same year, the Zimbabwean government embarked on testing the efficacy of the *Bhanan'ana* powder through the Medical Research Council of Zimbabwe (MRCZ). The MCRZ also indicated that it had tasked more than one hundred researchers across the country to conduct rigorous checks on the use of various herbs before they could be granted both ethical and scientific approval. In the year 2021, Chinhoyi University of Technology announced that it had managed to come up with a COVID-19 treatment premised on indigenous knowledge systems. Its remedy had initially been termed "Covid"[58] made from a herb called *zhombwe*, which is found in abundance in Chiredzi (an area in the south of Zimbabwe). All these were endeavors from the academy to try and authenticate the efficacy of ATM/AIM.

While the path to ascertain the efficacy of ATM continues in a COVID-19 context in Zimbabwe, voices of pessimism also continue to reverberate. For example, when it was announced that the Zimbabwean government had authorized herbalists to treat patients against COVID-19, some in the medical fraternity were sceptical. For example, Fortune Nyamande, who is the chairperson of the Zimbabwe Association of Doctors for Human Rights, was of the view that this would derail the gains that had been realized by putting the country on lockdown. He appeared to insinuate that the use of herbs in response to the pandemic would lead people to stop following the WHO guidelines. He also called for caution in the use of herbs because for him this was not grounded in science. His analysis brings to the fore the historical conflict that exist between religion and science. Hence, while the role of traditional medicine was acknowledged, calls were being made to ensure that this was subjected to rigorous testing in order to come up with evidence-based scientific solutions. However, Humbe[59] argues that "taking time to finalise researches on the efficacy of some of the traditional herbs in managing the coronavirus is fuelling suffering in Zimbabwe for its health delivery system has collapsed." Onias Ndoro, the director in the Ministry

because of its strength as comparable to a bolt of lightning.

58. It appears that Chinhoyi University of Technology has taken down the name from the internet because of intellectual property rights issues. The name Covid already existed for a pill before COVID-19 happened. We await to see how they will rename it. Some academics have suggested that they make use of indigenous Shona terms.

59. Humbe, "Living with COVID-19," 82.

of Health, in concurrence with Humbe bemoaned the lack of funding for research and the manufacture of traditional medicines, which he said results in the lack of recognition in the health sector.[60]For him, the way forward is to strengthen the Traditional Medical Council so that it spearheads the manufacturing of traditional medicines. He also challenged the secrecy that surrounds ATM/AIM, where practitioners do not want to disclose important herbs or to pass on their knowledge to others, resulting in the hindrance of the traditional medical practice being standardized.[61] However, the encouragement to disclose needs to be accompanied with a clear policy on intellectual property rights. The government may need to educate traditional health practitioners on patent law.

Conclusion

The intention of this paper was to explore the significance of indigenous knowledge systems in a COVID-19 context in Zimbabwe. In other words, the focus of the paper was on the intersection of religion, culture, and health. The paper therefore highlighted the debate surrounding the relationship among these concepts. It then showed that the COVID-19 pandemic resuscitated interest in ATM/AIM in Africa in general and Zimbabwe in particular. With the formal health systems in dire straits, ATM/AIM provided an important alternative to dealing with the pandemic. Zimbabweans were forced to reconsider the utility of ATM/AIM in the face of an unconfirmed cure for coronavirus. Despite the scepticism from conventional medicine, Zimbabweans continue to deploy indigenous knowledge systems as they endeavor to combat the pandemic. The paper also highlighted the role that is being played by research institutions and universities in searching for solutions and remedies to the pandemic; solutions and remedies that are grounded in African religio-cultural beliefs and practices. The tug-of-war that exists between Africa and its erstwhile colonizers on the former's ability to contribute meaningfully to global health discourse became evident in the Madagascar case. The case is clear evidence of the continued marginalisation of African epistemology. However, the increased utilization of ATM/AIM in the COVID-19 context is clear evidence of the resilience of Indigenous African Religion(s) and culture. This is a pointer to the fact that any future

60. Sibanda et al., Religion and the COVID-19," 15.

61. Sibanda et al., Religion and the COVID-19," 15.

responses to pandemics need to be cognizant of specific and contextual religio-cultural health practices for the quick containment of viruses. As Sibanda, Muyambo, and Chitando[62] posit, "investing in greater understanding of the role of indigenous knowledge systems among Africans from diverse backgrounds remains highly strategic." In this case, Zimbabwe needs to find ways of operationalizing the existing legal instruments on traditional medicine so that the clamor for it to be mainstreamed in the formal health system does not end on paper but in deed.

Bibliography

Abrams. Andrea. L. *Legislative Landscape for Traditional Health Practitioners in Southern Africa: A Scoping Review.* BMJ Open, 2020. 10:e029958. doi:10.1136/bmjopen-2019–29958

Advent Health University. "Religion and Healthcare: The Importance of Cultural Sensitivity." Blog entry, December 29, 2020. https://www.ahu.edu/blog/religion-and-healthcare-the-importance-of-cultural-sensitivity.

Asante, Molefi. K. *An Afrocentric Manifesto: Toward an African Renaissance.* Cambridge: Polity. 2007.

Beyers, Jaco. "Religion and Culture: Revisiting a Close Relative." *HTS Theological Studies* 73/1 (2017). https://doi.org/10.4102/hts.v73i1.3864.

Bensonn, Jill, Jill Thistlethwaite, and Pascale Moore. *Mental Health across Culture: A Practical Guide for Health Professionals.* New York: CRC, 2018.

Bhui, Kamaldeep. "Culture, Religion and Health Care." *International Journal of Integrated Care* 10 (2010) 57–59.

Cavender, Tony. *The Professionalisation of Traditional Medicine in Zimbabwe.* Human Organisation, 1988.

Chatters, Linda. M. *Religion and Health: Public Health Research and Practice.* Annual Review on Public Health, 2000.

Chawane, Midas. *The Development of Afrocentricity: A Historical Survey.* Yesterday & Today, 2016.

Chirimuuta, Chipo, and A. Chirimuuta. "The Preparedness of Africans for the Fourth Industrial Revolution and for COVID-19." In *Global Capital's 21st Century Repositioning: Between COVID-19 and the Fourth Industrial Revolution on Africa,* edited by R. Makamani, A. Nhemachena, and O. Mtapuri, 19–43. Cameroon: Langaa, 2021.

Chitando, Ezra. *Living with Hope: African Churches and HIV/AIDS.* Geneva: WCC, 2007.

Eckersley, Richard. M. "Culture, Spirituality, Religion and Health: Looking at the Bigger Picture." *Medical Journal of Australia* (2007) 54–56.

Foege, William. H. "Positive and Negative Influences of Religion, Culture and Tradition in Public Health." *American Journal of Public Health* 109/3 (2019) 378.

Haya, Hassan O. "Promotion of Public Health Care Using African Indigenous Knowledge Systems and Implications for IPRs: Experiences for Southern and

62. Sibanda et al., Religion and the COVID-19," 15.

Eastern Africa." *African Technology Policy Studies* Special Paper Series 30. Nairobi: ATPS Communicating Department, 2007.

Hordern, Joshua. "Religion and Culture." *Medicine* (2016) 589–92.

Humbe, Bernard.P, "Living with COVID-19 in Zimbabwe: A Religious and Scientific Response." In *Religion and the COVID-19 Pandemic in Southern Africa*, edited by F. Sibanda, T. Muyambo, and E. Chitando, 72–88. London: Routledge 2021.

Le Roux-Kemp, Andrea. "A Legal Perspective on African Traditional Medicine in South Africa." *The Comparative and International Law Journal of Southern Africa* 43/3 (2010) 273–91.

Maeda, Justin M., and John N. Nkengasong. "The Puzzle of the COVID-19 Pandemic in Africa." *Science* 371/6524 (2021) 27–28.

Motsi, E. "COVID-19 Pandemic and Personal Protective Equipment Production: The Search for Sustainable Solutions—A Zimbabwean Experience." In *COVID-19 and the Dialectics of Global Pandemics in Africa: Challenges and Opportunities and the Future of the Global Economy in the Face of COVID-19*, edited by M. Mawere, B. Chazovachii, and F. Machingura, 211–30. Cameroon: Langaa, 2021.

Nlooto, Manimbulu, and Hassan O. Kaya. "Editorial: African Indigenous Knowledge Systems and Public Healthcare." *Journal of African Studies* 31/1 (2007) 1–3.

Rwodzi, Aaron. "COVID-19 and Southern Africa Development Community (SADC): A Litmus Test for Regional Solidarity." In *Global Capital's 21st Century Repositioning: Between COVID-19 and the Fourth Industrial Revolution on Africa*, edited by R. Makamani, A. Nhemachena, and O. Mtapuri, 77–110. Cameroon: Langaa. 2021.

Sibanda, F., T. Muyambo,and E. Chitando. "Introduction: Religion and Public Health in the Shadow of COVID-19 Pandemic in Southern Africa." In *Religion and the COVID-19 Pandemic in Southern Africa*, edited by F. Sibanda, T. Muyambo, and E. Chitando, 1–24. London: Routledge, 2022.

"Traditional Healers Mourn Underfunding towards Research, Manufacture of Traditional Medicines." *Newsday*, 11 March 2021.

World Health Organisation. "Promoting the Role of Traditional Medicine in Health Systems: A Strategy for the African Region." AFR/RC50/R3. 31 August 2000.

Yehya. Nadine A. and Mohan J. Dutta. "Health, Religion and Meaning: A Culture-Centred of Druze Women." *Qualitative Health Research* 20/6 (2010) 845–58.

Chapter 9

Conceptualizing Life and Death among the Krobo of Ghana

A Phenomenological Perspective

George Ossom-Batsa

Introduction

Life and death are two polarities of human existence that all human cultures and religions struggle to explain.[1] Different people offer different meanings and significance to them. This suggests that what constitutes life and death is not the same in all cultures. The difference reflects the various attitudes that people have toward life, especially human life, in their worldview.[2]

Furthermore, whereas biological sciences view human life from the physical or material point of view, religion and indigenous cultures, on the contrary, normally appeal to myths to explain the mysteries of

1. Cf. Suri and Pitchford, "Gift of Life", 128–34; see also Penoukou, "Christologie au Village," 69–109.

2. Refer to the following for detailed discussions on the issue: Gundani, "Roman Catholic Church"; Gyekye, "Beyond Cultures"; ID, "Tradition and Modernity"; Heckert, "Beyond Identity"; Ilogu, "Transition—Igbo Burial Customs"; Kraft, *Christianity in Culture*; Leach, "Ritual"; Kewku-Nuako, "Enigma of Life"; Badham, and Badham, *Death and Immortality*.

life and death, which are, however, concrete realities.[3] For example, for Christianity, Islam, African traditional religions and cultures, and, in fact, most world religions, life and death are real, and they are interpreted in reference to the supernatural being (God).[4] These resonate in Krobo philosophy and ritual life.[5]

In Krobo philosophy, life may be summarized in a tripartite scheme: life–community–continuance.[6] This tripartite scheme is inextricably connected with the goal of life, which for the *Krobo* is ancestorship. Furthermore, the scheme suggests that human life has a beginning but has no end. For this reason, in *Krobo* anthropology, a human being is composed of three elements: spiritual shadow *(kla),* soul (*susuma*), and body (*nomlotso*). Once a person is born, the living principle (*susuma*) infused in the body (*nomlotso*)[7] by the divine continues to exist forever. This living principle, known as *susuma,* leaves the body only at death and enters the spiritual world, where it continues to exist.[8] The *kla*, on the other hand, may depart from the body momentarily.

3. Compare the collected essays in Obayashi, *Death and Afterlife*, where all the contributors stress this point. See also Izreel, *Adapa and the South Wind*; Orr, "Fullness of Life," 565–75.

4. Cf. Kizilabdullah, "Pre and Post-Death Rituals," 117–35. See also Anderson, *Death and Dying*; Jones, *Approaching the End.*

5. For a detailed treatment of the Krobo culture, we refer you to the standard work, Huber, *Krobo: Traditional Social and Religious Life of a West African People.* Bibliographical material on the topic is, however, very limited. According to our knowledge, there is no extant monograph or article that has dealt with our theme. Our work therefore is the first in this direction. The author writes from his experience as a native and also his seven years of pastoral work among the people. Some of the data used for the work was collected during the seven years of ministry in the area. This is complemented by recent interviews and surveys conducted. Besides interviews, the following fundamental articles have been resourceful: Huber, "Outlines of Ultimate Reality", "Ultimate Reality and Meaning," 245–55; ID, "L'afrique de L'oeust."

6. Huber, "Outlines of Ultimate Reality," 246–47.

7. *Nomlotso* comes from two words: *nomlo*, which means "person," and *tso,* which means "tree." Etymologically, *nomlotso* means "the tree that contains the person." The human identity (*nomlo*) is the imperishable part of the person, and is referred to by the Krobos as *susuma.*

8. Similar ideas are present in other cultures in Ghana. For example, Gyekye notes that in Akan culture, the human person is composed of three elements: *ɔkra* (soul), *sunsum* (spirit), and *honam* (body). The *ɔkra* is the element that constitutes the innermost self, the essence of the individual person. *ɔkra* is the individual's life for which reason it referred to as *ɔkrateasefo*, that is, the living soul. Gyekye, "Essay on African Philosophical Thought," 85. For a critique of Kwame Gyekye's ideas refer to Majeed, "Analysis of Kwame Gyekye's Conception," 137–49.

In the light of the above, what makes human life meaningful is the relationship that exists between the living principles on the spiritual level, on the one hand, and the social ties established because of birth, on the other hand, and union with the supreme being. Consequently, human life, which is born into a family, is never to be lived in isolation; it must always be lived in relationship with other people, in the family and the larger community.[9] A community is formed not on a code of law, but on the consciousness of being human and being in union with the divine. In other words, the awareness of being human ought to prompt in the individual a desire to relate to his like in an authentic loving encounter. This sense of community is key in Krobo thought, and it may be termed as "existence-in-relation"; you are because you are related to others.

From the cultural anthropology outlined above, it means that to the Krobo human life does not come to an end with death but continues in the world of the dead.[10] Earthly existence comes to an end with death, but the life principle (*susuma*) of the person continues to exist in another form. In between the two forms of existence is the transitional stage, death. The new form of existence is believed to be spiritual and, though not perceptible to the naked human eyes, real. Special spiritual powers are required to see the dead, talk to them, and experience them. It is believed that union with a person is not broken by death. In fact, the deceased still belong to their families and communities as integral members. Culturally, without the deceased members, a family is not complete. That life begins in the divine, that life ought to be lived in a community, and that life has no end are, therefore, fundamental in Krobo cosmology and anthropology.

To maintain a balance in the tripartite structure, the Krobo have recourse to rituals,[11] which are mirrors of the conceptual world of any culture because they provide the means to view the behavior of a people concerning the divine, and also the people's total outlook on the world around

9. The importance of the community aspect of life is witnessed by the many elaborate public rituals in which the role of the community is primary.

10. This idea is not clearly defined in the Krobo worldview. Sometimes one comes across belief in reincarnation as a mode of continuing to live after death. When a newborn baby resembles a dead relative, the dead relative is said to be reincarnated in the child. In such a case, the baby is immediately marked with a small cut on the face for fear that if they didn't do that the child would not stay and would return to the world of the dead.

11. For a discussion on rituals in Krobo culture, refer to Ossom-Batsa, "Ritual as Mechanism for Averting Evil," 143–60.

them.[12] Furthermore, "ritual is capable of addressing truths that language alone, however eloquent or even poetic, is inadequate to express."[13]

Against this background, this paper examines Krobo rituals concerning birth and death to establish a philosophical understanding and theological meaning of life and death in the culture. The first part of this article discusses the geographical location and historical background of the Krobo. This analysis of their religious beliefs opens the window unto their philosophical and theological anthropology. Engaging insights from the study of two rituals, the final part provides an anthropological, philosophical, and theological reflection on what it means to live and to die in the Krobo culture.[14]

Geographical and Historical Setting

Geographical Setting

The Krobo tribe is one of the seven Adangme-speaking tribes,[15] which occupy the southeastern part of Ghana. They share boundaries in the east with the Ewe tribes[16] and on the west with the Akan-speaking tribes. The whole area that stretches from the Volta River to the west and towards the interior part of the country is a fertile farming land. Because of this, most of the people were farmers, producing mainly cereals (millet and maize), which were their staple foods. Other food crops grown included various types of tubers (yams, cassava, sweet potatoes, etc.). Since the livelihood of the tribe depended on the land, farming came to acquire, in addition to the social and economic dimensions, a spiritual dimension as a process of maintaining and promoting human life. This has resulted in the development of specific and elaborate rituals associated with planting and harvesting.

12. The centrality of ritual in the religious experience of any religion is summed up by Dhavamony, *Christian Theology and Religions*, 227, in the following words: "The cultic re-presentation of religious experience is central to the life of the religious community; it is a symbolic performance". Compare ID, *Phenomenology of Religion*, 166. See also Brody, "Materiality of Religion," 212–21; Bell, *Ritual*, 109.

13. Murray, "Cultures and Faith," 26.

14. Ott, "Globalization and Contextualization," 43–58.

15. The seven Adangme tribes are: Krobo, Osudoku, Se, Ningo, Kpone, Pampram, and Ada.

16. The language of the Ewe tribes is called "Ewe." Part of this tribe is found in southern Togo. They speak a similar language and also have a similar culture.

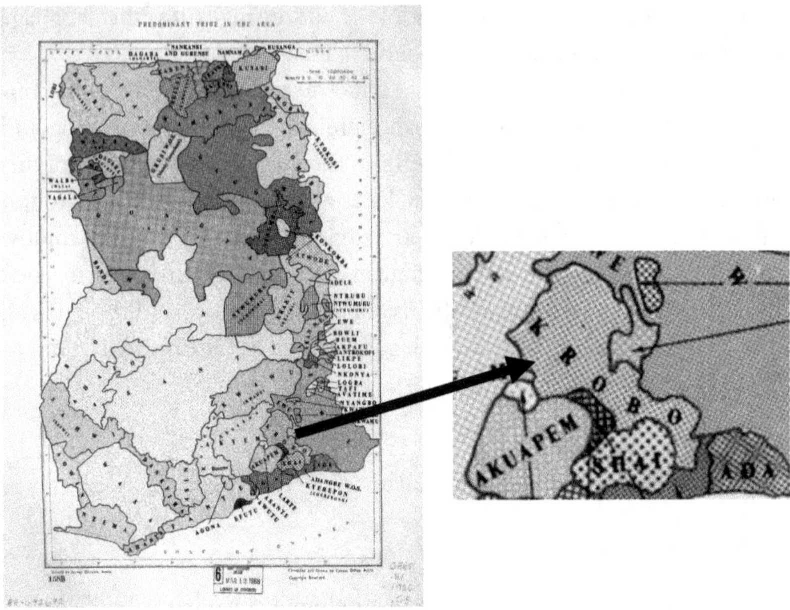

Figure 5: The Krobo[17]

Historical Setting

According to oral tradition, the original home of the Adangme-speaking tribes was *Same* or *Saberma*,[18] a grassland between Benin and Nigeria. Due to frequent attacks from invaders, they were forced to migrate from their ancestral homes.[19] They moved downwards until they reached the banks of the Volta River. After they had crossed over to the other bank at *Lolovo*,[20] the tribes separated and moved in different directions un-

17. Ghana Statistic Service, "Tribes-Ghana-Maps," 1966; https://www.loc.gov/item/88692692.

18. *Same* and *Saberma* are variants of the name of the original home of the Krobos that one finds transmitted in the oral traditions.

19. Existing manuals on Krobo history give no dating of when this exodus from *Same* took place. Consistent dating of the history of the Krobo begins from 1892, the descent from the Krobo mountain.

20. *Lolo* (love)-*vo* (is finished) is the place where the Adagme tribes who journeyed together separated and each went their own way. The separation was seen as the end of love, hence the name *Lolovo*.

der their leaders. The Krobo tribe, under the leadership of their priests, moved northwards and came to settle on a mountain, which later became known as "the Krobo mountain."

Figure 6: The Krobo mountain 1

Figure 7: The Krobo Mountain 2

The Krobo mountain rises above any other hill in its vicinity. From the highest point, one gets a panoramic view of the plains on all sides. It offered a strategic position, shielding the people from frequent attacks by enemies. This mountain home, where the tribe had lived for over a century, is referred to in traditional history as the ancestral home of the Krobo. In the year 1892, under the orders of the British colonial administrators, the people abandoned their mountain dwelling and came to live in the nearby plains, which later developed to be Somanya and Agomanya, the two traditional centers of the Yilo and Manya,[21] respectively.

Narrating the history of the Krobo, Huber and other scholars have noted that the Krobo were influenced significantly by the neighboring Akan and Ewe tribes. This is seen mostly in the development of kingship with its elaborate court regalia, an institution that was absent among the Krobo before their arrival at their mountain home.[22] It has been scholarly documented that the Krobo initially practiced "priestdom"; they were governed by a council of priestesses and priests called *djemeli.*[23] Kingship in its present form is a recent development, modeled on Akan culture.

Initially, priests and priestesses were the sole authority-holders in the community; they were also the custodians and preservers of the customs. Because of their unique position, public rituals and the cyclic rites of the year were performed under their jurisdiction and authority for them to gain public recognition and acceptance, and thus be observed by all. In addition to this role, the priests and priestesses were also the mediators between the gods and the people. Therefore, both political and religious power resided in them.

However, with the introduction of kingship on the pattern of the neighboring Akan tribes, the political role of the priests was assumed by the chiefs. As has been noted by G. K. Nukunya, any significant alteration or change in any constituent part of society leads to a readjustment of the parts to maintain a balance.[24] This was also the case in the traditional social structure of the Krobo, where chiefs came to assume part of the function of priests and priestesses.

21. The Yilo and Manya are the two groups of people who form the Krobo tribe.

22. Huber, "Outlines of Ultimate Reality," 246.

23. The etymology of *djemeli* is not very clear. It probably derives from *djemi*, which means "in the world". The suffix *eli* normally is reflexive and could be translated as "those" or "elders." Thus *djemeli* could means "those in the world" or "elders in the world." These are not exclusive but the latter appropriately describes the identity and function of the *djemeli*. Their spiritual maturity put them in closer relationship with divine realities to be able to mediate between the people and the spirits.

24. Nukunya, *Tradition and Change in Ghana*, 1.

The Social Structure

To appreciate the nexus between religious beliefs and daily living among the Krobo, it may be opportune to examine the social structure of the Krobo tribe. The Krobo tribe has a tripartite structure. The smallest segment is the *we* or *weku* ("home" or "union of homes"). The *we* is the extended family, and it is made up of several nuclear families related to a common ancestor. Several *weku* of the same descent line together form the *kasi*,[25] and a group of *kasi* in the same descent line forms the *wetso*[26] (literary meaning "family tree"—homes related to the same parent tree).

Unlike the neighbouring Akan, the people practice the patrilineal system, which means children belong to, inherit property and office from, and owe allegiance to the family of their fathers. Continuance or growth of the descent group is largely what every member seeks. One is said to be alive when his lineage grows, meaning an increase in the number of children born into the component families. Additionally, the dead are said to live on in their descendants, suggesting a close bond between the living and dead members of the family.

The Belief System[27]

Based on the fact that religious practices permeate every aspect of their lives, from the *weku* to the *wetso*, ethnographers such as Huber describe them as deeply religious.[28] They believe in a creator God (*Mau*), the presence of evil and good spirits, and a multiplicity of divine beings and ancestral spirits.[29] Notably, the deities are hierarchically conceived in their

25. The word *kasi* is composed of two different words: *ka*, which means an oval traditional dish for eating, and *si*, a shortened form of *sisi*, which means "under." So *kasi* literary means "under the same eating dish." It appears the word was used in ancient times to express the consanguine affinity among a group of homes (*we*). Their relationship is symbolically expressed by the image of the dish.

26. The Krobo *wetso* in anthropological terms is the equivalent of the clan.

27. The two important components of religion are the belief system and the ritual system. The belief system articulates the theoretical formation of faith, that is, the people's relationship with the divine and relationship among themselves. Ritual, on the other hand, is the practice of belief. In other words, ritual is belief in action. The meaning of ritual is explained by the belief system, and the belief system is concretely lived in ritual behavior.

28. Huber, "Outlines of Ultimate Reality," 245–55.

29. A similar belief pattern is found among other tribes of Ghana, for example,

relationship to one another, and this, to some extent, shows the level of their powers as well.

For example, the creator God or supreme being stands over and above all the divinities. Beside him are the minor gods or deities (*wo* or *djemawo*), the spirits (good and bad), and finally the ancestral spirits. Each divinity is independent of the other, but all of them are under the supreme being. Though all the divinities are spiritual beings, they are believed to have been created by *Mau*, the origin of all life. In other words, except *Mau*, all other spiritual beings are creatures.

The Supreme Being

Let us now examine belief in the supreme being, whom they refer to as *Mau*.[30] He is the creator God, and he is neither approached nor worshipped directly because although he is believed to be everywhere, he is also perceived to be remote. Recourse to him is only through the minor gods or divinities and the ancestors, whom the people consider closer to them in their everyday life. As a result of this, *Mau* has neither shrines nor images in the Krobo culture. For this reason, first-time visitors to the place, who see only shrines of minor gods in Krobo villages and towns may be misled to conclude that Krobo do not know a creator God. The absence of a shrine or sanctuary for *Mau* is because of the greatness and grandeur with which he is viewed among the Krobo. *Mau* is believed to be ubiquitous and, therefore, cannot be localized in a static object like the deities. Besides, the *Krobo* maintain that *Mau* is fullness in himself; he does not need anything to complement his being, nor does he need offerings to act. And he is always benevolent toward his creatures.[31]

Nevertheless, prayers that accompany rituals show that *Mau* is worshipped every time. For example, no ritual is performed without first soliciting the blessings of *Mau*. Furthermore, every libation begins by

the Akan. For detailed discussion on the Akan belief system refer to Sarpong, "Sacred Stool of the *Akan*," 23–29.

30. Refer to an explanation of the etymology of the word *Mawu* (*Mau)* among the Ewe-speaking tribes in Riviere, "*Mawu*, l'insurpassable chez les *Evé* du Togo," 27. The word *Mau*, used by the Krobo to refer to the supreme being, may be a loan word from the Ewe tribes, as a result of the association the Krobos have had with the Ewe on their journey to the Krobo mountain.

31. A similar idea is found among the Ewe-speaking tribes in Togo and Ghana. See Riviere, "*Mawu*, l'insurpassable chez les *Evé* du Togo," 25–39.

first invoking *Mau*. Rituals performed at the various sanctuaries of other deities and the prayers in other circumstances and ceremonies nominate *Mau* first before any other deity. These observations suggest that the people see *Mau* as the supreme being.

The Deities/Spirits

In their day-to-day living, the Krobo deal much more directly with the gods (*wo*) of their clans, who have images or are visibly represented, and with the ancestors than with *Mau*. The minor gods are normally clan deities, whose origins have been lost in the transmission of the tradition. In the past, every adult Krobo poured libation many times during the day. Before and after taking any beverage (local gin, *akpetesi*) or water, a small amount of the liquid is poured on the ground for the ancestors and the spirits. Some older people still do it, and they claim that the practice has become so much a part of them that they do it involuntarily without even reflecting on it. Some consciously do it, justifying it merely as a cultural practice to remove from it any pagan interpretation.

Since the minor deities are familial, they are often represented with various images or items. Some of these include a piece of stone, a piece of clay moulded into a human form, or a combination of different items (stones and clay mouldings). An extraordinary big tree, a big stone with a strange form, a river, a hill, or the skeleton of some animal (mostly serpents) are often used to represent the minor gods. These items are believed to be imbued with the spiritual forces of the deities and are therefore considered sacred.

Furthermore, the minor deities, as well as ancestral spirits, have the power to bless or punish bad behavior in families and society. They bestow blessings and fortunes when the cultural prohibitions and regulations are observed, and they punish in the event of transgression. To pacify them for transgressions and to secure their blessings for long life and protection against evil, sacrifices are constantly offered. Furthermore, an individual's or the community's misconduct is redressed through ritual offering in the form of a material item, for example, a sheep or a white fowl. These items are normally offered to the minor gods or deities concerned, together with some amount of local gin, *apketeshi*, for libation.

The Ancestors (*Nimeli*)

The word *nimeli*[32] is the plural form of *nomo*, which means an elder. Elderly members of the community, both women and men, are called *nimeli*. Thus, etymologically, the ancestors are considered elderly members of the family and their community. The respect and honor that is accorded elderly living members of the family are also given to the deceased members of the family and the community. Just as families relate to each other in their communities on earth, so also the *nimeli* live a similar communion in the world of the dead. In this light, the ancestors of a family could be regarded as ancestors of the whole community, even though in a strict sense ancestorship is by blood relationship.

The Krobo have a strong belief in ancestral spirits,[33] but they make a difference between the deities and other spirits and the ancestral spirits. For the Krobo, the ancestors are not gods. They are human beings who have lived good lives in their earthly sojourn and acquired spiritual powers in the world of the dead. Consequently, the ancestors become models in their families and communities, and at the same time custodians of the moral order.

Not all dead persons become ancestors. The way a deceased person has lived determines whether he/she passes into the world of the ancestors or not. Normally, three basic qualifications must be met: first, the person must have led a good life on earth; second, he/she must have had a good death, that is, not death through an accident or any tragic event, as these are often interpreted as a punishment from the ancestors. The deceased must have left a progeny to succeed him/her. The question then arises, what about people who die childless but have led good lives, or children? According to tradition, they cannot be considered ancestors. But this does not mean that such people are lost. No, they are considered as being in the spiritual world of the dead, not as ancestors, but as *kpade* ("spirit"/"ghost").[34]

32. The word *nomo* means an old man or elderly man; the plural form is *nimeli*. A female elderly person is called *yomo*; the plural is *yimeli*. But when we have female and male elderly persons together, the Krobos refer to them with the masculine plural, *nimeli*.

33. The traditions concerning ancestors are widespread in Ghana. Some tribes, for example, the Ashanti, have specific cults for the dead.

34. An interview conducted at the Agavenya, Somanya traditional area suggests that *nemeli* refers to a state of being, whereas *kpade* refers to both a state of being and the spirit of the dead in general.

Notably, the *kpade* are equally as powerful as the ancestral spirits. The *kpade* may bless members of their families but may also inflict punishment in the form of sickness or death. At this point, it appears that the difference between *nimeli* and *kpade* is one of honor. Whereas the *nimeli* are generously remembered by all people, the *kpade* are often forgotten even by their close relatives.

Dead relatives in general are believed to be close to members of their families and clans. They can either bless them or punish them, for the transgression of the taboos of the clan or tribe, or when they have not administered the property inherited by the clan or family. The concern with ancestors and their relationship with the living is a dominant theme in numerous African traditional religions.[35]

Among the dead relatives, only the ancestors are informed ritually of any major event—for example, initiations, marriages, tapping of palm wine—that takes place in their families. This is normally done to solicit their blessings and protection.

As can be seen in the above survey, the relationship between the divinities and the spiritual beings has a dual purpose: to secure blessings in this earthly life and to avert evil. It appears the Krobo worship the divinities and venerate the ancestors not for what they are, but for what they can offer them. Belief in the power of evil spirits that threaten human existence and many times bring suffering and sickness strengthens and motivates constant recourse to the divinities and the ancestors.

Consequently, issues of life and death (evil) permeate every aspect of the existence of the Krobo. At any given moment, the preoccupation of the Krobo is to have well-being, to live in the absence of misfortune and evil and to prosper. For this reason, life and death are important aspects of the Krobo cosmology or religion. To understand and adequately interpret the essence of human existence in Krobo perspective—relationships with the other and the environment—one must first understand what it means to live and to die in the culture.

The Concept of Life and Death

Life and death are two realities in the existence of human beings.[36] These two concepts have raised many existential and ontological questions

35. Burton, "Living with the Dead."

36. Kizilabdullah, "Pre and Post-Death Rituals," 119.

throughout the centuries: What is life? What is its origin? What is death? What happens after death? Is there life after death? In what form? These questions have occupied philosophers and religious thinkers across all cultures around the globe. An examination of Krobo culture reveals that similar questions have been posed and dealt with within the anthropo-cosmological matrix of their worldview. In the Krobo worldview, there are two worlds: the spiritual and the physical/material world. Life and death are intricately related to these two realities. Life is an entrance into the physical world from the spiritual world and death is a departure from the physical world into the spiritual world. This hatching is transformative. For this reason, entrance into life (birth) and departure (death) are accompanied by ritual activities that underline the complexities of existence in the different modes and explain the diverse social and religious links.

What It Means to Live

The Krobo word for life is *wa*. This same word assumes verbal forms such as *wami* (growth) and *wae* (growing). We find the same word in the polysyllabic word *yi-wa-nam*, which literary means "receiving life for the head" but is often translated as "salvation." A sick person, for example, describes his or her state as follows: *I be he-wami*, "I have no life in my body." This same idea may be expressed about death. The sick person may say, *I nge gbo e*, which literary means "I am dying" but is ordinarily taken to mean "I am sick."

The brief semantic study above shows that for the Krobo life means well-being, growth, and absence of sickness. Well-being implies blessing and fertility. In their self-understanding, the Krobo realize that well-being and the absence of sickness are values one cannot buy or acquire by personal effort but are bestowed by the gods on those who observe the norms and precepts of Krobo culture. The incapacity of human beings to overcome evil in their efforts is compensated for among the Krobo by frequent recourse to the gods for protection and well-being.

A rite of passage is a ceremony performed to facilitate a person's change in status, for example, at birth, at puberty, at marriage, and at death.[37] Birth, puberty, marriage, and death are normally held to be the four principal stages in a person's life. Through gestures and accompanying

37. For a foundational and comprehensive discussion of the question refer to van Gennnep, *Rites de passage*; see also Turner, *Ritual Process*.

words, the neophyte is conferred with a new status and is thus introduced into a new group or unit of society. The ritual of birth has been selected to demonstrate the theological basis and articulation of the Krobo understanding of human life.

The Birth Ritual[38]

The ancient Krobo knew that biological life begins with the coming together of woman and man; however, they still attributed the origin of the new life to *Mau*. For example, a pregnant woman is said to have "gone to draw water from the cistern of the gods" (*e ho Mau aje pa ya*). Conception is perceived as originating from the divine. Hence, childbirth is considered not only a physical capability but also a spiritual reality. There is always a spiritual dimension to birth since the newborn baby is seen as a blessing from the gods and the ancestors. The ancestors and gods are believed to have the power to either seal the womb of a woman to prevent childbirth or bless the woman with a child. This underlines the spiritual nature of pregnancy.

From the moment of conception (expressed in Krobo as *sidami*, which literary means "standing up"), the woman is bound by ritual observances to protect the seed in her womb. The first requirement is that she must keep the news of the pregnancy secret, telling only her husband, since people with bad intentions could harm the baby and cause miscarriage. The news becomes public only when the pregnancy advances and the woman's stomach begin to protrude out.

During the time of pregnancy, the woman observes ritual sanctions or prohibitions, such as the following: she must not quarrel with anybody, she must not be involved in any mischievous deed, she must not steal, etc. All these are meant to protect the baby in her womb from any harm and secure good health. Furthermore, the ritual observances are also meant to protect the woman and prepare her for safe delivery.

Immediately after delivery, the newborn is washed by an elderly woman with warm water mixed with special spices. Then the newborn is wrapped in a piece of cloth, usually part of an old cloth of the father and placed on a prepared bed. Neighbors, nearby relatives, and friends, upon hearing the news, join the family in merrymaking. The joy that accompanies the birth of a baby is captured in expressions such as these:

38. Golo, "Ritual as Mechanism," 143–60.

bi gno, ("child sweet"); *Maule hano* ("It is God who gives"); *Mau lede* ("God says"); and *Hueni* ("It belongs to the intimate one"). These expressions are used on the occasion by those gathered to rejoice at the safe delivery, to indicate the fact that a child is the joy of its parents. No other joy surpasses this for a couple. On account of this, childless marriages are normally considered a misfortune. Sometimes such marriages are even interpreted as a punishment from the gods for offenses committed in the family, not necessarily by the couple.[39]

For the Krobo, the birth of a child is, first, a blessing from the gods, and, second, a victory for the woman who delivers safely. As can be seen from some cradle songs, the child, right from its appearance in this world, is entrusted to the protection of the gods. We reproduce one such cradle song that explains our point:

> *Asilokoto*![40]
> God has given it to me,
> that I may play with it.
> *Asilokoto*!
> God has given it to me,
> that I may carry it on my back
> Asilokoto!
> If I carried gold on my back
> I truly, carry nothing!
> *Asilokoto*!

An Interpretation of the Cradle Song

The two important ideas in the prayer are the child as God's gift and the preciousness of the child's life. Though not explicitly stated, we may deduce from the phrase "God has given it to me" in its context as referring to God being the creator of human beings. The awareness that the child comes from God lays on the parents the task of seeing to the child's spiritual growth. Spiritual growth implies recommending the child to God for his protection and putting the child in continuous relation with God and the spirits.

39. Gatti and Ossom-Batsa, "Drama of Infertility," 115–41.

40. *Asilokoto* is an exclamatory remark that means, "Look, how broad and beautiful!"

The preciousness of the child's life is underlined by comparing it with gold. Among the Krobo, gold is one of the most precious items a person can possess. Only a few people can afford to acquire gold. The worth or importance of a person or a family is normally measured by the number of gold ornaments they exhibit during public festivals and feasts. Gold, with all its value and the air of importance it bestows on the owner, has nothing to equal begetting a child. The lyrics of the song audaciously proclaim the deep satisfaction of a mother in carrying a child on her back. In other words, to nurse a baby is an expression of the fulfillment of motherhood for the Krobo woman.

Related to the fact that a child is God's gift is the understanding that the child does not belong to the mother as property. God, who is the dispenser of all life, gives or entrusts the child to the mother as a companion (God has given me that I may play with it). Any idea that a child belongs to the parents and so they can do whatever they like with it runs contrary to this understanding. The above prayer, therefore, affirms the sacredness of human life and consequently the need to preserve it.

The newborn is solemnly introduced into human society on the eighth day, when it is given a name. Hitherto, the newborn is in a transitory state: between the spiritual world and earthly existence.

Related to the idea of life is death, which stands at the opposite end of the spectrum. Though there is a strong belief in the community of the living dead, death is nevertheless looked at by the Krobo as an enigma. The desire of the Krobo to live to a ripe old age and receive abundant blessings in this world, especially through surviving offspring, makes death a tragic event and an enemy.

What It Means to Die

The word for death, *gbe-no*, belongs to the same semantic field of "to kill," *gbe*. Death is regarded as that which kills a person (*gbe-no*), in other words, that which brings an end to physical well-being. For this reason, death must be kept afar from human beings.

It is to be noted that the ancient Krobo were ritualistic. There is, in fact, no separation between religion and social or political life. Living by itself is a ritual! It is therefore understandable why there are many rituals in Krobo culture. Attempts to overcome the perils of life have led to the development of many rituals. All the rituals have one major purpose, namely, to avert evil, to prevent sickness and premature death, and finally to implore the divine for fertility.[41]

To overcome the malefactors in life, each stage of life has accompanying rituals to maintain a happy equilibrium between the community and the divinities, especially the living dead, the ancestors. Among the most important rituals are rituals during pregnancy, at birth, adolescence, old age, and death. For this paper, I examine only the ritual concerning death.

Rituals in Krobo culture are directed toward individual and social integrity.[42] Both the well-being of the individual and that of the community at large are guaranteed by ritual action. Sumer has stressed the fact that initiation in both indigenous and modern society is directed toward the welfare of the individual, his/her integration into the community, as well as the harmony of the entire society.[43] Often the misconduct or bad behavior of an individual also affects the harmony in the community, and this needs to be redressed. For example, when an individual violates a taboo, such as going to the riverside at night to fetch water, the whole community becomes contaminated. And not only the transgressor of the taboo suffers its effect, but the whole village or town community. Purification is achieved only when the spirit of the river is pacified by slaughtering a sheep and sprinkling its blood on the road leading to the river. If this ritual is not performed, all in the village and not only the sinner run the risk of punishment. In this case, the entire river may dry up and the village will suffer a water shortage.

Preparing for Death

Notwithstanding the awareness of the Krobo that death can come to anybody at any moment, their ritual behavior suggests that they view the old and very sick as those on the way to death. That is why in the past when people reached a certain age, they began to prepare for their death in several ways: by distributing their property to their children (*blonya*

41. See Izre'el, *Adapa and the South Wind*, 136, who notes that "our inner convictions come out when we utter blessings and curses." See also D'alveilla, "Initiation," 314–17.

42. Bond, "Living with the Spirits," 5, expresses a similar idea when he states, "rituals, however, constrain the disruption [of death] and make it part of the social construction." We agree with Bond that death is disruptive but differ from him that life after death is only a social construction.

43. Sumer, "Initiation Ceremony," 70–77.

tomi), undergoing the *blomi pomi* ritual, an expiatory ritual, and holding on more strongly to the values of upright living.

a. *Blonya tomi* literary means "putting things right." This implies reconciliation with members of one's family and giving to each what is due to her or him. However, this term is used mainly to refer to the act of a father sharing his property or belongings (fixed or movable property, money, etc.) with his children so that after his death each has something on which to continue to live.

   Though the act appears to be a social one, it has religious overtones in that it helps to avoid conflict and struggle among the progeny when their genitor is no more. The soul of the deceased is believed to be at rest when the family (his children) he leaves behind him are at peace with one another and have a good memory of him.

   Another aspect of the *blonya tomi* appears to be the idea of putting oneself right before *Mau.* Partiality is regarded as an evil act. Thus, by sharing the property among the children, which sometimes is not fairly done, the old man or father seeks righteousness before God. Generally, *blonya tomi* is guided by justice for peace to reign in the family. Since sometimes not all children show the same love and care for their fathers, those more faithful to their fathers are rewarded in the *blonya tomi* by receiving more items than the others.

b. The ritual of *blomi pomi* ("crossing the road"). This ritual is performed for a sick person who is at the point of death or for a person who has had a serious accident, for example, falling from a palm tree. The aim is to cleanse the person of any sins committed so that at death he/she may pass smoothly to the world of the ancestors. When the health of a family member is seriously deteriorating, the family head or any adult male member of the family quickly gathers some elders for the ritual. They carry the sick person to the entrance of the house, where they pour libation, using these or similar ones:

   [Name of person], *I gne mo blomi po e,*
   no ye bu ne ya se ne blono ne dzo hamo.
   Translation:
   [Name of person], I am crossing you the road;
   may evil be far away from you, and the be blessed for you.

   With this prayer of libation it is believed that if the person should die, there is no obstacle in the way to entering the world of the dead. If this ritual is not performed, especially in the case of an accident, and the victim dies, the death is seen as a bad death. Both *blonya tomi* and *blomi pomi* show how an individual implicitly or explicitly prepares and is prepared for death.

The Death and Funeral Rituals

Prayers and petitions in other rituals are centered on the preservation of life, averting evil, and keeping death away. But at last, death strikes. When this happens, death is interpreted only as physical separation, since the dead are believed to be alive in one form or another. However, the Krobo do not think of their dead as coming back into earthly life. They only say the dead enter a new mode of existence not visible to the naked human eye. Nevertheless, the dead are close to their kinsmen; they bless them but also punish them when they misbehave.

Although the Krobo reckon that death may strike at any moment, they still believe that some deaths are premature. Did a person die naturally? Was a person killed by an evil spell cast on him/her by an enemy? Or is death the result of the transgressions of the rules of the ancestors? These and many other questions arise out of the belief of the Krobo about evil and death. For this reason, the family elders try to find the cause of the death of a person before they begin to make the funeral arrangements. Often, diviners are consulted, who in one way or the other always offer some reason. In the past, much weight was given to this practice such that it led to strife in many families if a member of the family was pointed out as the cause of the death.

From the moment of the death of a person until the burial and the funeral rites, the Krobo demonstrate through ritual actions that the deceased is not lost but alive in another mode of existence. Some of the relevant moments are the preparation of the dead body for burial and the rituals of separation and incorporation before and after the burial.[44]

a. The preparation of the corpse for burial. As soon as the death occurs, the family head or the eldest male member of the family is informed of the event. In ancient times, the family head, on receiving the news, would inform the whole family, beginning with the ancestors. Using some amount of the local gin (*akpetesi*), he would pour out libation. In the prayer, he informs the ancestors of the family and asks for the

44. Opong, "Some Aspects of Basotho."

blessing that the funeral proceed peacefully. After this, messengers are sent to announce the death to family members around and those in other places. While this takes place, the dead body is ritually prepared for a wake-keeping. The body is first bathed in warm water, smeared with aromatic pomades, and nicely dressed in a newly made garment or one of the best dresses the deceased possesses.[45] The corpse is then laid in state and the funeral begins.

The wake is kept in the home of the deceased or where the corpse is laid in state (sometimes in the family home or another suitable place). The evening preceding the burial, the family members, friends, and sympathizers gather around the corpse and sing funeral dirges to express their grief for the death and to show their love for the dead person. Sometimes the singing of funeral dirges continues throughout the whole night until the following day.

b. Ritual of separation. Before the body is carried away for burial, the ritual of separation takes place. Normally, the family of the deceased is ritually separated from him or her. The separation is understood as the freeing of the surviving members of the family from the pangs of death but not from the person.[46] In order words, the household in which death occurs is believed to be defiled, and the people and the entire compound must therefore be purified. The purification is an attempt to keep death always far away from them.

c. Post-burial rituals. When the crowd returns from the cemetery, the head of the family of the deceased announces the period of mourning (*ya sitremi be*), which may be in weeks or months. This period in the terminology of Van Gennep is the "liminal period."[47] This is a transition period for members of the family to come to terms with the loss of their family member and adjust themselves to living in his or her physical absence. In the case of adults and married persons, the period begins with the ritual shaving of the hair of the widow or widower, the children, and close relatives. This group of persons continues to wear the black cloth/dress, the traditional mourning attire, until the end of the period. On the appointed day, the bereaved family and well-wishers gathered for the final funeral rites,

45. Van Gennep, *Rites of Passage*, 153–54. See also Opong, "Some Aspects of Basotho Funeral Rituals," 32–33.

46. Huber, "Outlines of Ultimate Reality," 253–54.

47. Van Gennep, *Rites of Passage*.

which include *ni yimu jiemi*, literary "removal of the black dress," and a communal family meal. With this, members of the bereaved family have been reintegrated into their routine life.

d. Significance of the rituals. The funeral rituals have a dual purpose: to introduce the deceased into the world of the dead[48] and to protect the living members of the family against the pangs of death. The belief that the dead person continues to live is expressed symbolically in the items with which they are normally buried and in the words of the funeral dirges sung. Some items the deceased are fond of in their earthly life, for example, a hat or a walking stick, are put in their coffins or on their graves with the idea that they will need these things in their next life.[49]

Conclusion

In the preceding pages, I have demonstrated through a phenomenological analysis what it means to live and to die in Krobo culture. I have pointed out that life and death, the two end points in a continuum, originate in the divine and lead to the divine. To live a meaningful life, the transition stage, death, as well as the goal of life must be always kept in view.[50] Some significant points from the study are the following.

Firstly, to the Krobo, to live implies both material and spiritual welfare. Since life originates from the divine, it is spiritual. But it has to be lived in the material world, with all its exigencies. For this reason, both the material and spiritual must always be kept in view as the individual journeys back towards the divine. It is in the light of this that the Krobo seeks a constant relationship with the divine daily.

Secondly, the ultimate meaning of life is the attainment of a fruitful life. This is understood as a realization of a blissful life here and now, but this ought to continue in the life after death. This presupposes that there is more to the human person than the corporeal reality of the individual. Therefore, well-being and prosperity should begin in this worldly

48. Imasogie, *Guidelines for Christian Theology*, 58–59, notes a similar ritual among the Igbos in Nigeria.

49. Van Gennep, *Rites of Passage*, 153–54.

50. Compare with the three stages of ritual (separation, transition/liminality, and incorporation/ reaggregation) outlined and discussed by Van Gennep, *Rites of Passage*. See also Opong, "Some Religious Aspects," 25–45; Ayinbora, "Absence of a Post-Burial Christian Funeral Liturgy," 52–75.

existence through the fight against sickness, misfortune, evil, and other earthly disasters. To achieve this, the Krobo have constant recourse to the divinities and ancestors for protection and blessings.

Lastly, the search for a fruitful life should create an opening for a systematic religious and moral formation that will promote the dignity of the person in the face of the exigencies of human realities. Life and death will then be seen as inseparable constitutive elements of humans.

Bibliography

Anderson, Ray S. *Theology, Death and Dying*. Oxford: Basil Blackwell, 1986.

Ayinbora, Samuel A. "The Absence of a Post-Burial Christian Funeral Liturgy: A Case for a New Funeral Ritual for the Frafra of Northern Ghana." *Questions Liturgiques* 88 (2007) 52–75.

Badham, Paul, and Linda Badham, eds. *Death and Immortality in the Religions of the World*. New York: Paragon House, 1987.

Bell, Catherine. *Ritual: Perspectives and Dimensions*. Oxford: Oxford University Press, 1997.

Bond, George C. "Living with Spirits: Death and Afterlife in African Religions." In *Death and Afterlife: Perspectives of World Religions*, edited by Hiroshi Ōbayashi, 3–18. New York: Greenwood, 1992.

Brody, A. J. "Materiality of Religion in Judean Households: A Contextual Analysis of Ritual Objects from Iron II Tell en-Naṣbeh." *Near Eastern Archaeology* 81 (2018) 212–21.

Burton, John W. "Living with the Dead: Aspects of the Afterlife in Nuer and Dinka Cosmology (Sudan)." *Anthropos* 73 (1978) 141–70.

D'alveilla, Goblet. "Initiation: Introductory and Primitive." In *Encyclopaedia of Religion and Ethics*, edited by James Hastings, 314–17. Edinburgh: T. & T. Clark, 1914.

Dhavamony, Mariasusai. *Christian Theology and Religions: A Systematic Reflection on the Christian Understanding of World Religions*. Berne: Peter Lang, 2001.

———. *Phenomenology of Religion*. Rome: Gregoriana, 1973.

Gatti, Nicoletta, and George Ossom-Batsa. "The Drama of Infertility: Reading Isa 56:1–8 from Krobo Perspective." *Horizons in Biblical Theology* 40 (2018) 115–41.

Gundani, Paul, H. "The Roman Catholic Church and the Kurova Guva Ritual in Zimbabwe." In *Rites of Passage in Contemporary Africa: Interaction between Christian and African Traditional Religion*, edited by James L. Cox, 198–223. Cardiff: Cardiff Academic, 1998.

Gyekye, Kwame. *Beyond Cultures: Perceiving a Common Humanity*. Accra: Ghana Academy of Arts and Sciences, 2000.

———. *An Essay on African Philosophical Thought: The Akan Conceptual Scheme*. Philadelphia: Temple University Press, 1995.

———. *Tradition and Modernity: Philosophical Reflections on the African Experience*. Oxford: Oxford University Press, 1997.

Heckert, Jamie. "Beyond Identity: Questioning the Politics of Pride." *The Politics of Contesting Identity*, edited by Craig J. A. Stewart et al., 12–32. Edinburgh: University of Edinburgh Press, 2003.

Huber, Hugo. *The Krobo: Traditional Social and Religious Life of a West African People.* Studia Instituti Anthropos 16. Fribourg: St. Paul, 1993.

———. "L'afrique de L'oeust: Reflexion sur le Patrimoine Culturel." *Séminaire 'Présence des Cultures Africaines*, 37–41. Fribourg, 19–23 October 1988.

———. "Outlines of Ultimate Reality and Meaning in Krobo Ritual." *Ultimate Reality and Meaning* 3 (1980) 245–55.

Ilogu, Edmund. "Transition—Igbo Burial Customs." In *Traditional Religion in West Africa*, edited by Ebenezer A. Ade Adegbola, 109–11. Ibadan: Sefer, 1998.

Imasogie, Osadolor. *Guidelines for Christian Theology in Africa.* Imasogie, Osadolor. Achimota: Africa Christian, 1983.

Izre'el, Shlomo. *Adapa and the South Wind: Language Has the Power of Life and Death.* Winona Lake, IN: Eisenbrauns, 2001.

Jones, David A. *Approaching the End: A Theological Exploration of Death and Dying.* New York: Oxford University Press, 2007.

Kewku-Nuako, Kwame. "The Enigma of Life: Death Rites among the Akans of Ghana and Christian Eschatology." *The Journal of Religious Thought* 56 (2001) 1–19.

Kizilabdullah, Sahin. "Pre and Post-Death Rituals in Christianity: A Phenomenological Analysis." *Turkish Journal of Theological Studies* 3 (2019) 117–35.

Kraft, Charles H. *Christianity in Culture: A Case Study Dynamic Biblical Theologizing in Cross-Cultural Perspective.* Maryknoll, NY: Orbis, 1989.

Leach, Edmund R. "Ritual." In *Ritual and Belief: Readings in the Anthropology of Religion*, edited by David Hicks, 176–213. Boston: McGraw-Hill College, 1999.

Majeed, Hasskei M. "An Analysis of Kwame Gyekye's Conception of 'Sunsum'in Akan Philosophy." *Ghana Journal of Religion and Theology* 7 (2017) 137–49.

Nukunya, Godwin K. *Tradition and Change in Ghana: An Introduction to Sociology.* Accra: Ghana University Press, 1992.

Opong, Kofi A. "Some Aspects of Basotho Funeral Rituals." *Journal for the Study of Religion* 17 (2004) 25–45.

Orr, John T. W. "The Fullness of Life: Death, Finitude, and Life-Philosophy in Edith Stein's Critique of the Early Heidegger." *Heythrop Journal* 55 (2014) 565–75.

Ossom-Batsa, George. "Ritual as Mechanism for Averting Evil and Securing Life among the Krobo." *Acta Theologica* 28 (2008) 143–60.

Ott, Craig. "Globalization and Contextualization: Reframing the Task of Contextualization in the 21st Century." *Missiology* 43 (2015) 43–58.

Penoukou, Efoé J. "Christologie au Village." In *Chemins de la Christologie Africaine*, edited by François Kasabélé et al., 69–109. Paris: Desclée, 1986.

Riviere, Claude. "*Mawu*, l'insurpassable chez les *Evé* du Togo." *Anthropos* 74 (1979) 25–39.

Sarpong, Peter K. *The Sacred Stool of the Akan.* Tema: Ghana Publishing, 1971.

Smith, Edwin W. "Religious Beliefs of the Akan." *Africa* 15 (1945) 23–29.

Sümer, Necati "Initiation Ceremonies in Primitive Tribes and some Religions." *Dini Arastirmalar* 21 (2018) 61–80.

Suri, Rochelle, and Daniel B. Pitchford. "The Gift of Life: Death as Teacher in the Aghori Sect." *International Journal of Transpersonal Studies* 29 (2010) 128–34.

Tunner, Victor W. *The Ritual Process: Structure and Anti-Structure.* Ithaca, NY: Cornell University Press, 1969.

Van Gennep, Arnold. *The Rites of Passage.* London: Routledge, 1997.

Part VI

Christianity and Mission Work

Chapter 10

Revisiting Missionary Work in Zimbabwe[1]

A History of the United Baptist Church of Zimbabwe

Elijah Elijah Ngoweni Dube

Introduction

There has been little research on the history of South Africa General Mission (SAGM) missionaries' work in Zimbabwe. The United Baptist Church (UBC) of Zimbabwe, which was formed out of the work of these SAGM missionaries, is also sparsely documented. This article seeks to address this knowledge gap. The SAGM missionaries evangelized the Chimanimani district of Zimbabwe, which happens to be a Ndau people's territory. SAGM evangelized the Chimanimani district (then part of British Gazaland) and the church that was born out of this mission bears the name: the Association of the United Baptist Churches of Zimbabwe (UBC).[2] The chapter follows a historical approach. It comprises of several parts. The first deals with missionaries in Africa in general. The second is on missionaries' work in Zimbabwe. The third focuses on South

1. "Revisiting" here pertains to missionary work in Zimbabwe in general, not specifically the SAGM work in Zimbabwe. Since there has been a lot written on missionary work in Zimbabwe, the revisiting concerns that aspect. The emphasis on SAGM is my contribution, which adds to what is already known about mission work in Zimbabwe. "Revisiting" seems appropriate to me in this regard.

2. Dube, *Getting Married Twice*, 117–74.

Africa General Mission, with particular emphasis on its founders (Andrew Murray, Martha Osborne, and William Spencer Walton). The rest of the chapter will address other related issues, including the Holy Spirit's visit at Rusitu (1915), later years in the mission/church, the United Baptist Church (UBC), and Serving in Mission (SIM).[3]

Missionaries in Africa

The SAGM missionaries were one small component of a much broader involvement of missionaries belonging to different bodies in Africa. SAGM was arguably a smaller mission group compared to some of the other missionary groups. It is in this light that this chapter seeks to situate SAGM missionaries among the missionaries in Africa in general.

A lot has been written on missionaries in Africa in general. Mercy Amba Oduyoye avers, "the story of missionary engagement with Africa has been told and retold."[4] Compared to the story of missionaries in Africa in general, the history of SAGM missionaries in Zimbabwe is less well known.[5]

An irrefutable fact of history is that missionaries of different affiliations and from far afield were driven to go to faraway lands with the conviction that they had a message of salvation to share in order to rescue those who were deep in "darkness." Although around 1750 there were very few (three or four) small Protestant groups who were interested in missionary work in Africa, this was to change after a great revival in Europe and America between 1700 and 1790, which caused many more people to want to spread God's word to other parts of the world. It was this desire to reach out to the unreached that many different Protestant missionary groups were formed.[6] This desire drew people from different denominational affiliations to team up in one society in order to reach out to those far afield and win them for Christ. The SAGM missionaries that evangelized the Chimanimani district in Zimbabwe were a good example of this mix.

3. Dube, *Getting Married Twice*, 117–74.

4. Oduyoye, "Christian Engagement," 91.

5. Dube, *Getting Married Twice*, 117–18.

6. Hildebrandt, *History of the Church*, 80; Dachs, *Christian Missionary*, 53; Dube, *Getting Married Twice*, 118.

The relationship between missionaries and settler colonialists has always been a critical discussion point. Some conflate the two and consider each one of them to have been one side of the same coin, with the other being the reverse side of the coin. On the contrary, they were separate entities, with the presence of missionaries preceding that of colonialists.[7] This, however, does not mean that they did not cooperate with each other on the ground. SAGM missionaries enjoyed some cordial relationships with settler farmers, for example, and benefitted from their hospitality. The settler government also collaborated and/or worked with missionaries in a number of ways as this chapter will later shed more light on. As Dube puts it, "It would be inappropriate . . . to perpetuate a perception that the missionaries served just as a 'front' for colonialists. Missionaries are almost always thought to have been part of a grant scheme by the white colonialists to, in some way, sedate or blindfold Africans with religion while the colonialists were busy colonising African territories . . . the missionaries and the colonisers were on different undertakings although the lines separating them were blurred in the eyes of onlookers."[8]

Apart from the quest to win the unreached for Christ, missionaries believed themselves to have been on a civilizing mission. The Western world understood itself to have been in the highest form of civilization and therefore saw the need to civilize those in "primitive" forms of development.[9] Bhebe argues, ". . . Civilization in its simplest and most radical form meant the adoption by Africans of European behavior, clothing and other western customs . . ."[10] What they perceived to have been the highest form of civilization was one and the same thing with Christianity. This explains the penchant drive to castigate African religions and to instill a new civilization that could be nothing other than Christianity. This also further explains the negative attitude that missionaries had toward everything that was African.

The missionaries sought to teach new methods of trade, agriculture, and industrial skills in the different regions where they were located.[11] Although they most probably genuinely wanted to improve the lives of the people, they had other aims as well. Dube notes, "As they introduced

7. Paas, *Faith that Moves*, 126; Dube, *Getting Married Twice*, 118–19.

8. Dube, *Getting Married Twice*, 119.

9. Mugambi, *African Heritage*, 38–41.

10. Bhebe, "Missionary Activity," 44–45.

11. Mugambi, *African Heritage*, 41.

the African to the new methods of trade, agriculture and skills they also sought to erase the African's civilisation and create Africans 'in the missionaries' image.'"[12] This issue of mimicking white people has lingered on in many African contexts. Africans would need to take an honest look at themselves and question why they do what they do, especially in postcolonial contexts.

The attitude of the missionaries toward Africans and their culture and/or religion was to change toward the end of the nineteenth century. According to Mugambi:

> Towards the end of the nineteenth century there developed in Europe a great interest in the study of the African religions and cultures. The previous view that African peoples did not have any religion or culture was modified in that development so that early in the twentieth century the popular view was that African peoples had their own religions and knew something about God. However, these religions were considered to be in the primitive stages of evolution, and the objective of Christian missionary activity would be to erase the religious understanding of those peoples and replace it with the highest religion which was thought to have been attained in Christianity.[13]

In practice, therefore, the attitude of the missionaries toward African traditional practices and cultures remained negative.[14] The dominance of Western culture remained intact. African traditional religion(s) and African cultures were not studied for what they were but for what the Westerners wanted them to be.[15] Missionaries and Westerners missed an opportunity to appreciate that which was good in the cultures of Africans. They perpetuated an attitude that was anti-African and sought to denigrate anything that was African. Any postcolonial studies of African Christianity should admit these flaws and seek to wean African Christianity from its intricate association with Western culture.

It is to be noted that some missionaries went to India, a move that enthused their fellow Westerners to venture out as missionaries to other parts of the world. Before 1800, four different missionary societies tried to establish work in Sierra Leone, a colony of freed slaves, which was

12. Dube, *Getting Married Twice*, 120.

13. Mugambi, *African Heritage*, 42.

14. Dube, *Getting Married Twice*, 120.

15. Dube, *Getting Married Twice*, 120.

presumed to have been the safest place to use as a base for reaching the rest of Africa with the good news of Christ.[16]

South Africa was another base that the missionaries also attempted to use, especially the Cape region.[17] This is more relevant for the purposes of this chapter, for it was from South Africa that the various missionary groups were to go up north to places such as Botswana, Malawi, and Zimbabwe (then Southern Rhodesia) to evangelize.[18]

Contrary to common sentiments and/or perceptions, establishing missions and winning converts was never easy for missionaries. Jenkins and Stebbing note that Robert Moffat and other missionaries to the then Matabele kingdom labored for years without any converts around the 1850s.[19] The same challenges were to be encountered by later missionaries, including SAGM missionaries.[20]

Missionaries' Work in Zimbabwe

Different missionary bodies went to different regions in Zimbabwe. They had an arrangement that forbade competing for souls. Chitando refers to this when he avows, "For a long time, the Dutch Reformed Church was the only denomination which held sway in the area (Masvingo). This was in line with the early missionaries' tacit arrangement of not jostling for souls in the same field."[21] This explains why SAGM was the only missionary body involved in the evangelization of the Chimanimani district in Zimbabwe. The same is true of other regions as well, where only one missionary body had a presence in a single region at a time.

In cities these arrangements were non-existent. Those who relocated to the cities formed and met in close proximity to other denominations, which would have been formed by members who relocated to the cities as well. According to Murphree:

> The greatest multiplication of denominations was found in the urban areas. When members of the various churches left their homes to work in the towns they set up congregations of their

16. Hildebrandt, *History of the Church*, 81–82; Dube, *Getting Married Twice*, 121.
17. Hildebrandt, *History of the Church*, 82.
18. Dube, *Getting Married Twice*, 121.
19. Jenkins and Stebbing, *They Led the Way*, 2–12.
20. Dube, *Getting Married Twice*, 145–49.
21. Chitando, "What's in a Name?," 107.

> own denominations in their new environment. Thus, those which had been carefully separated by comity agreements in the rural scene, found themselves side by side. Conflict between them, however, was not particularly severe since they drew their adherents from distinct tribal and geographical units, and there was no great tendency for their members to cross the lines of demarcation set thereby. The strongest conflict was between these groups as a whole and the younger proselytizing denominations which did not draw their members from a rural base.[22]

Referring to the same phenomenon, Weinrich proffers a different reason for its occurrence. The other reason for missionary bodies going to different regions was because they were given tracts of land in those regions by the colonial government.[23] The fact that missionary bodies went to different regions in Zimbabwe is incontestable.

The Ndebele were first to have contact with the missionaries before the Shona. The Shona, like the Ndebele, reacted negatively with the result that the missionaries labored for many years without winning a single convert.[24] The Catholic, Anglican, and Dutch Reformed Churches, among others, were among the beneficiaries of the colonial government's land apportionment to missionary bodies. Precisely because of this alienation from the land, most Shona people viewed the missionaries as the same as the white settlers and colonialists.[25] To date, the lines separating the white colonial government and the white missionaries have remained blurred.

The late nineteenth century was quite critical as far as the quest for the evangelization of Africa is concerned. The 1870s, 1880s, and 1890s were the time of the European rush into Africa.[26] The Church of England began work in Rhodesia (now Zimbabwe) in 1891. Several other Protestant missions were soon to be drawn into the evangelization of Zimbabwe: the Wesleyan Methodists (1891), the Dutch Reformed Church (1891), the American Board of Commissioners for Foreign Missions (1893), the Seventh Day Adventists (1895), the American Methodist Episcopal Church (1896), the Brethren of Christ (1897), the SAGM (1897) on which this chapter focuses, and later the Presbyterian Church, the Salvation Army,

22. Murphree, *Christianity and the Shona*, 12.

23. Weinrich, *African Marriage*, xii; Murphree, *Christianity and the Shona*, 11–12; Dube, *Getting Married Twice*, 122.

24. Dube, *Getting Married Twice*, 122.

25. Weinrich, *African Marriage*, 4; Dube, *Getting Married Twice*, 123.

26. Ranger, "Invention of Tradition," 211; Dube, *Getting Married Twice*, 123.

and the Church of Sweden. Roman Catholics also established works in Zimbabwe (then Rhodesia) during this time (from the late nineteenth into the early twentieth century) but the number of their converts did not rise quickly.[27] Gaining converts was a major challenge. This chapter will stress this when it discusses the work of the SAGM missionaries in Zimbabwe.

The Ndebele and Shona uprisings (1896–1897) disrupted missionary work in Zimbabwe just as the Chimurenga wars later in the 1970s would as well. Zvobgo notes that Christian missionaries founded new mission stations from the end of the Shona rising in 1897 up to 1923.[28] 1897 was the very same year that the SAGM missionaries trekked into Chimanimani, Zimbabwe, from South Africa.[29]

Many missionary groups were involved in the evangelization of Zimbabwe. Hildebrandt,[30] Smith,[31] and King[32] give the names of the missionary societies that worked in Zimbabwe as: the London Missionary Society (LMS); the Roman Catholic Mission (RC); the Church of England (CE; the Anglican Church; the Wesleyan Methodist Missionary Society (WMMS); the Dutch Reformed Church of South Africa (DRCSA); the American Board of Commissioners for Foreign Missions (ABCFM); the Board of Foreign Missions of the Methodist Episcopal Church (MEFB); the South Africa General Mission (SAGM); the Brethren in Christ Church (BC); the Presbyterian Church of South Africa (PCSA); the Church of Central Africa-Presbyterian; the Free Presbyterian Church of Scotland; Svenska Kyrans Mission (SKM); the Swedish Free Mission (SFM); the Salvation Army (SA); the Seventh-Day Adventists (SDA); the South African Baptist Missionary Society (SABMS); the Church of Christ (CC); and the Free Methodist Church (FMC). Some of the above are alternatively given the names: the Methodist Church (UK); the Methodist Church (USA); and the African Methodist Episcopal Church.[33]

This chapter turns its focus now on the SAGM missionaries who evangelized the Chimanimani district of Zimbabwe.

27. Hildebrandt, *History of the Church*, 177–78 ; Dube, *Getting Married Twice*, 123.

28. Zvobgo, *History of Christian Missions*, 66.

29. Dube, *Getting Married Twice*, 123.

30. Hildebrandt, *History of the Church*, 177–78.

31. Smith, *Christian Mission*, 52–71.

32. King, *Missions in Southern Africa*.

33. Dube, *Getting Married Twice*, 124.

South Africa General Mission (SAGM)

The fact that has already been noted above is crucial in a consideration of the SAGM missionaries' presence in Chimanimani, Zimbabwe. It was exclusively this missionary body that was involved in this region. SAGM established two mission schools in Chimanimani, at Rusitu and Biriiri, in the region in which they were involved and somewhat restricted to. It also established a hospital and Bible school at Rusitu mission station. This missionary organization was later to be called Africa Evangelical Fellowship (AEF), a name that also was later dropped for the current United Baptist Church (UBC).[34]

The Ndau people are to be found in the Chimanimani and Chipinge districts of Zimbabwe, and in Mozambique. The American Board of Commissioners for Foreign Missions (ABCFM) evangelized the Chipinge district of Zimbabwe, while SAGM concentrated on the Chimanimani district. In 1893, ABCFM established their first station at Mt Selinda, and in 1894 another at Chikore,[35] both in the Chipinge district.

There is evidence of the fact that the missionaries of these two missionary groups (ABCFM and SAGM) were conscious of the presence of the other group and would cooperate in certain works. Even today, members of the denominations that emerged as a result of these two missionary organizations sing songs or hymns from the same Ndau hymn book.[36] Just like SAGM, ABCFM also changed the mission name to a church name. The ABCFM of Mt Selinda is now called the United Church of Christ in Zimbabwe (UCCZ).[37]

What was to be commonly known as the SAGM) (3 January 1894), later Africa Evangelical Fellowship (AEF) (16 June 1965), and today Serving in Mission (SIM), began as Cape General Mission (CGM) in South Africa on 12 March 1889. It was a result of the acts of three prominent figures: Martha Osborn (sometimes spelled Osborne or Osborn-Howe), Dr. Andrew Murray, and William Spencer Walton (sometimes called just W. Spencer Walton or simply Spencer Walton).[38]

34. Dube, *Getting Married Twice*, 124.

35. Smith, *Christian Mission*, 64–65.

36. Dube, *Getting Married Twice*, 124–25.

37. Dhube, *Association of the UBC*, 26; Dube, *Getting Married Twice*, 125.

38. Kopp, *God First*, 17, 28; Serving in Mission website, https://www.simsg.org/our-history; Fuller; Dube, *Getting Married Twice*, 125.

Each one of the three words in 'Cape General Mission' carried some significance. Huntingford reports that, ". . . The new Mission would be called the Cape General Mission: 'Cape' because that is where its activities were to be centred; 'General' because it was intended to minister to a wide variety of peoples; 'Mission' because its workers were to be sent by God to do His work . . ."[39]

The Founders

The three cofounders are described as "dominant, charismatic individuals." It is also said that they shared many similarities. They emphasized holiness of life, evangelistic fervor, and missionary zeal.[40] Beckett submits that "The roots of the SAGM . . . were firmly established 'in the lives, convictions and leadings' of four devout 'servants of God,'" adding George Howe, who is omitted by the others.[41]

The name Cape General Mission could not be retained for long because the mission's sphere of influence had become broader than was originally envisaged. According to the Serving in Mission website, "After Martha Osborn married George Howe, they formed the South East Africa General Mission (SEAGM) in 1891. CGM and SEAGM merged in 1894, forming the South Africa General Mission. Because their ministry had spread into other African countries, they changed their name to Africa Evangelical Fellowship (AEF) in 1965."[42] Dhube concurs and mentions that the name Cape General Mission was changed to South Africa General Mission (SAGM) and remained so until it was given the name Africa Evangelical Fellowship (AEF).[43] As a result, the mission's name kept on changing several times, depending on its sphere of influence.[44]

According to Beckett, the Cape General Mission started with the following being members of its first council:

- President—Dr. Andrew Murray

39. Huntingford, *History of the Southern Field*, 9.

40. Dhube, *Association of the UBC*, 1; Kopp, *God First*, 28; Dube, *Getting Married Twice*, 125–26.

41. Beckett, 'Handmaids of Imperialism', 16–17; Dube, *Getting Married Twice*, 126.

42. Serving in Mission website, https://sim.org.za/wp-index.php/history/.

43. Dhube, *Association of the UBC*, 2.

44. Dube, *Getting Married Twice*, 126.

- Director—Spencer Walton
- Associate Director—Dudley Kidd
- Honorary Secretaries—Martha Osborn and George Howe
- Treasurer—P. G. H. Wilmot
- Council Members—Mrs. Walton and Miss Ferguson[45]

Although the purpose of this chapter is not necessarily to give a profile of its founders, I agree with Kallam that "To discover the beginning of the Africa Evangelical Fellowship, it is necessary to trace three lives as they joined together in working for the peoples of South Africa, which resulted in the founding of the Mission."[46] The three lives referred to here are those of the three cofounders (Martha Osborn-Howe, Andrew Murray, and W. Spencer Walton) that have already been mentioned. We turn, therefore, to brief accounts of their lives.

Andrew Murray

Andrew Murray, who was born in South Africa at Graaff Reinet (Eastern Cape) on 9 May 1828, was a critical figure in the founding of the mission. He was involved, from the very beginning, with Mrs. Osborn and Mr. Howe. Later he was involved with Mr. Walton in the "on-going work." In other words, his involvement was before, during, and after the formation of the mission.[47]

He is said to have been a man of many talents. The conversion of this very influential figure took place in 1845, according to Murray himself. He considered missions as "the chief end of the church" and he found seminaries, a university, and a missionary training institute. He was a great Bible teacher with his teachings subsequently published in some 250 books.[48]

45. Beckett, "Handmaids of Imperialism," 24; Dube, *Getting Married Twice*, 126–27.

46. Kallam, *History of the AEF*, 34.

47. Huntingford, *History of the Southern Field*, 8; Dube, *Getting Married Twice*, 127–28.

48. Dube, *Getting Married Twice*, 128.

Murray was not a missionary himself but he was a great promoter of missions who helped to found the SAGM in 1894. Dhube calls Dr. Andrew Murray "the most influential of the three."[49]

Martha Osborne

It is remarkable to note that a mission and later a church that would later somewhat downplay the role of women in church leadership had a woman as one of its cofounders. Women today are not allowed to assume any "elder" roles in the United Baptist Church. Although women have gradually been allowed to take up pastoral roles in the church, they are regarded as unfit and/or unqualified to conduct certain functions like presiding over the Eucharist and baptism. They also cannot bury the dead. They spend their whole lives serving as "evangelists", the term UBC uses to refer to new entrants into the pastoral ministry, those who have not yet been ordained as ministers in the church. Based on their gender, women are never ordained within the UBC setting.

The only woman among the cofounders, Martha Osborn-Howe was definitely vital to this mission in a number of ways. In fact, Dhube[50] and Kallam[51] are of the opinion that Martha should be acknowledged much more than she has been. Dhube argues that ". . . the South Africa General Mission was founded on the works of Mrs Martha Osborn-Howe. In that sense, she is the undisputed founder of the Mission—though that honour was not to be conferred on her in actual words."[52] For Kallam, "The Africa Evangelical Fellowship owes a great debt to Martha Osborn–Howe as a cofounder with Spencer Walton and Andrew Murray, a fact not fully acknowledged in the history of the Mission. The contributions of Dudley Kidd and Frank Huskisson to the growth of the Mission have also failed to get the recognition they should receive."[53] Kopp likewise maintains that "SAGM . . . owes its inception chiefly to a lady worker, Mrs Osborne."[54]

Like Andrew Murray, and unlike William Spencer Walton, Martha was born in South Africa. She was born at Sandfontein Farm near

49. Dhube, *Association of the UBC*, 2.
50. Dhube, *Association of the UBC*, 2–3.
51. Kallam, *History of the AEF*.
52. Dhube, *Association of the UBC*, 1.
53. Kallam, *History of the AEF*, i–ii.
54. Kopp, *God First*, 17.

Uitenhage in Port Elizabeth in 1846.[55] Having been raised in a Christian family, Martha had great interest in Christian work. She was married first to a soldier, Captain Osborn, from India. When he died in 1877, she subsequently married Rev. George Howe, which is why she had the name Osborn-Howe.[56]

To sum up Martha's great work, Huntingford asserts, "Martha Osborn was indefatigable in her work for God . . ."[57]

William Spencer Walton

Unlike the first two, William Spencer Walton was born in London on 15 January 1850. The other two were both born in South Africa. He had difficult health challenges as he was growing up. He had voyages on ships to Australia (1865) and to South Africa (1867), hoping that his health would improve. At the age of twenty-two, on 18 February 1872, he received Christ at an evangelistic meeting. For the next ten years he was involved in ministering the word of God wherever he was invited, although he continued his secular employment. In 1882 he was included in the panel of speakers for the Keswick Convention, where he met with Dr. Andrew Murray for the first time. Within the same year he gave up his secular employment and joined the Church Parochial Mission as an evangelist. This he did until he resigned in 1884 so as to engage in a wider interdenominational ministry. In mid-1880 he was invited to conduct meetings for soldiers in Papillon's Soldiers' Institute, and this is interesting because one of the earliest thrusts of Mrs. Osborn and Mr. Howe was amongst troops in South Africa.[58]

Although Mr. Howe is not quite acknowledged in SAGM history, Dhube mentions that "William Spencer Walton (often simply, W. Spencer Walton)—a Baptist minister from England . . . was recruited to come to South Africa by Mr and Mrs Osborn-Howe."[59]

55. Dhube, *Association of the UBC*, 1; Dube, *Getting Married Twice*, 129; Huntingford, *History of the Southern Field*, 5.

56. Dhube, *Association of the UBC*, 1.

57. Huntingford, *History of the Southern Field*, 6; Dube, *Getting Married Twice*, 129.

58. Dube, *Getting Married Twice*, 130; Huntingford, *History of the Southern Field*, 7.

59. Dhube, *Association of the UBC*, 2.

Spencer Walton had many talents. Apart from preaching he had strength in recruiting other workers for the mission. Even at a time when others in Europe felt that resources were not available, he was quite instrumental in raising awareness and support for the mission. Unsurprisingly, he was not always in agreement with some of his colleagues on the field in South Africa. He was, nonetheless, the first director of the SAGM in Cape Town.[60]

Kallam remarks that "Walton arrived in South Africa in 1888 for a series of meetings set up by Andrew Murray, Howe, and Mrs Osborn. By the end of these meetings, the plan for the Cape General Mission had been conceived in their minds."[61] According to Kopp, "Following W Spencer Walton's second entry into South Africa, and with the help of co-founders Martha Osborn-Howe and Dr Andrew Murray, the Cape General Mission was launched in 1889."[62] It is remarkable that the mission started right from the very beginning with an international flavor to it. This international flavor has remained with the mission to date. Kopp adds, "Like other faith missions, SAGM/AEF became internationalized by virtue of the fact that the USA, Canada, the United Kingdom, Australia, New Zealand, and South Africa provided both its missionary personnel and its support bases."[63] Although the latter may be more relevant to missionary personnel at a later stage in the mission, the fact remains that the mission had an international element to it right from its inception.[64] In addition, the mission drew, from its inception, missionaries from diverse denominational backgrounds. It was, therefore, not founded by missionaries who had a homogenous denominational affiliation.

The sphere of influence of SAGM was much broader than just its involvement in Chimanimani, Zimbabwe. Glen avers, "Mr and Mrs Spencer Walton pioneered the work in Swaziland in 1891. In 1894 . . . work was opened up in Zululand, Tembuland, Pondoland, Bomvanaland (all three in the Eastern Cape), amongst the Indian people of Natal, the tribes of Gazaland, the Vanyanja of Nyasaland (Malawi) and as far North as the Kaonde tribe of Northern Rhodesia (now Zambia)."[65] In Zimbabwe, the

60. Dube, *Getting Married Twice*, 130; Dhube, *Association of the UBC*, 2.

61. Kallam, *History of the AEF*, 41.

62. Kopp, *God First*, 18.

63. Kopp, *God First*, 39.

64. Dube, *Getting Married Twice*, 131.

65. Glen, *SAGM*, 48.

SAGM missionaries were to influence and change the human landscape of Chimanimani.[66]

Geographical Expansion of the Mission

As has already been established, the mission's work was not to be confined to Cape Town, where it had started. Its influence was to be felt in other places in South Africa and outside the borders of South Africa as well. As Huntingford puts it, "The work increased tremendously in scope and geographical location and the number of workers increased correspondingly. The SAGM was now based in three centres: the original one in Cape Town, and Durban and Johannesburg."[67] Beckett concurs: "The SAGM was based in three centres; Cape Town, Durban and Johannesburg, from where it spread into much of Southern Africa."[68]

The change of its name was necessitated by the gradual change of its sphere of influence. It could not continue to be called the Cape General Mission when its scope had become broader. Its name, therefore, changed to SAGM. It would have been even better to call it Southern Africa General Mission if it had been known that it was going to have much wider influence in southern Africa.[69]

The change of the name was not simply that; it was also a coming together of two missions. The South East Africa Evangelistic Mission (SEAEM) and Cape General Mission (CGM) came together on 1 January 1894 under the name South Africa General Mission.[70]

The original mandate had been ministry among the whites. Work among black people began in the compounds of Kimberley (northern Cape) and Johannesburg (Transvaal). Beyond this, work was started among blacks in Swaziland, KwaZulu Natal, the Orange Free State, and south Mozambique. Underlining the fact that missionaries benefitted from the development put in place by colonial settlers, Dhube mentions that ". . . with the extension of British colonial rule northwards, missionaries of the SAGM also penetrated with freer access to Zimbabwe (then Southern Rhodesia), Malawi (then Nyasaland), Zambia (then Northern

66. Dube, *Getting Married Twice*, 131.

67. Huntingford, *History of the Southern Field*, 13.

68. Beckett, "Handmaids of Imperialism," 28; Dube, *Getting Married Twice*, 131.

69. Dube, *Getting Married Twice*, 132.

70. Dube, *Getting Married Twice*, 132.

Rhodesia) and Angola."[71] Implicitly mentioned here is the close connection between imperialism and/or colonialism and mission work.

Its eschatology, which emphasized the imminent return of Christ, spurred it further and further. They had a sense of urgency regarding reaching the unreached with the gospel. It appears that these missionaries had a genuine zeal for the spread of God's word—something that cannot be taken away from them irrespective of how much criticism is leveled against them.[72]

"God First—Go Forward" was the mission's motto.[73] Huntingford adds, "'God First' is the watch word of the Fellowship; 'Go Forward' is its motto, desire and intention, to whatever work, in whatever place, amongst whatsoever people God chooses to send."[74] This is greatly evident in the SAGM missionaries that evangelized Chimanimani in Zimbabwe. Not even the unfavorable terrain of this region and the malaria-bearing mosquitos could stand in their way. Right from the beginning and later, there were fatalities due to these adverse conditions.[75]

The missionaries to Gazaland in Zimbabwe (then Southern Rhodesia) were sent from the Johannesburg office.[76] According to Kopp, ". . . Zimbabwe was entered in 1897, then Malawi (1900), Zambia (1910), Angola (1914), and Mozambique (1936)."[77] Kopp further reports that "In the years that followed the name change (with reference here to a later change of name to Africa Evangelical Fellowship), the Mission continued to expand by establishing work in Mauritius (1969), Namibia and Reunion (1970), Botswana (1973), Gabon (1986), Madagascar (1987), and finally Tanzania (1989)."[78]

Reasons for the second change of name are outlined by Dhube, who notes that "The main reason behind the change of the name of the Mission from South Africa General Mission (SAGM) to Africa Evangelical Fellowship (AEF) and, with it, as was the case in Zimbabwe, the automatic change of the name of the Church from South Africa General

71. Dhube, *Association of the UBC*, 3.

72. Dube, *Getting Married Twice*, 134.

73. Kopp, *God First*, 28.

74. Huntingford, *History of the Southern Field*, 4.

75. Dube, *Getting Married Twice*, 137.

76. Huntingford, *History of the Southern Field*, 15.

77. Kopp, *God First*, 33.

78. Kopp, *God First*, 33; Dube, *Getting Married Twice*, 133.

Mission Church to Africa Evangelical Fellowship Church, was a growing feeling within the Mission that the words 'South Africa' were becoming too limited for the sphere of the Mission's activities (which now extended virtually over all of Southern and Central Africa and the Islands) and that with the rise of black nationalism the words were beginning to cause political problems outside South Africa . . ."[79] Procter states that this change of name to Africa Evangelical Mission took place at the international conference held in South Africa in 1963.[80]

Kopp agrees with the aforementioned and summarizes the developments as follows: "The SAGM/AEF was initially aimed at the Cape Province of South Africa as portrayed by its original name Cape General Mission. The later expanded aim of the Mission in southern Africa in general, including Angola, Zambia, Malawi, Mozambique and southwards, was reflected by the name South Africa General Mission. Eventually as the Mission expanded further northwards, and more and more countries gained independence from colonial rulers, the name was again changed to Africa Evangelical Fellowship to more accurately indicate its scope."[81]

The Trek into Zimbabwe

The term Gazaland was a very broad term used to refer to the Ndau territory in Zimbabwe and in Mozambique (Portuguese East Africa). The Melsetter district included what are called Chimanimani and Chipinge districts today. The whole area was known as Gazaland or British Gazaland, to differentiate it from Portuguese (Mozambique) Gazaland. The name Gazaland had a lot to do with the Gaza Nguni of the nineteeenth century.[82] It is in this sense that any study of the history of the Ndau people cannot be complete without making reference to the connection that the Ndau people have with Soshangane, who fled (South Africa) from Tshaka in the nineteenth century.

I have already alluded to the fact that the conditions that the missionaries had to go through in order to evangelize the Chimanimani district of Zimbabwe were not easy. In 1896, Dudley Kidd proposed the idea of establishing a mission station in British Gazaland and this vision

79. Dhube, *Association of the UBC*, 49.

80. Procter, *Fools for Christ*, 12.

81. Kopp, *God First*, 38–39.

82. Dhube, *Association of the UBC*, 4.

was shared by Harry Raney, an engineer, who would accompany Kidd into this territory.[83]

Difficult as it was, Kidd and Raney remained resolute with their plan to evangelize Gazaland. The urgency that they felt to evangelize Gazaland was not shared by the British Council of the SAGM, which felt that if this work was to be done, it needed to be done by African evangelists. The latter were against the missionaries' exposing themselves to unhealthy climate coupled with the prevalence of malaria.[84]

Harry Raney, John Coupland (Jack), and Dudley Kidd were the three pioneers into Gazaland. According to Beckett, "In December, 1897, three pioneer missionaries, Raney, Coupland, and Kidd, embarked upon a mission into a potentially volatile human landscape, rumblings of the 1896/97 Shona/Ndebele rebellions against Imperial domination and subordination still shaking the unsettled 'white' community of Gazaland."[85] They definitely entered Zimbabwe at a very volatile period but not even this volatility could stand in their way. They were determined to reach the unreached and with that vision they embarked on the mission.

When we talk about missionaries today, we do not seem to do justice to the hardships they had to endure. It almost always seems as if they enjoyed very smooth transitions from their places of origin and as if they likewise ministered without any form of hardship. On the contrary, they suffered, and Fuller asserts that "All the pioneers faced physical rigors, oppressive spiritual darkness, and violent opposition."[86] There was a great deal of walking involved and difficulties in moving luggage from one place to another, among other challenges. Many missionaries lost their lives in missionary endeavors and many suffered ill health. Some had to watch colleagues die and others had to abort work in certain locations.[87] King, who compiled accounts from different missionary bodies who were involved in work in Zimbabwe, admits:

> As I have read these stories I have been impressed again at the cost in life and health of bringing the Gospel to Southern Rhodesia (Zimbabwe). Missionaries have died or watched loved ones die, stricken with fever and other diseases. Sometimes a

83. Dube, *Getting Married Twice*, 134 ; Beckett, "Handmaids of Imperialism," 31.

84. Beckett, "Handmaids of Imperialism," 32.

85. Becket, "Handmaids of Imperialism," 58.

86. Fuller, Serving in Mission, http://images.sim.org/pdfs/history/whfuller-sim-history.pdf.

87. Dube, *Getting Married Twice*, 135–36; King, *Missions in Southern Rhodesia*, 9.

> start was made with work in a certain area but fever drove the Missionaries out. This sacrifice of life and health has not only been faced by European Missionaries, but also by African Christians. From the time of Makhaza, the first African Christian in Rhodesia to die because he was a 'follower of the Book', to the present day African Christians—Ministers and Evangelists and their families and others—have faced dangers to health and strength to preach the Gospel to people settled in backward, unhealthy areas of the country.[88]

Writings by Glen[89] and Beckett[90] are particularly important for the purposes of this chapter because they are by people who either were right on the ground in Gazaland or who had an opportunity to interview the missionaries on the ground. Reginald Glen was an SAGM missionary who responded to King's call to submit an account of SAGM work in Gazaland. Beckett, on the other hand, is himself the son of another SAGM missionary, Rev. Haward Beckett, whom I had an opportunity to interview when I was in Zimbabwe from 18 April to 18 May 2016 conducting fieldwork for my doctoral studies, from which I have extracted the information for this chapter. It is important to mention that the dissertation by Beckett was given to me by his father, Rev. Haward Beckett, after I had interviewed him. It proved to be very significant in giving me the perspectives of the SAGM missionaries themselves and the reflection of them by an SAGM missionary's son.[91]

Along the same lines, Dhube account is, of course, not by a missionary or missionary's son but by the leader of the United Baptist Church, Dr. Bishop Joshua Dhube, from the 1960s (transitional years) to around about 2004.[92]

Having left Johannesburg in March 1897, the three pioneers travelled by ship to Beira and by rail to Chimoio. From there they trekked in on foot with African carriers who deserted them, carrying off most of their food and equipment. They lost a lot of time in trying to recover these necessities and were physically very weak when they finally reached Dzingire, near the border with Portuguese East Africa. The late Chief Dzingire, then a young man, was very averse to these strangers

88. King, *Missions in Southern Rhodesia*, 9.

89. Glen, "South Africa General Mission (Rusitu)."

90. Beckett, "'Handmaids of Imperialism.'"

91. Dube, *Getting Married Twice*, 136.

92. Dube, *Getting Married Twice*, 136.

invading his country. However, they built huts and prepared for the rainy season. In November it was decided that John Coupland should stay with the remaining supplies while the other two returned to the railhead to obtain more. On reaching the railhead they decided that Mr. Kidd should return to the headquarters to give a report, while Raney returned to Coupland.[93]

Raney found John Coupland very ill with malaria fever. This illness would take Coupland's life on 14 November 1897, and Raney buried him the following day. Raney placed a stone on Coupland's grave, on which he carved one word, "Promoted" (from the conversation they had few days before in which Coupland referred to death as "promotion"), and the date.[94]

It is important to note that these pioneers were young men who sacrificed their careers to go on the trek. Beckett points out, "Harry Raney was twenty-eight years old when the trek into Gazaland was undertaken . . . At the time he offered himself as a missionary to Gazaland, he was chief engineer of the Mayer and Charlton mines . . . John Coupland was a mason . . . Neither man, however, could boast of any prior training to prepare them for what lay ahead . . ."[95] Dhube mentions that Dudley Kidd was an able administrator from the founding of the mission in 1889 and that Kidd used his abilities in the siting of Rusitu Mission in 1897. Of the three pioneers, the third was not committed to staying in Gazaland.[96]According to Dhube, the actual volunteer pioneers among these three were Raney and Coupland.[97] Kidd only accompanied them to select the spot for the first station and see them properly started.

The lines separating missionaries and white settler farmers and/or colonialists were always blurred. They remain blurred even today in the thinking of many Africans. The fact that there was a lot of cooperation and collaboration between them does not make it any easier. There is evidence of close relationships between the SAGM missionaries and the settlers and colonialists. Beckett details how Coupland and Kidd benefitted from the hospitality of Mr. Martin and Mr. Human.[98] The latter was a

93. Dube, *Getting Married Twice*, 136.

94. Dube, *Getting Married Twice*, 137.

95. Beckett, "'Handmaids of Imperialism,'" 35.

96. Dhube, *Association of the UBC*, 4–5.

97. Dhube, *Association of the UBC*, 6.

98. Beckett, "'Handmaids of Imperialism,'" 42.

settler farmer. It was perhaps because of this close relationship between the missionaries and the settlers that the Ndau found it difficult to distinguish between them.[99]

Since Kidd had returned to the SAGM offices in Johannesburg, the task of finding a site for the mission in Gazaland rested on Raney's shoulders. Raney was a fighter in many respects. Alone in Gazaland, Raney undertook, with extreme difficulty, the task of establishing a proper site for the mission station. Recorded in his diary are six periods of fever that sent him to bed, and twice what he called a "breakdown," including mental confusion as a result of fever. The mission site had to be moved from Dzingire to Chingwekwe (Rusitu), the current site. Coupland had died on the first site in Dzingire village. The new site was at a high elevation, with good water supply.[100]

There was undeniable suspicion about each other between the SAGM missionaries and the Ndau people in Chimanimani. Raney writes:

> We have been a good time here, and yet how little there seems done; the natives have not yet learnt to put much confidence in us, but still have the idea that we want to get something out of them, or, in some way or other, mean them ill. We hear of some places where the people long to be taught the Word of Life, but here their core idea is what they can get out of us in the way of limbo or salt, and they will beg for matches, cotton, needles, etc. Only yesterday I visited the chief, N'Garema [Ngorima], and though he was friendly and gave me milk, yet there still was suspicion on his part and he wanted to know if we were to take his land. But, praise God, the people are better than they were when I first pitched my tent here; then the children fled in terror at my approach and the women got out of the way, and all the time seemed in fear; now the children come round here to play or ask to be allowed to grind for us, the mill being a novelty to them, and the women show much more confidence in coming to sell their grain and eggs, etc. But when I ask them to learn a Zulu hymn or chorus, or suggest any learning, they say they are afraid and don't want to, the evil spirits will harm them if they do; even those who live and work here with us say the same. And so we have just to live down their superstition, and the effects of ill treatment they have experienced at the hands of some whites, and therefore pray for grace to live the Christ life before them

99. Dube, *Getting Married Twice*, 139.

100. Dube, *Getting Married Twice*, 138.

> which must eventually tell. This will, perhaps, help our friends to pray for us in a definite way, for we need your prayers.[101]

Two years into the mission's existence at Rusitu in Chimanimani, Zimbabwe, Raney expressed the desperate situation that the SAGM missionaries found themselves in.[102]

It has already been stated that the SAGM missionaries lacked appreciation of the Ndau people and their ways of life. Raney gives credence to this assertion when he mentions that "This people are as mean a race as one can imagine, bound by the sins of lying, idleness and drunkenness, and with little, or no natural affection even for their own flesh and blood. Gratitude seems to be an unknown quality. And yet, this is the material we have to work upon, and these are the people among whom we are sure God has some chosen ones. Workers have been labouring here for nearly five years, and though we cannot yet point to one who has been born again, we know God is working, and we can see a difference in them. They know about God, they have often heard His Word, but as yet prefer to go their own evil way . . ."[103] Raney represents sentiments shared by many other missionaries of his time. They evidently were too quick to judge the people they had come to evangelize. A close study of the Ndau would have shown that they had their own ways of showing gratitude, for example, compared to those that Raney was used to.[104]

Apart from Raney and Kidd, more missionaries were to be involved in the work at Rusitu Mission, and later at Biriiri Mission (both in Chimanimani and under SAGM). Beckett[105] and Procter[106] mention Mr. James Middlemiss and Mr. A. E. Estall, who arrived in Mutare (then Umtali) on 16 June 1898 to assist Raney in the mission work in Rusitu. Beckett remarks that "In constructing the mission station in Gazaland, the SAGM missionaries were to have an enduring impact upon the physical landscape . . ."[107] Moreover, the site for the mission station was "central to many kraals," a clear indication of the missionaries' desire to "interact" with the Ndau in an effort to "Christianize" the human landscape. As such, they

101. Raney, "Gazaland," 36–37.

102. Raney, "Gazaland," 84.

103. Raney, *From Different Points*, 60.

104. Dube, *Getting Married Twice*, 143.

105. Beckett, "'Handmaids of Imperialism,'" 52–53.

106. Procter, *Fools for Christ*, 18–19.

107. Beckett, "'Handmaids of Imperialism,'" 53.

differed greatly from their "non-Christian" contemporaries, the latter practising a policy of residential segregation from the "natives."[108]

The language issue was always a barrier for the missionaries, who had not learned the local languages. The locals also found it difficult to express themselves to the missionaries who did not speak their language. To add to this, there was also a challenge in the fact that the two had different worldviews. This further confounded the situation.[109]

The missionaries labored for a long time at Rusitu without any converts to show for it. Douglas Wood can be said to have been God's blessing to the mission at the time that he was at Rusitu. Wood, who appreciated the importance of learning the people's language, had spent some time learning the Zulu language in Zululand. A fair grasp of the Zulu language was critical in understanding the ChiNdau tongue owing to the similarities in the framework of the two languages. Wood was a most important influence at Rusitu, together with James Middlemiss and Estall. Douglas Wood's language skills were an immense help. He and Estall could speak with the Ndau people in their language and he translated some hymns into Ndau. Wood also translated the Gospel of Mark into Ndau. They were joined by Japheth, a Zulu evangelist from Durban.[110] Dhube mentions that "By Christmas Day, 1901, Wood reported for the first time that there were 120 men, women and children who attended a Christmas party at the Mission."[111]

Apart from learning the people's language, Wood knew that meeting with the people in their homes would make a big difference. He would go out of the mission station to meet the Ndau people in their homes and in their communities. He is also said to have been in the habit of walking around on Saturdays calling out *Mangwani iSondo* ("Tomorrow is Sunday") as a way of inviting people to come for church services on Sundays.[112]

The blurred lines separating the missionaries from the settler colonialists were something Wood himself was conscious of. About the difficulty that the Ndau people had in distinguishing between the missionaries and the interpreters from the settler colonialists and the police, Wood

108. Dube, *Getting Married Twice*, 143–44.

109. Dube, *Getting Married Twice*, 144.

110. Dube, *Getting Married Twice*, 145.

111. Dhube, *Association of the UBC*, 13–14.

112. Dube, *Getting Married Twice*, 146.

writes, "It seems that we are often mistaken for the police, the Native Evangelist being dressed in European clothing as none of the other natives about here are, and that would account in great measure for the general helter-skelter that takes place, when we are beheld approaching."[113]

Eventually, in 1902, there were to be some few converts, beginning with three, two young men, one of which was called Chiwanguwangu (a nickname), and a girl called Mutendi (or Murutendi, both shortened forms of Amutendi Zvendinoereketa, daughter of Chief Mushayanembeu Ngorima). The other convert was Chiwanguwangu's older brother, Marijeki Chiuya Dhliwayo. The efforts of Wood and other fellow workers were evidently not in vain. It had taken many years though for them to see these first converts. After the three above, and not long afterwards, Mwathetha Samuel Nkomo (Sithole or Unzemwoyo) and Ruka Bwerudza (older brother of Rev. Mackinase Bwerudza) also converted to Christianity.[114]

The mission was to face other difficulties. Later, in 1905 and early in 1906, the future of the mission became uncertain. Wood had relocated to Johannesburg. The British Council were considering passing the work over to another mission. They felt that, owing to the several challenges the mission was faced with, it would be better for SAGM to concentrate its efforts in other fields. John Hatch, who carried on with work during this tenuous period, offered to resign in June 1907. By divine providence, the mission at Rusitu experienced nothing short of a blessing from God, resulting in the growth in the school and more young men converting to Christianity. In light of these developments, the mission recommitted to work at the station and Hatch stayed.[115]

Japheth, the interpreter was to sadly pass on due to malaria, together with other interpreters had been very handy in the evangelization of the Ndau people. Owing to their efforts, the numbers of converts was on the rise.[116]

When the SAGM missionaries ventured into Zimbabwe, they had their focus on evangelizing Mozambique as well but the Mozambique work did not take off because the Chartered Company did not give them permission to carry the work out.[117]

113. Wood, "Gazaland," 226.

114. Dube, *Getting Married Twice*, 148–49.

115. Dube, *Getting Married Twice*, 149.

116. Hatch, "Blessed Are They," 98–99; Hatch, "Gazaland Progressive," 53.

117. Procter, *Fools for Christ*, 144.

The descending of the Holy Spirit at Rusitu Mission Station on 10 October 1915 helped bolster the mission. Mr. and Mrs. G. E. Barnes had arrived at the station in 1910, followed by Mr. and Mrs. Howells, who arrived from England in 1914. The presence of the Howells seems to have been instrumental in the kind of revival that was seen and experienced.[118]

The details about how the event happened are given by Rees Howells:

> We arrived at Rusitu in August, 1915 . . . we soon discovered that God, His Son Jesus, and the Holy Ghost were the same; and because they never change we could count on the same results in dark Africa as we witnessed in Wales. We went through the Welsh Revival and witnessed remarkable 'demonstrations of the Spirit.' We told the people about that revival (language was no hindrance as we have many interpreters), and we, the missionaries, agreed as to the conditions of revival, and were willing to comply with them: On the people's side the conditions were: 1. Confession of all known sin. 2. Full surrender to the will of God. Thursday evening, we (missionaries) not only prayed definitely for a revival, but had the assurance that the prayer was answered. Sunday evening, October 10th, the heavens opened. The Holy Spirit descended, and there was no room for the blessing. We witnessed the same results as in Wales. Rusitu was a transformed church, many young men had entered the 'School of Faith.' An Evangelist Class of about fifteen was started, and our boarding school was more than doubled.[119]

The visitation was to spur on the mission station. Dhube[120] and Kallam[121] agree that the church at Rusitu experienced a great revival and that many young people (men and women) offered themselves as "evangelists" and were deployed as "teacher-evangelists" to preach and establish churches and schools in the Chimanimani district. The missionaries had come to a realization that the instrumentality of the African evangelists was critical to the growth and expansion of the mission. They had realized that "Africans were best fitted to carry the message to their fellow Africans." The missionaries attested to the fact that after the visitation

118. Dhube, *Association of the UBC*, 15; Howells, "New Environment," 55.

119. Howells, "Great Expectations," 130–31.

120. Dhube, *Association of the UBC*, 19.

121. Kallam, *History of the AEF*, 189.

they could see that the Holy Spirit was convicting the Ndau people when the missionaries and the interpreters went out to evangelize.[122]

With reference to a later occurrence, Dhube notes, "Back home at Rusitu in the great influenza of 1918 which took many lives worldwide after World War 1, no one died at Rusitu. In fact, people found refuge at the Mission as they came to stay there and escape death which was wreaking havoc even in Chimanimani District."[123] God's Spirit can be said to have significantly influenced and shaped events at Rusitu. In other words, the Holy Spirit's power was manifest in numerous ways at Rusitu. It is important to note that all these occurrences were taking place in Ndau territory that had been, before the advent of missionaries, under the influence of Ndau traditional religion. Such great demonstrations of the power that Christianity wielded should have shifted the Ndau's perceptions in a tremendous way. It is in this sense, among others, that the missionaries can be said to have greatly influenced the Ndau people's beliefs and lifestyle.[124]

In line with the above, Procter asserts that, "Although somewhat restricted territorially by the presence of other Missions in that part of Rhodesia, the station at Rusitu became a centre for Gospel witness in and around the Reserve where the station was located on a narrow ridge . . ."[125]

Later Years in the Mission/the Church

The missionaries, apart from evangelizing, also established a central primary school at Rusitu, a teacher training school at Biriiri (1956), out-schools, medical work at Rusitu, an orphanage (founded in March 1921, but it closed down in 1957 due to lack of funding) and a Bible college (both at Rusitu).[126]

Much of the history of the later years of the mission and of the church (UBC) can be gleaned from Dhube (*UBC. The Highlights*). As already established, more and more missionaries were to be involved in mission work both at Rusitu and at Biriiri (the two SAGM stations in Chimanimani). According to Dhube, "Among the missionaries of these two

122. Dube, *Getting Married Twice*, 152.

123. Dhube, *Association of the UBC*, 18.

124. Dube, *Getting Married Twice*, 152.

125. Procter, *Fools for Christ*, 145.

126. Dube, *Getting Married Twice*, 153.

decades who were involved in the orphanage were: Rev and Mrs Hatch, Miss Alma Gahm, Miss Lilian Taylor . . . , Miss Elmina Doner, Mbuya Katie Allen (later Mrs Legg . . .), and Rev and Mrs Reginald Glen . . . Others at the Mission were the McGills and their daughter Jessie and Miss Chapman, the first missionary nurse in the clinic as well as Mrs Margaret Evans, wife of Rev David Evans, when the orphanage was closed."[127]

The two mission stations (Rusitu and Biriiri) have remained standing to this day. Dhube points out that "Rev Smith, together with Rev Merritt the Principal, was the builder of Biriiri Mission—first as a teacher training college from 1956 to 1964 when it was gradually turned into a secondary school. Rev Smith did all the older stone work at Biriiri and designed the outlook of the Mission. He was later to be joined by Rev Roy Davey also from Rusitu who was also a construction man and a mechanic."[128]

As mentioned in the foregoing discussion, the autonomy of the church was not an event but rather a process. As Dhube recalls:

> Before this period of thirty years ended (1930–960), the seeds of church autonomy which were to reach their full blossom in the 1970s were sown in earnest. The Mission now wanted the Church to learn to support the work itself and move away from giving the penny which had been generally the norm till now . . . . Meanwhile, the Church began wondering as to why the Mission was trying to leave the Church to carry its work alone when the Mission and the Church were supposed to be one thing—the church. The Church waged an all-out struggle against the Mission to have one constitution and one name. But the Mission replied that that was impossible as the Mission was interdenominational and international whereas the Church was indigenous with no "mother" Church overseas as was the case with other denominational Missions such as Anglicans, Methodists, Presbyterians, Dutch Reformed and even Baptists which the Rusitu Church was even not at that time. After the Church insisted to become one thing, the Mission gave the Church a constitution which was in the main the Mission's constitution. It was the Constitution of the South Africa General Mission, with 'church' added at the end to read Constitution of the South Africa General Mission Church.[129]

127. Dhube, *Association of the UBC*, 22.

128. Dhube, *Association of the UBC*, 35.

129. Dhube, *Association of the UBC*, 45; Dube, *Getting Married Twice*, 153.

For Dhube, "The leading players in this saga were, on the Mission side, the Reverends Glen, Merritt and Evans, as this was after Rev Dotson left Rusitu on the baptism issue (which he wanted nothing but immersion and disagreed with his fellow missionaries)."[130]

Between 1930 and the 1960s the missionaries' work was both consolidated and expanded to cover more of the pockets that had been left untouched so far.

Other missionaries of this time included Rev. and Mrs. Ernest Barnes, Misses Jenks and Lilian Taylor (the first principal of Rusitu Primary School up to Standard VI), Rev. and Mrs. Judson Merritt (the intellectual who opened Biriiri Teacher Training College in 1956), and Rev. and Mrs. David P. Evans (who came in 1949). Mr. Evans became the first Rusitu Bible School principal from its beginning in 1953, with one student, John Semwayo, who was to be joined in his second year in 1954 by Simon Mundeta from the American Board Mission of Chikore and Joshua Dhube. Still another missionary couple were Rev. and Mrs. Edward W. (E. W.) Smith, who was nicknamed "Kupupira" from the chorus "It's bubbling in my heart," which he taught and translated into ChiNdau together with his friend evangelist Reuben Magaa Mutisi while still at Rusitu.[131] Procter records that ". . . In 1963 there were twenty-one day students and five evening class students, while the staff has been increased by the addition of the African pastor, Mr Makinase Bgwerudza, and Messrs. Gordon Crofts and Haward Beckett."[132] The latter, Rev. Haward Beckett, now an old man, lives in Harare, Zimbabwe, today and I had the privilege of interviewing him for my doctoral studies, the thesis on which this chapter is based.

SAGM autonomously ministered in the Ndau area of Chimanimani for a long time and its influence in the area cannot be underestimated. To date the church that was born out of this mission in Chimanimani, Zimbabwe, maintains a significant stronghold in the Chimanimani district although other churches are also now present.[133]

130. Dhube, *Association of the UBC*, 45–46.

131. Dube, *Getting Married Twice*, 155.

132. Procter, *Fools for Christ*, 125.

133. Dube, *Getting Married Twice*, 156.

United Baptist Church (UBC)

Joshua Dhube was the bishop and church chairman of the United Baptist Church of Zimbabwe (UBC) for decades from the late 1960s to around 2004.

The phenomenon of SAGM founded churches gaining autonomy was not unique to Zimbabwe. According to Huntingford, "Nationalism was to become a powerful force and, one after another, countries under colonial rule were to become independent political entities. In the late 1950's discussions were begun which were to lead to independence from the Mission and autonomy being both recommended and offered to the various church groups associated with the SAGM in the different countries of the field."[134] As a result of many discussions and negotiations about church autonomy, the SAGM was to allow the mission-founded ministries to function under black ministers. Several churches, under different names, were born out of the SAGM in different countries.[135] The same happened in South Africa and in Swaziland, for example.

A layman, Mr. Time Zabanyana Dube, led the church now called UBC at a time when there were no clergy to lead it, through the difficult 1960s into the early 1970s, when Joshua Dhube (now Dr. Bishop Joshua Dhube) was studying in Swaziland and the United States of America. Joshua Dhube returned in 1971 and resumed the chairmanship in 1972. Zabanyana, who died at Biriiri in 1976, was the only layman to have led this church. In 1969, during Zabanyana's time, the church adopted the Africa Evangelical (Fellowship) Church constitution but that constitution was superseded at Joshua's return by the United Baptist Church constitution.[136] Without knowing how much was different in these two constitutions, it is clear that the UBC constitution retained a lot of what the former constitution had.

The missionaries and the indigenous Ndau Christians in Chimanimani, as established, did not agree "overnight" or "over dinner" to let the church be autonomous. Dhube records that "The years of dispute between the church and the mission over becoming one entity stretched over a period of about 20 years—from the mid-1950s to the first half of the 1970s. This period, which was to end with the Church adopting a new United Baptist Church, UBC (formally, The Association of United Baptist

134. Huntingford, *History of the Southern Field*, 20.

135. Kopp, *God First*, 60.

136. Dube, *Getting Married Twice*, 157.

Churches of Zimbabwe) Constitution in 1973, saw three name changes of the Mission and the Church."[137]

The church had to change its name after parting with the mission for the reasons that follow. According to Dhube, the leading argument for a further name change for the church was that the church could not continue to change its name whenever the mission changed its name.[138] The church needed a name independent of the influence of the mission because the former had the desire to become completely Baptist. As Dhube expresses it, "The desire to continue in partnership with the Mission was strong, just as it has remained to be so today. We were 'born' by a Mission 'parent' body; how could we change that history."[139] It should be mentioned that although UBC and AEF (now Serving in Mission) parted ways, the two have continued to be in partnership, with the latter supporting different projects that are run by UBC.[140]

Dhube mentions 1974 as "the first full year of UBC as an autonomous Church . . ."[141] It is important to follow this closely, as has been done here, because one needs to understand that even after autonomy was achieved, UBC never reconsidered its position on several issues regarding Ndau indigenous practices and their connection or non-connection to Christianity.

The church has continued to thrive to date. According to Dhube, "Only the war years from 1975 to 1979 were to be a disrupting factor in seeing the rejuvenated Church thrive to full bloom. But all was God's 'order'. And after the war was over, contrary to all human fears of never seeing the church thrive again, what was a parochial church confined to Chimanimani District in the main with a handful of workers became a nationwide church with an ever increasing number of workers . . ."[142]

Serving in Mission (SIM)

The SAGM/AEF lives on but now under the name Serving in Mission (SIM). Consequently the church that was born out of this mission in

137. Dhube, *Association of the UBC*, 49; Dube, *Getting Married Twice*, 158.
138. Dhube, *Association of the UBC*, 50.
139. Dhube, *Association of the UBC*, 50.
140. Dube, *Getting Married Twice*, 158.
141. Dhube, *Association of the UBC*, 56.
142. Dhube, *Association of the UBC*, 57.

Zimbabwe is now known as the United Baptist Church of Zimbabwe, while the mission itself is now called SIM. Fuller[143] and Kopp[144] note that Africa Evangelical Fellowship (AEF) (formerly SAGM) merged with Society for International Ministries (formerly Sudan Interior Mission) on 1 October 1998.[145]

The SIM website asserts that "A union of several organizations founded over 100 years ago, SIM works today with the same passion as its founders."[146] It adds that "In the 1980s, Andes Evangelical Mission (AEM), International Christian Fellowship (ICF), and Soudan Interior Mission (SIM) joined forces to become SIM, which then stood for the 'Society for International Ministries.' AEF joined with SIM in 1998. In 2000, SIM adopted the trade name (or slogan) 'Serving In Mission,' for English–speaking countries, but our official name around the world today is simply SIM."[147]

Conclusion

The chapter has dealt with the SAGM missionaries that evangelized the Ndau people. It has focused particularly on the SAGM missionaries that evangelized the Chimanimani district (then part of British Gazaland) and the church that was born out of this mission, UBC. It has been divided into several parts. The first dealt with missionaries in Africa in general. The second was on missionaries' work in Zimbabwe. The third focused on SAGM. A brief history of the latter years of the mission or the church in Zimbabwe was considered. South Africa was shown as a central base as far as the evangelization of Zimbabwe is concerned. SAGM missionaries' history, especially regarding the evangelization of the Chimanimani district, is somewhat little known compared to that of other missionary bodies that evangelized other parts of Zimbabwe. This is the gap that this chapter has intended to fill. The chapter may also serve to open further avenues through which more research and publications can be pursued regarding

143. Fuller, Serving in Mission, http://images.sim.org/pdfs/history/whfuller-sim-history.pdf.

144. Kopp, *God First*, 2.

145. Dube, *Getting Married Twice*, 158–59.

146. Serving in Mission, https://www.simsg.org/our-history.

147. Serving in Mission, https://www.simsg.org/our-history; Dube, *Getting Married Twice*, 159.

the history, life, and work of the United Baptist Church of Zimbabwe, including its connection and relationship with Ndau indigenous religion.

Bibliography

Beckett, J. "'Handmaids of Imperialism' or 'Servants of God'? Interaction of the South Africa General Mission with the Landscape of British Gazaland 1897–1905." PhD diss., Loughborough University, 1994.

Bhebe, N. M. B. "Missionary Activity among the Ndebele and Kalanga—A Survey." In *Christianity South of the Zambezi*, edited by A. J. Dachs. Gwelo: Mambo, 1973.

Chitando, Ezra. "What's in a Name? Naming Practices among African Christians in Zimbabwe." In *Theology Cooked in an African Pot*, edited by K. Fiedler et al. Zomba, Malawi: Association of Theological Institutions in Southern and Central Africa (ATISCA), 1998.

Dachs, A. J. "Christian Missionary Enterprise and Sotho-Tswana Societies in the Nineteenth Century." In *Christianity South of the Zambezi*, edited by A. J. Dachs. Gwelo: Mambo, 1973.

Dhube, Joshua. *The Association of the United Baptist Churches of Zimbabwe Commonly called United Baptist Church of Zimbabwe (UBC). Celebrating 100 Years of Gospel Witness (1897–1997). The Highlights.* Harare: United Baptist Church, 1997.

Dube, Elijah E.N. *Getting Married Twice: The Relationship between Indigenous and Christian Marriages among the Ndau of the Chimanimani Area of Zimbabwe.* Pretoria: University of South Africa, 2017. http://hdl.handle.net/10500/23809.

Fuller, W. H. *Serving in Mission: Linking Hands around the Globe. 2007.* http://images.sim.org/pdfs/history/whfuller-sim-history.pdf.

Glen, Reginald. "The South Africa General Mission (Rusitu)." In *Missions in Southern Rhodesia*, edited by P. S. King. Centenary: Inyati Centenary Trust, 1959.

Hatch, John E. "Blessed Are They." *The South African Pioneer: The Official Organ of the South Africa General Mission* 18/4 (April 1905). http://archives.sim.org/pdfs/CGM%20SAGM%20AEF%201889%20-%201998/South%20African%20Pioneer%201885%20-%201964/SA%20Pioneer%20Cape%20Town%201886%20-%201918%20OCR/SA%20Pioneer%201905%2018%204%20April%20CT%20OCR%20.pdf.

———. "Gazaland, Progressive." *The South African Pioneer: The Official Organ of the South Africa General Mission* 20/3 (March 1907). http://archives.sim.org/pdfs/CGM%20SAGM%20AEF%201889%20-%201998/South%20African%20Pioneer%201885%20-%201964/SA%20Pioneer%20Cape%20Town%201886%20-%201918%20OCR/SA%20Pioneer%201907%2020%2003%20March%20CT%20OCR%20.pdf.

———. "Gazaland Rusitu." *The South African Pioneer: The Official Organ of the South Africa General Mission* 29/8 (August–September 1916). http://archives.sim.org/pdfs/CGM%20SAGM%20AEF%201889%20-%201998/South%20African%20Pioneer%201885%20-%201964/SA%20Pioneer%20Cape%20Town%201886%20-%201918%20OCR/SA%20Pioneer%201916%2029%2008%20Aug%20Sept%20CT%20OCR%20.pdf.

Hildebrandt, J. *History of the Church in Africa.* Nairobi: Africa Christian, 1996.

Howells, Rees. "Great Expectations. Rusitu, Gazaland." *The South African Pioneer: The Official Organ of the South Africa General Mission* 29/10 (November 1916). http://archives.sim.org/pdfs/CGM%20SAGM%20AEF%201889%20-%201998/South%20African%20Pioneer%201885%20-%201964/SA%20Pioneer%20Cape%20Town%201886%20-%201918%20OCR/SA%20Pioneer%201916%2029%2010%20Nov%20CT%20OCR%20.pdf.

Howells, Lizzie H. "New Environment. Rusitu, Gazaland." *The South African Pioneer: The Official Organ of the South Africa General Mission* 30/7 (July 1917). http://archives.sim.org/pdfs/CGM%20SAGM%20AEF%201889%20-%201998/South%20African%20Pioneer%201885%20-%201964/SA%20Pioneer%20Cape%20Town%201886%20-%201918%20OCR/SA%20Pioneer%201917%2030%2007%20July%20CT%20OCR%20.pdf.

Huntingford, A. C. F. "History of the Southern Field. AEF. The First One Hundred Years in the Southern Field 1889–1989." http://archives.sim.org/pdfs/CGM%20SAGM%20AEF%201889%20-%201998/A%20Publications,%20Theses,%20Manuscripts/Huntingford,%20History%20of%20[th]e%20Southern%20Field%201989%20(AEF).pdf.

Jenkins, D., and D. Stebbing. *They Led the Way: Christian Pioneers of Central Africa.* Cape Town: Oxford University Press, 1966.

Kallam, J. G. "A History of the Africa Evangelical Fellowship from Its Inception to 1917." PhD diss., New York University, 1978.

King, P. S., ed. *Missions in Southern Rhodesia.* Centenary: Inyati Centenary Trust, 1959.

Kopp, T. J. "God First—Go Forward: The Impact of the South Africa General Mission/Africa Evangelical Fellowship on the Africa Evangelical Church, 1962–1994." PhD thesis, University of South Africa, 2001.

Mugambi, J. N. K. *African Heritage and Contemporary Christianity.* Nairobi: Longman Kenya, 1989.

Murphree, M. W. *Christianity and the Shona.* London: Athlone, 1969.

Oduyoye, Mercy A. "Christian Engagement with African Culture: Religious Challenges." In *Uniquely African? African Christianity Identity from Cultural and Historical Perspectives*, edited by James L. Cox and Gerrie Ter Haar. Trenton: Africa World, 2003.

Paas, Stephan. *The Faith that Moves South: A History of the Church in Africa.* Zomba, Malawi: Kachere Series, 2006.

Procter, J. *Fools for Christ's Sake.* Africa Evangelical Fellowship (SAGM), 1965. http://archives.sim.org/pdfs/CGM%20SAGM%20AEF%201889%20%201998/A%20Publications,%20Theses,%20Manuscripts/Procter,%20Jack%20Fools%20For%20Christ's%20Sake%20OCR%20low.pdf.

Raney, Harry. "Gazaland." *The South African Pioneer: The Official Organ of the South Africa General Mission* 12/3 (March 1899). http://archives.sim.org/pdfs/CGM%20SAGM%20AEF%201889%20-%201998/South%20African%20Pioneer%201885%20-%201964/SA%20Pioneer%20Cape%20Town%201886%20-%201918%20OCR/SA%20Pioneer%201899%2012%20%20ALL%20CT%20OCR%20%201.pdf.

———. "Gazaland. From Different Points of View." *The South African Pioneer: The Official Organ of the South Africa General Mission* 16/3 (March 1903). http://archives.sim.org/pdfs/CGM%20SAGM%20AEF%201889%20-%201998/South%20African%20Pioneer%201885%20-%201964/SA%20Pioneer%20Cape%20Town%201886%20-%201918%20OCR/SA%20Pioneer%201903%2016%2003%20March%20CT%20OCR%20%201.pdf.

———. "In Gazaland." *The South African Pioneer: The Official Organ of the South Africa General Mission* 13/6 (June 1900). http://archives.sim.org/pdfs/CGM%20SAGM%20AEF%201889%20-%201998/South%20African%20Pioneer%201885%20-%201964/SA%20Pioneer%20Cape%20Town%201886%20-%201918%20OCR/SA%20Pioneer%201900%2013%206%20June%20CT%20OCR%20%201.pdf.

Ranger, Terrance. "The Invention of Tradition in Colonial Africa." In *The Invention of Tradition*, edited by E. Hobsbawm Ranger Terrance. Cape Town: Cambridge University Press, 1983.

Serving in Mission. "History of SIM." https://sim.org.za/wp-index.php/history/.

———. "Our History." https://www.simsg.org/our-history.

Smith, E. W. *The Christian Mission in Africa: A Study Based on the Work of the International Conference at Le Zoute, Belgium, September 14th to 21st, 1926*. London: International Missionary Council, 1926.

Weinrich, Anna K. H. *African Marriage in Zimbabwe and the Impact of Christianity*. Gweru: Mambo, 1982.

Wood, Douglas. "Gazaland." *The South African Pioneer. The Official Organ of the South Africa General Mission* 13/12 (December 1900). http://archives.sim.org/pdfs/CGM%20SAGM%20AEF%201889%20-%201998/South%20African%20Pioneer%201885%20-%201964/SA%20Pioneer%20Cape%20Town%201886%20-%201918%20OCR/SA%20Pioneer%201900%2013%2012%20Dec%20CT%20OCR%20%201.pdf.

Zvobgo, Chengetai J. M. "The Influence of the Wesleyan Methodist Missions in Southern Rhodesia, 1891–1923." In *Christianity South of the Zambezi*, edited by A. J. Dachs. Gwelo: Mambo, 1973.

Chapter 11

African Christianity

A Dialogue between Religion and Culture

Joel Mokhoathi

Introduction

Much has been said on the need for contextual theologies for Africa and/or for Africans. This is because "Christianity in Africa continues to carry a burden, a veritable incubus, which it has to come to terms with and, if possible, seek to overcome and lay to rest."[1] This is the burden of infusing Christianity with the African cultural life. In his book *Christianity in Africa: The Renewal of a Non-Western Religion*, Kwame Bediako highlights some philosophical debates and the progress that has been made so far by African intellectuals on the problem of African Christianity. He writes:

> [I]f the Christian way of life is to stay in Africa, then African Christianity should be brought to bear on the fundamental questions of African existence in such a way as to achieve a unified world-view which finally resolves the dilemma of an African uncertain of its identity, poised between the impact of the West and the pull of its indigenous tradition.[2]

1. Bediako, *Christianity in Africa*, 4.
2. Bediako, *Christianity in Africa*, 5.

Bediako alludes to the dichotomy that is inherent in the acceptance of Christianity by indigenous converts. He insists that it should be able to address the fundamental question of existence for Africans, and this pertains to the issue of identity, which is overshadowed by Western influence but, at the same time, based on indigenous knowledge systems and traditions. He then postulates:

> If the Christianising of African tradition may be considered to have been largely concerned with resolving a basically religious [italics in original] problem—in that it had to do with making room in the African experience of religious powers for Christ and the salvation he brings—the Africanising of Christian experience can be seen as being concerned with resolving as essentially intellectual problem—how African Christianity, employing Christian tools, may set about mending the torn fabric of African identity and hopefully point a way towards the emergence of a fuller and unfettered African humanity and personality.[3]

It is clear that the acceptance of Christianity by indigenous converts is not purely a matter of faith but also of practice and identity. It is a reflective action that requires one to seriously ponder how they locate their sense of self or identity in relation to their conviction. In this case, being Christian directly impacts against one's natural (indigenous) identity—this is because being Christian, in itself, is an identity. At this instance, two identities are at war and continue to fight for recognition until one finds an appropriate way in which to consolidate them. This is not an easy process as some Christian converts find it difficult to merge the two together—like nominal Christians do. Hence, there are those who profess to be Christian by day and proponents of African traditional religion (ATR) by night. The intension of this paper, therefore, is to provide an overview of the emergence of Christianity in Africa, focusing in Africa south of the Sahara; trace the origins of Christianity in South Africa; look at the development of "African Christianity" as the contextualization of Christianity; briefly reflect on the contextuality of the gospel; and debate the need for contextual theologies.

3. Bediako, *Christianity in Africa*, 5.

Africa—South of the Sahara

The geographical region south of the Sahara was largely judged from the outside by European explorers.[4] Unable to visit the region, many explorers and historians gathered secondhand information about the sub-Saharan desert, which had a great share of errors and fables.[5] Around that time, the great African desert was not even given a name. It was not until the Arabs came along in 6 BCE that the desert was termed the Sahara. The term was used by Arabs to refer "to that vast region which was like an enormous basin."[6] In consequence, the geographical region beyond the northern part of Africa seemed to possess a vague historiography and was therefore described by means of fables and myths. Providing the historical narrative of the time, Mokhtar noted that this mystic region was described by explorers in the following manner: "The Greeks, and later on the Romans, spoke only of Inner Libya, a very vague geographical expression signifying what lay beyond the North African territories, or Inner Ethiopia, a zone still farther south which derived its name from the dark skins of its inhabitants."[7]

Accordingly, the sub-Saharan part of Africa possessed a vague historiography. This situation only changed with the arrival of Arabs in the territory around 6 BCE. Before the arrival of Arabs, the sub-Saharan desert was a region that frightened many generations of explorers by its sheer mysteriousness, and yet captured the imagination of Europeans for many centuries due to its depiction as a region full of fabulous tails in which men and animals took upon the forms of absurd or terrifying monsters. For the Portuguese of the Age of Discovery, this part of Africa was presented as "the land of white Moors and black Moors, of fabulous gold mines and of mysterious Christian monarch, the fabled Prester John of the Indies."[8]

To the Europeans of the age of Romanticism, the Saharan part of Africa carried the image of "parching deserts and lion-infested wilderness and barbarous monarchs disporting themselves with savage magnificence."[9] Therefore, Africa south of the Sahara Desert remained a

4. Hallett, *Africa to 1875*.

5. Mokhtar, *General History of Africa*.

6. Mokhtar, *General History of Africa*, 513.

7. Mokhtar, *General History of Africa*, 513

8. Hallett, *Africa to 1875*, 1.

9. Hallett, *Africa to 1875*, 1.

great mystery for the Western world until the era of imperialism, around the sixteenth to the eighteenth centuries.[10] During this time (around the sixteenth century), the main contact of Europeans with the sub-Saharan part of Africa was through the traffic of slaves for commercial gain in the "New World" of imperialism.[11] At this time, the historiography of Africa was still vague. It changed in the middle of the nineteenth century with the growth of humanitarian efforts, and as Christian missionaries and explorers began to present Africa in a different guise.

The mysticism that had entranced the imagination of Europeans for many centuries was now being replaced by the representation of Africa as the "theatre of the blackest ignorance and crime, where brutal slave traders and tyrannical chiefs held sway over the suffering millions of heathendom."[12] Africa was now perceived to be the beneficient of the white man, shouldering his burden as he brought the blessings of civilization to the newly caught, sullen peoples. According to Oduro, Pretorius, Nussbaum, and Born, this "burden" was characterized by three Cs—Christianity, Commerce, and Civilization.[13] The idea behind these Cs was that all three should go together and promote each other: Christianity must prepare the way for commerce so that Western civilization can replace African culture, that is, the Africans' supposed lack of civilization. In that manner, the Sahara became the grand stage for Christianity, colonization, and Western civilization as was initially intended by European powers in the nineteenth century.[14] Even though it became one of the major religions of Africa, Christianity had to contest for converts with other major faiths like Islam, African traditional religion, Hinduism, and Judaism. These are the foremost-practiced faiths in Africa.

The Spread of Christianity in the Sahara

The earliest period of evangelization in Africa south of the Sahara began with the influence of Diogo Gomez, a leader of an expedition that was sponsored by the Portuguese king in 1458.[15] Diogo Gomez began the pro-

10. Lenin, *Imperialism.*
11. Pawliková-Vilhanová, *Christian Missionary Enterprise.*
12. Hallett, *Africa to 1875*, 1.
13. Oduro, et al., *Mission in an African Way*, 37.
14. Oduro, et al., *Mission in an African Way*, 37.
15. Denis, *African Indigenous Christianity*, 3.

cess of evangelism by converting the Gambian prince, Nomimansa, who was later baptized by the abbot of Soto de Casa, a Portuguese priest.[16] This is the era that was commonly known as the "padroádo period" (1450–790 CE). It was referred to as such because it was a period that was characterized either by the influence of the Portuguese throne over missionary work or activities in territories that were under the jurisdiction of Portugal.[17]

After the conversion of Nomimansa, Portuguese men started marrying indigenous women, and built villages that were modeled after European forms of architecture. In each of these villages, there was a church. Portuguese missionaries or priests (which maintained a staff of twelve friars) from the Cape Verde Islands often visited these village churches on a regular basis to ensure their sustainability.[18] According to Sundkler and Steed, a convent (monastery) was established at Cachau on the Rio Grande, which is about eighty miles south, around that same time (1450–790 CE).[19] From there, the Portuguese missionaries duplicated what they did in Gambia and at Cachau on the Rio Grande (starting village churches and establishing monasteries), with small variations, in other parts of Africa. Denis describes this process in the following manner:

> The pattern was duplicated, with small variations, in the kingdom of Warri; a small enclave in the kingdom of Benin; the kingdom of Congo, the territory between Sofala and the island of Mozambique on the Indian Ocean coastline; along the Zambezi River in the kingdom of Monomotapa; Lamu, which is on the coast of present day Kenya and in Kilwa off the coast of the Comoros Islands.[20]

In consequence, Christianity spread to various African nations, including the ones mentioned above. Nevertheless, in Denis' view, it was in the ancient kingdom of Congo that Portuguese missionary efforts proved to be most successful. Around the seventeenth century, an extensive network of mission stations was established in Congo. Dominicans or Jesuit priests ran these mission stations. Walston and Stevens further note that

16. Sundkler and Steed, *History of the Church in Africa*; Denis, *African Indigenous Christianity*.

17. Kalu, "African Christianity."

18. Denis, *African Indigenous Christianity*, 3.

19. Sundkler and Steed, *History of the Church in Africa*, 45.

20. Denis, *African Indigenous Christianity*, 3.

King Afonso I further promoted the new Christian faith antagonistically.[21] Therefore, by 1619 the bishop of Saõ Salvador could count on the support of eighty priests and canon chanted services that followed European custom. The Portuguese missionary efforts at Congo seemed to yield good returns, as Christianity became the most popular religion in the continent. These efforts, however, were later undermined by the commercial interests of Portuguese merchants, who saw potential gain in slave trade.

Walston and Stevens postulate that because of Portuguese merchants, the missionaries came to be despised and looked upon with scorn, which was initially directed at the Portuguese merchants.[22] Thus, the missionaries, to some extent, inherited the dishonor and contempt with which the Portuguese merchants were treated. At the dawn of the eighteenth century, two great forces combined to regenerate the process of evangelization in Africa south of the Sahara, namely, abolitionism and evangelical revival. According to Kalu,these two forces worked together to revive evangelism and to end slave trade.[23] Through the social activist component of evangelism, missionaries proposed to end slave trade by involving the chiefs, who most probably controlled the supply side of the trade. From this a number of legitimate trading arrangements were made, new administration policies enforced, and Christianity was used as a civilizing agent, enabling the environment.

With this traction, humanitarian efforts began to grow, as missionary bodies, individuals, theologians, explorers, and historians, with various modes of funding and training, flocked to Africa. Pawliková-Vilhanová asserts that this

> [P]hase of the expansion of the missionary movement in Africa, which continued throughout the nineteenth century up to the present day, may conveniently be dated from 1792 and the publication of William Carey's Enquiry into the Obligations of Christians to use any means for the Conversion of the Heathens, which was called a landmark in Christian history, "the first and still the greatest missionary treatise in the English language" (italics and inversion in original).[24]

21. Watson and Stevens, *African-American in World mission*, 143.
22. Watson and Stevens, *African-American in World mission*, 143.
23. Kalu, *African Christianity*, 33.
24. Pawliková-Vilhanová, *Christian Mission in Africa*, 250.

Consequent to Carey's publication, the Baptist Missionary Society was formed on 2 October 1792 for reaching out to non-Western worlds.[25] Soon after, many missionary bodies were established. For instance, in 1795, the Interdenominational London Missionary Society was formed. In 1799, the Evangelical Church Missionary Society, the Religious Tract Society, and many other missionary bodies were established. The establishment of these various missionary bodies therefore seemed to convey a central message, that the "task of leading Africans on the path of civilization by the expansion of moral and religious instruction and converting the pagans to the true religion fell on the newly established mission societies."[26] This is how Christianity spread throughout the African continent, particularly in Africa south of the Sahara—it was advanced by the efforts of various missionary bodies that engaged in evangelical activities in non-Western worlds.

Christianity in South Africa

The arrival and development of Christianity in South Africa is very contentious. Kruger, Lubbe, and Steyn, for instance, trace it back to the late sixteenth century epoch.[27] They argue that the development of Christianity occurred in various but successive phases. The first phase was marked by the arrival of the Dutch colonies around 1652. The second phase was characterized by the arrival of the French Huguenots, who had fled persecution in France around 1688. The last was characterized by the arrival of the British settlers in 1820. As these European settlers moved into the interior of the country, Kruger et al. assert that "they took Christianity—a Christianity adapted to their needs in a new environment—with them."[28]

Hastings, on the other hand, traces the origins of Christianity in South Africa to the arrival of Georg Schmidt around 1737, a lone Moravian layman who was later ordained by post.[29] At his arrival, Schmidt attempted for some few years to find a mission station at Baviaanskloof in order to begin his missionary work among the "Khoikhoi" or "Hottentots,"

25. Pawliková-Vilhanová, *Christian Mission in Africa*, 250.
26. Pawliková-Vilhanová, *Christian Mission in Africa*, 250.
27. Kruger, Lubbe, and Steyn, *Human Search for Meaning*.
28. Kruger, Lubbe, and Steyn, *Human Search for Meaning*, 12.
29. Hastings, *Church in Africa*, 197.

as they were commonly called by Europeans.[30] Finding the Khoi language too difficult to learn, Schmidt resolved to teach the Khoi people the Dutch language. He read them Zinzendorf's *Berlin Discourses* and instructed them on the theology of Paul in the Epistle to the Romans.[31]

According to Hastings, Schmidt "even baptized a few of the people who had listened to his teaching, in a nearby stream."[32] His performance of baptism over indigenous converts, however, spurred some arguments with his Dutch clergies. His Dutch predikant claimed that he had no authority and the permission to baptize indigenous converts because he was just a layman. However, they were later shocked to discover that "though he arrived at Cape Town a layman, he had since been ordained by post."[33] According to Hutton, Schmidt died forty-one years later in Silesia "with a prayer for South Africa on his lips."[34]

A Dutch tailor, a Moravian by denomination who was in the company of Germans in 1792, followed Georg Schmidt. These Moravian missionaries arrived at Baviaanskloof, where Georg Schmidt had worked for few years, to begin mission work among the native peoples of South Africa. Hastings states that the "Moravians of 1792 received more of a welcome and ongoing support in their missionary endeavour than had Schmidt."[35] Isichei further states that "[w]hen more Moravians arrived in 1792, they met one of his converts, an eighty-year-old Khoi woman called Helena, with a cherished Dutch New Testament."[36] For that reason, these are the two versions of the arrival and development of Christianity in South Africa.

Both speak to a particular context in the history of Christianity in South Africa. One traces Christianity to the arrival of the Dutch colonies around 1652,[37] while the other traces it to the arrival of Georg Schmidt in 1737.[38] Schmidt was later followed by Johannes Van der Kemp in 1792, but there were already Khoi converts like Helena around that time.

30. Isichei, *History of Christianity in Africa*, 105.
31. Hutton, *History of the Moravian Missions*, 129.
32. Hastings, *Church in Africa*, 197.
33. Hastings, *Church in Africa*, 197.
34. Hutton, *History of the Moravian Missions*, 130.
35. Hastings, *Church in Africa*, 198.
36. Isichei, *History of Christianity in Africa*, 105.
37. Kruger, Lubbe and Steyn, *Human Search for Meaning*, 12.
38. Hastings, *Church in Africa*, 197.

Nevertheless, whether one perceives Kruger's version or that of Hastings as the starting point of Christianity in South Africa, it is not essential. What matters is the fact that Christianity reached the natives and became one of the major religions of South Africa. As such, the move towards the interior of the country can be perceived as an aspect that fast-tracked the work of missionaries, who spread the Christian gospel among the Khoikhoi/San and indigenous peoples.

Missionaries often built communal facilities such as schools or colleges, hospitals, and churches, and established mission stations. These facilities were used as a platform to evangelize while serving the natives. By the end of the nineteenth century, Christianity had gained a strong footing among the indigenous peoples, and African traditional religion (ATR) was on the wane. ATR was being "outshone by the package of European religion (Christianity), culture (science) and political and military strength."[39] As the primary religion of indigenous peoples, ATR had existed long before the advent of Christianity, and other religions in Africa south of the Sahara. This implies that ATR is one of the earliest religions of Africa, particularly south of the Sahara. Thus, the development and spread of Christianity in South Africa was largely associated with missionary work, from various missionary societies, and the European colonial expansion.

What of African Christianity?

Any remark on the question of African identity seems to be an important matter for indigenous converts to Christianity. This is because the church in Africa has intrinsically been grappling with and hoping to overcome the issue of identity crisis. It has been a long-standing pursuit by African theologians in order to redefine what being an African Christian means. Tinyiko Maluleke, for instance, noted that "African theologians have needed to come to terms with and give a coherent definition of what it meant to be an African Christian—which is, in other words, the question of identity."[40] Redefining what an African Christian is, however, is not an easy task. Rather, it is a strenuous exercise, laden by historical and colonial underpinnings.

39. Kruger, Lubbe, and Steyn, *Human Search for Meaning*, 12.

40. Maluleke, "Identity and Integrity," 28.

From this viewpoint, "[i]t is clear that the agony of African questions of identity is rooted in the tragic encounter between Africa, Europe and America in all its dimensions. Outside this encounter the quest for African identity might not have been so agonizing and not nearly so elaborate and so self-conscious."[41] That is why I refer to the "redefinition" rather than the "definition" of what it means to be an African Christian. There is a vast gap between the archaic past of the earliest Africans and the present. Moreover, African Christians were often pressured, if not conditioned, to despise their own heritage.

Desmond Tutu described this pressure in the following manner: "We cannot deny too that most of us have had an identical history of exploitation through colonialism and neo-colonialism, that when we were first evangelized often we came through the process having learned to despise things black and African because these were usually condemned by others."[42] This is where the problem is. How can Africans resuscitate and call for a return to what they have learned to despise for so long? In order to be able to despise their own heritage, Africans must acknowledge that they have been in agreement with another—joining hands with outsiders in condemning their own heritage.

Their consent and participation in this process made it possible for their heritage to be marginalized. It is, therefore, not only the fault of the colonizers but of the colonized as well. They readily accepted Western ideals without painstaking resistance, thereby depriving themselves of the opportunity to experience Christianity and Christ within their cultural heritage. Rather, they used their newly found Christian knowledge to suppress their own heritage. That is probably why Joseph Galgalo portrayed African Christianity as a paradox. He argued that "it is vibrant and growing, but at the same time shallow and superficial."[43] It is characterized by the struggle for authenticity and uniqueness. On the one hand, it is a form of resistance against early missionary activities and their presentation of Christianity in Western apparel; on the other, it is a search for self-actualization in a convoluted interplay between African religious heritage and African culture.

With this interplay in mind, one feels obliged to enquire: What makes African Christianity Christian? In addition, is the distinction

41. Maluleke, "Identity and Integrity," 36.

42. Tutu, "Black Theology/African Theology," 26.

43. Galgalo, *African Christianity*, 5.

often made between "African Christians," on the one hand, and "Christian Africans," on the other? Evidently, there are various answers and interpretation to these questions. However, in whatever way one might look at this, the expressions "African Christian" and "Christian African" seem to imply different connotations. The term "African Christian" seems to denote a Christian convert who is fully aware of the religio-cultural demand that is aligned to his or her African identity, whereas the term "Christian African" seems to imply a convert who is primarily Christian, but who also happens to be an African.[44] An African Christian, therefore, is a Christian convert that lives within the world that is referenced by the religio-cultural underpinnings of his or her African heritage and acknowledges them as his or her own.

A Christian African, on the other hand, is a convert that upholds the teachings of Scripture without giving due regard to his or her religio-cultural heritage and leaves it behind as if it were not his or her own. The fact that he or she might also be an African happens to be a mere coincidence, which has no bearing on his or her Christian status. Against these contrasting ideas, it is worth asking another question: How do African Christians practice their Christianity within the African context without betraying their heritage? Alternatively, is it the betrayal of their African heritage that makes them authentically Christian?

Can the Gospel Be Contextualized?

The gospel is the hallmark of Christian theology. It is the central message by which Christianity is communicated. The English word "gospel" is translated from the Greek *euangelion*, meaning "a reward for bringing of good news" or the "good news" itself.[45] The term appears about seventy-seven times in seventy-four verses of the New Testament. The undertone of the word and its etymological root cannot be more pronounced than found in Matthew 4:23: "And Jesus went about all Galilee, teaching in their synagogues, and preaching the gospel (euangelion) of the kingdom . . ." The word implies authoritative news regarding the impending judgment.

Even though it is the central feature of Christianity, the gospel has been understood and interpreted differently under different circumstances. For instance, there is the prosperity gospel, the liberation gospel, the

44. Mokhoathi, "African Christianity," 1–2.

45. Prill, "Gospel on the Mission Field," 137.

feminist gospel, and other variations of the gospel. These are but a few examples. They all fall within the broader segments of Christianity. As its central message (the gospel), Christianity is also denominational. There are three main branches of Christianity. These are, namely, (1) Eastern Orthodoxy, (2) Roman Catholicism, and (3) Protestantism. The Eastern Orthodoxy version of Christianity is largely found practiced in Russia and Eastern Europe, whereas Roman Catholicism and Protestantism are found everywhere. In this paper, the specific focus is on Protestantism, where one may find a plethora of denominations all claiming to be Christian.

Throughout the centuries, there has not been one universal gospel designed to fit all contexts. Rather, the gospel has always been understood and transmitted in relation to a specific people and background. Proclaimed by Jesus, the founder of Christianity, the gospel was at first directed to the Jews.[46] Jesus and his first disciples were Jews, and for several centuries after his death Christians of Jewish origin were a significant presence both inside and outside the land of his birth.[47] The entire psychological makeup of the Jews had taught them that, by divine right, they belong to God and are his chosen people (Deut 14:2). Not only did they regard themselves as the possession of God, but they also thought that God was their rightful possession (Deut 32:9). After Jesus' death, however, things began to change.

The book of Acts, for instance, provides a historical account of early Christians who had primarily addressed their fellow Jews, and saw the extension of the gospel to the Gentiles (non-Jews) as a divine surprise.[48] The rapid transmission of the gospel among non-Jews in Antioch (Acts 11:19–21), Cyprus, and Asia Minor (Acts 13–14) gave rise to a new problem: Do the Gentile believers in Jesus need to convert to Judaism? Various answers were given, but all were situated within the view of a particular group. Some Jews who had embraced the Mosaic law, such as Peter and James, insisted that the Gentiles should take upon themselves "the yoke of the Torah" and, for practical purposes, become Jewish (Acts 15:1). Other Jews, such as Paul, thought that the Mosaic law belonged to the old covenant, which was set aside by the death and resurrection of Jesus.

The Gentiles who were converted under the influence of such leaders were not required to uphold the Mosaic law. They were therefore free

46. Cohen, *Ways that Parted*, 1.

47. Marcus, "Jesus Movement," 87.

48. Marcus, "Jesus Movement," 87.

from the requirements of the Old Testament such as food laws, circumcision, and Sabbath observances.[49] In a letter to the assemblies of Galatia, Saint Paul recounts of a meeting in Jerusalem around the 40s between himself and other Christ-believing preachers (Gal 2:9). He reports that Peter, James, and John (the so-called pillars of the Jerusalem church), on the one hand, and himself, Barnabas, and Titus, on the other, executed a formal agreement, sealed by handshake, that called for two distinct but equally divinely mandated and empowered missions.[50] This agreement regarded the transmission of the gospel—one for the circumcised, and another for the uncircumcised.

In calling them "the gospel of the uncircumcised" and "the gospel of the circumcised" (Gal 2:7–8), these early Christian missionaries seemed to be plotting a new definition of the term *euangelion* ("good news") into a fixed dichotomy between the Jews and Gentiles. They instituted an absolute polarity among believers and this was characterized by the distinction between us versus them. It became a case of us for the Jews and them to the Gentiles. The Jewish worldview, which became a template for all early Christians, used such biblical distinctions as "Jews" versus "the nations"—*ta ethnē*, meaning "Gentiles."[51] Circumcision was a cultic marker of difference, rooted in God's covenant with the Jewish ancestor Abraham (Gen 17).

The covenant had provided a long list of regulations from which "living like a Jew" (*ioudaikōs zēn*) was mandatory for everyday life, and set apart from the standard of "living like a Gentile" (*ethnikōs zēn*). This kind of polarity became a point of contestation between Saint Peter and Saint Paul: "But when I saw that they walked not uprightly according to the truth of the gospel, I said unto Peter before them all, if thou, being a Jew, livest after the manner of the Gentiles, and not as do the Jews, why compellest thou the Gentiles to live as do the Jews?" (Gal 2:14). The contrast between the Jews and Gentiles was a marker from which the dichotomy could be made between those who worshipped the God of Israel and those who embraced other religions—often perceived as idolatry.

This complex cartography of us against them provides the backdrop and vocabulary for the debate among early Christians about who could be included in the Christian community and under what conditions. The

49. Marcus, "Jesus Movement," 88.

50. Mitchell, "Gentile Christianity," 5.

51. Mitchell, "Gentile Christianity," 103.

gospel was for the Jews and, as the circumcised, God was their possession. The Gentiles, on the other hand, as the uncircumcised, were a divine surprise. For that matter, the gospel was dichotomized. An interesting development occurred, however, with the apostleship of Saint Paul. He opened up a third category against the polarity of Jews (the circumcised) versus Gentiles (the uncircumcised). He combined these polar opposites into a composite view. That is, he preached an inclusive gospel—that of both the Jews and Gentiles.

Saint Paul introduced a gospel of the "called ones": "But we preach Christ crucified, unto the Jews a stumbling block, and unto the Greeks foolishness; But unto them which are called, both Jews and Greeks, Christ the power of God, and the wisdom of God" (1 Cor 1:23–24). He extended his missional mandate to non-Jews who were uncircumcised, spoke Greek, worshipped idols, and lived outside the land of Judea. In so doing, Saint Paul preached a new, inclusive gospel. The success of the mission to these "called ones" among the Gentiles, which could hardly have been predicted during the life of Paul (let alone Jesus), by all indications was so great as to eclipse and far outrun the mission to Jews.[52]

The conversion of Cornelius served as an example that convinced Peter that "God does not show partiality" (Acts 10:34), a decision that was indorsed and authorized by the apostles and elders in Jerusalem in a formal session (Acts 15). This was a turning point for Gentile Christians. Gentile Christianity refers "to a theological orientation that regards the conversion of the Gentiles as an apocalyptic sign of the culmination of God's decisive plan for human history and salvation for the whole world."[53] Saint Paul insisted that Gentile converts should not undergo circumcision because they would be accepting an entirely different economy of divine salvation, a mistake that could nullify their faith in Christ and symbolize their return to slavery to the flesh (Gal 3:3; 5:13). Saint Paul's argument became a Magna Carta of Gentile Christianity as his views moved beyond the polarity between Jews and Gentiles to consider "those who are from faith" (Gal 3:7) as the true "children of Abraham." In his view, these received all the promises and blessings of the chosen people, but through a new route (faith) that evades the obligations of the Mosaic law. This became the one universal gospel for all nations.

52. Mitchell, "Gentile Christianity," 105.

53. Mitchell, "Gentile Christianity," 108.

The Need for Contextualization

Contextualization, as a subdivision of the various African Christologies—such as Christologies of inculturation, liberation, etc.—attempts to achieve two tasks. The first is the task of inculturation, which tries to explore different ways in which Christianity can be made to communicate with the African cultural heritage; the second is the task of praxis, which looks at how Africans can find meaning and gratification in the practice of Christianity.[54] Because these tasks are interconnected, they occasionally overlap. However, the essential thing is that they both seek to make Christianity communicative with the African cultural context. This is significant because African religious heritage and culture had no standing during the missionary epoch.

Hence, Laurenti Magesa noted that the monologist temperament of Christianity during the missionary epoch deprived Africans of their voice and constrained them from experiencing Christ within their cultural context.[55] He asserted that the "contact between Christianity and African religion has historically been predominantly a monologue, bedeviled by assumptions prejudicial to the latter, with Christianity culturally more vocal and ideologically more aggressive." Concurring with this, Aylward Shorter stated:

> In the colonial period Africans were made to feel ashamed of their culture. They were made to accept alien values and alien ways. They were completely passive. Their very being was conferred on them from outside. Today, there must be a complete break with the mentality of the past, with the inferiority complex of Africans in the colonial period. A deep decolonization must take place at the level of culture.[56]

This implies that Christianity, as presented by early missionaries, failed to find roots within the African cultural context. It was aggressive rather than amenable toward African religious and cultural heritage. African scholars nowadays are making significant strides in making Christianity communicable within the African religious and cultural context. This, however, is no easy task, as there is currently no consensus on how this can be achieved. So far, there are various opinions on the matter.

54. Moloney, "African Christology," 505–6.

55. Magesa, *African Religion*.

56. Shorter, *African Christian Spirituality*, 21.

Firstly, there are those African scholars who think that African religious heritage should be used as a starting point for inculturation.[57] They perceive of ATR as *praeparatio evangelica*, preparing Africans for the gospel of Christ.

Secondly, there are scholars who think that the contextualization of Christianity is an opportunity for the gospel to assess African cultures. They perceive of contextualization as a process that is necessary to allow the gospel to interrogate the viability of the African religious heritage and cultures.[58] Thirdly, there are those scholars who see no differences between Christianity and ATR and argue that both Christianity and ATR can mutually be used to enrich African religious and cultural heritage.[59] Regardless of their differing views, the most important thing to note is that these scholars are reminding us of the contextuality of the gospel and thereby theologies. Hence, one may speak of Jewish Christianity, Johannine Christianity, Gentile Christianity, and so forth. The context plays a central role in the transmission and interpretation of the gospel and, by default, in the formulation of theology. That is probably why Bénézet Bujo, as cited by Paulinus Odozor, argued that "we all speak from our various cultural caves as we open our mouths to theologize. [And that] God speaks to people in their various contexts."[60]

Conclusion

The contextualization of Christianity in Africa seems to have created a platform and an opportunity for Africans to reflect critically on how they can make Christianity more communicative to African religious and cultural heritage. This, however, does not go without challenges and contestations. But the most important thing is that African Christians continue to find means and ways in which to experience Christ within their cultural context. African Christianity is therefore that platform. It allows African Christians to use their cultural ideals and expression in order to live out their Christian faith. Moreover, this is an approach that does not seem to go against or challenge the validity of the gospel. Rather, it allows the gospel to find a meaningful place within the cultural setting,

57. Mbiti, *Bible and Theology*; Tutu, "Whither African Theology?"
58. Mugambi, *From Liberation to Reconstruction*; Mosala, *Biblical Hermeneutics*.
59. Setiloane, *African Theology*; Masoga, *Weeping City*.
60. Odozor, *From Theology in Africa*, 1.

where religion and culture mutually reinforce each other for the benefit of African converts to Christianity.

Bibliography

Bediako, Kwame. *Christianity in Africa: The Renewal of a Non-Western Religion.* Maryknoll, NY: Edinburgh University Press, 1995.

Cohen, Shaye. *The Ways that Parted: Jews, Christians, and Jewish-Christians ca. 100–150 CE.* Cambridge, MA Harvard University Press, 2013.

Denis, Philippe. "African Indigenous Christianity in a Geo-Historical Perspective." *Studia Historiae Ecclesiasticae* 38/2 (2012) 1–22.

Galgalo, Joseph. D. *African Christianity: The Stranger Within.* Kenya: Zapf Chancery, 2012.

Hallett, Robin. *Africa to 1875: A Modern History.* Grand Rapids: Michigan University Press, 1970.

Hastings, Adrian. *The Church in Africa 1450–1950.* New York: Oxford University Press, 1994.

Hutton, Joseph E. *A History of the Moravian Missions.* London: Moravian Publication Office, 1922.

Isichei, Elizabeth A. *A History of Christianity in Africa: From Antiquity to the Present.* Grand Rapids: William B. Eerdmans, 1995.

Kalu, Ogbu U. "African Christianity: An Overview." In *African Christianity: An African Story*, edited by Ogbu U. Kalu, 24–43. Pretoria: University of Pretoria, 2013.

Kruger, Jacobus S., Gerrie J. A. Lubbe, and Cornelius H. Steyn. *The Human Search for Meaning: A Multireligious Introduction to the Religions of Humankind.* Pretoria: Van Schaik, 2012.

Lenin, Vladimir I. *Imperialism: The Highest Stage of Capitalism.* Sydney, Australia: Resistance, 1999.

Magesa, Laurenti. *African Religion: The Moral Traditions of Abundant Life.* Maryknoll, NY: Orbis, 1997.

Maluleke, Tinyiko S. "Identity and Integrity in African Theology: A Critical Analysis." *Religion and Theology* 8/1 (2001) 26–41.

Marcus, Joel. "The Jesus Movement." In *The Cambridge History of Christianity: Origins to Constantine*, edited by Margaret M. Mitchell and Frances M. Young, 87–102. New York: Cambridge University Press, 2006.

Masoga, Mogomme A. *Weeping City, Shanty Town Jesus: Introduction to Conversational Theology.* Cape Town: Salty, 2000.

Mbiti, John S. *Bible and Theology in African Christianity.* Nairobi: Oxford University Press, 1986.

Mitchell, Margaret. 2006. "Gentile Christianity." In *The Cambridge History of Christianity: Origins to Constantine*, edited by Margaret M. Mitchell and Frances M. Young, 103–24. New York: Cambridge University Press, 2006.

Mokhoathi, Joel. "African Christianity: The Search for an African Personality." *Pharos Journal of Theology* 101 (2020) 1–9.

Mokhoathi, Joel. "Juxtapositioning of Christianity and African Traditional Religion: A Study of Christian Leaders and 'Sangomahood.'" PhD diss., University of the Free State, 2019.

Mokhtar, Ǧamāl al-Dīn. *General History of Africa (II): Ancient Civilizations of Africa.* Berkeley: University of California Press, 1981.

Moloney, Raymond. "African Christology." *Theological Studies* 48 (1987) 505–15.

Mosala, Itumeleng J. *Biblical Hermeneutics and Black Theology in South Africa.* Grand Rapids: Eerdmans, 1989.

Mugambi, Jesse N. K. *From Liberation to Reconstruction: African Christian Theology after the Cold War.* Nairobi: East African Education, 1995.

Odozor, Paulinus I. "From Theology in Africa to African Theology (Historical Notes); Impact of the Council on New Generation African TheologiansP." aper presented at "Celebrating 50 Years of Vatican II: Challenges/Contributions of African Church," Duquesne University, Pittsburgh, 28–29 September 2012.

Oduro, Thomas, Hennie Pretorius, Stan Nussbaum, and Bryan Born. *Mission in an African Way: A Practical Introduction to African Instituted Churches and Their Sense of Mission.* Wellington: Christian Literature Fund and Bible Media, 2008.

Pawliková-Vilhanová, Viera. "Christian Mission in Africa and Their Role in the Transformation of African Societies." *Asian and African Studies* 16/2 (2007) 249–60.

———. *Christian Missionary Enterprise in Africa: A Synonym for "Cultural Imperialism"?* Bratislava, Slovakia: Institute of Oriental African Studies, 2002.

Prill, Thorsten. "The Gospel on the Mission Field." *Haddington House Journal* 17 (2015) 137–55.

Setiloane, Gabriel M. *African Theology: An introduction.* Johannesburg: Lux Verbi, 1986.

Shorter, Aylward. *African Christian Spirituality.* London: Geoffrey Chapman, 1978.

Sundkler, Bengt, and Christopher Steed. *A History of the Church in Africa.* Cambridge: Cambridge University Press, 2000.

Tutu, Desmond M. "Black Theology/African Theology: Soul mates or antagonists?" *Journal of Religious Thought* 32(2) (1975) 25–33.

———. "Whither African Theology?" In *Christianity in Independent Africa*, edited by Edward W. Fashole-Luke, Richard Gray, Adrian Hastings, and Godwin Tasie, 364–69. London: Rex Collins, 1978.

Walston, Vaughn J., and Robert J. Stevens. *African-American Experience in World Mission: A Call beyond Community.* Pasadena, CA: William Carey Library, 2002.

Chapter 12

What Happened in Geneva?

The Semiosis of Sacramental Signs during the Pandemic

Lerato Mokoena

Introduction: The Eucharistic Controversy

The politics of semiotics dictate that signs and events must be qualified by speech and social worlds. These two collectives are then disseminated into performative elements constituted by their philosophy of language and representational media, either performative active, demonstrative, or symbolic. As a theoretical framework referential point, this article investigates the religious phenomena of sacramental signs and how their administration was affected by the pandemic (alcohol ban, no sharing of cups, and no water baptism). "Eucharist" denotes thanksgiving and is seen as the supreme act of Christian thanksgiving, convening to believers the body and blood of Christ.[1] Sacraments are, therefore, the hallmark sign of the Christian faith, lending believers a base that shapes and maintains religious identity and rituals in a social world through repetitive acts of verdictives (findings), expositives (affirmations), exercitives (orders), and commissives (vows). "What happened in Geneva" is an aphorism I use for the debate on sacraments between Zwingli and Luther at Marburg, Germany, in 1529 from a phenomenological semiotic point

1. Nmah, "Luther And Zwingli'S Eucharistic Controversy," 120–39.

of view, the study of signs and meaning, to examine how the administration of sacraments was affected by lockdown restrictions as an attempt at explaining the phenomena of religious rites and ritualistic performance. The aim is to prove through a dialectic preposition that signs and performative speech acts that exist simultaneously can also exist mutually, demonstrated as follows: the variable function (sacrament) equals the derivate of that function (performative and demonstrative speech), thus concluding that Zwingli and Luther were both right by way of the multi-evidentiality of events.

In October 1529, the disputation between Luther and Zwingli became public in the presence of Christ during the Eucharist. The meeting that has come to be known as the Marburg Colloquy in Reformation memory is one of the best debates to have taken place. Due mainly to the religious climate of the time, Luther had challenged the Catholic Church, inspired dialogue, and now had to face Zwingli, his contemporary in Zurich. Luther's pathway was his treatise *The Babylonian Captivity of the Church*; Luther rejected in this thesis the doctrines of transubstantiation and Christ's repeated sacrifice at mass. Leaving this Catholic tradition, he presented *Sola Scriptura*, which would be the hallmark of Luther's protestant Reformation, leading to the disputation between him and Zwingli and many other reformers as they battled with ideas. The scratching critique against the Catholic Church influenced contemporary reformers to relook at the significance of sacraments.

The pathway leading to the Marburg Colloquy are differences that arose in the eucharistic and liturgical differences as early as Wittenberg.[2] A few changes were considered to be introduced, such as Communion to the laity, simplifying liturgy in vernacular and eliminating both the vestments and elevation of the host.[3] It was these differences that caused an early stir and challenged the authority of doctrine. Although initially against the Catholic Church, Luther's reformation program also saw him stand in opposition to reformers who had originally endorsed his programs but later took a different ideological positioning on some issues. Zwingli would become one of the major contenders in that debate. Zwingli was not always in opposition with Luther, until 1524, when he appealed to Cornelius Hoen's symbolic interpretation of the words of institution, which Luther rejected. Zwingli's symbolic understanding of the

2. Chung, *Inventing Authority*, 15.

3. Chung, *Inventing Authority*, 15.

Eucharist surfaced in a letter he wrote to Matthew Alber of Reutlingen in November 1524, when he insisted that the words "this is my body" mean "this signifies my body."[4]

Transcripts of the Colloquy are unavailable as people routinely took notes and recollected them from memory. The most valuable and complete account is the *Itinenirium Hedios*. Hedio was a Zurich theologian who accompanied Zwingli to Marburg.[5] The report is not wholly accepted as objective, however, since the detailed accounts favor the Swiss reformation campaign. The details to follow are from the two theologians' earlier writings and secondary literature on the interpretations of the writings.

Luther and Zwingli: The Lutherans, "This is my body" (Matt 26:26); the Zwinglians, "The flesh is of no avail" (John 6:63)

The Zwinglians and the Lutherans arrived at Marburg, Zwingli with Melanchthon and Luther with Oecolampadius. The atmosphere might have been tense and eerie as the two theologians had only ever been interlocutors and were meeting for the first time, which would sadly be the only time. The two theologians and their accompanying compatriots had had brief private preliminary discussions before the actual debate began, detailed in *Du Marburger Religiougesprcaech*. In these accounts, Zwingli states that he and Melanchthon discussed the doctrine of original sin, the part that Word and sacrament play in the operation of the Holy Spirit, and the doctrine of the Lord's Supper. Both disputants state that they agreed on all tenets, save the Lord's Supper. Melanchthon, in his account, says that the doctrine was discussed and takes for granted that unanimity was not reached.[6]

To understand Luther's polemic writings, we first need to refresh our memory of his theology. According to Luther, after diverting from the Catholic tradition, there were only two sacraments; the Lord's Supper and baptism. Luther, like all the other reformers, drew interpretative inspiration from Scripture. However, the secondhand reader should refrain from saying that Scripture was the basis of confusion. Interpretative

4. Chung, *Inventing Authority*, 18.
5. Beto, "Marburg Colloquy," 73.
6. Beto, "Marburg Colloquy," 75.

methods and hermeneutical lenses were the driving force if we believe in the infallibility of Scripture. So it therefore can be argued that the two contrasting ideas of the Eucharist developed from the scriptural interpretation and hermeneutical approaches to the Bible, which is the principle by which somebody should understand Scripture.

Luther's interpretation of Scripture has no equal in German-language history. He is commended by my favorite philosopher and philologist, Friedrich Nietzsche, for having written such an excellent German translation of the Bible; Nietzsche called it "the best German book."[7] Even his sharpest opponents recognized the influence of his Bible translation skills. Luther detailed his academic, faith, and theological development as that first arose out of confusion and anger that God would judge him based on deeds and not justify him through grace in thhe detailed exposition below.

> I had conceived a most unusual, burning desire to understand Paul in his letter to the Romans; thus far, there had stood in my way not a cold heart but one single word that is written in the first chapter, "In it, the justice of God is revealed" (Rom 1:17) because I hated that word "justice of God." By the use and custom of all my teachers, I had been taught to understand it philosophically as referring to so-called formal or active justice, that is justice by which God is just and by which he punishes sinners and the unjust.—But I, an impeccable monk that I was, stood before God as a sinner with an extremely troubled conscience, and I could not be sure that my merit would assuage him. I did not love, no; I hated the just God who punishes sinners. In silence, if I did not blaspheme against God, I indeed grumbled with vehement anger against him. As if it isn't enough that we miserable sinners, lost for all eternity because of original sin, are oppressed by every kind of calamity through the Ten Commandments. Why does God heap sorrow upon sorrow through the Gospel, and the Gospel threatens us with his justice and wrath? This was how I was raging with a wild and disturbed conscience. Thus, I continued badgering Paul about that spot in Romans 1, seeking anxiously to know what it meant.[8]

The above quote serves as the precursor for Luther's critical discovery of the doctrine of justification by grace through faith alone and the basis of his rejection and extreme fear of hell punishment. This fear of a judgmental Christ was made acute during Mass. Luther's basis of

7. McKim, *Cambridge Companion*, 73.
8. McKim, *Cambridge Companion*, 89.

justification is that God lawfully abandons the debt of our sins and imputes Christ's righteousness to us when we place our faith in him. This interpretative model resolves all conflict between justification and sanctification for Luther.

The conflict between presence and absence refers to incarnational theology and the Trinity since the presence of Christ is the stronghold of the arguments. Corporeality and immateriality also feature as we ask whether it is indeed the incarnated body of Christ or the symbolic presence we are consuming during the Eucharist. Since the main focus of the disputation was corporeality and flesh, Zwingli brought up the argument from Augustine that "whatever exists in a certain place is a body," to which Luther responded, "While it is indeed true that whatever is contained in a place is a body, the converse is not necessarily true." Zwingli was propelled to further dig into his Augustine archives and quoted, "Take away space from bodies and you will have taken away the bodies."[9]

Calvin, in the *Institutes*, argued that although Christ cannot be simultaneously present, he can only be present spiritually during the sacrament while he is still at the right hand of the Father. Luther argued instead for consubstantiation, that while the bread and wine contain the body and blood of Christ, the elements don't change physically; Christ is present "with, in and under the elements."[10] In Luther's consubstantiation doctrine, the sacramental substance does not physically become (or transform) into the very body and blood of Christ (as it does in transubstantiation).[11] The Reformation, therefore, distinguished between three views of the Eucharist: transubstantiation, consubstantiation, and symbolic, and this is where Zwingli's view finds ideological positioning.

Llorente and Feldmeth propose that we must use the Aristotelian dialect method to trace Zwingli's deductive logic on the Eucharist to separate it from that of Luther.[12] Zwingli had had earlier influence from predecessors, whether aware or not. A considerable part of his influence can be traced to Erasmus, although we find that the Eucharist controversy was already in full swing as early as the ninth and sixteenth centuries. The Western church was already influenced by Augustine of Hippo's thesis of consecrated elements, who did not believe

9. Chung, "Inventing Authority," 24.

10. Enns, *Moody Handbook of Theology*, 250.

11. Llorente and Feldmeth, "Zwingli on the Symbolic Eucharist," 8.

12. Llorente and Feldmeth, "Zwingli on the Symbolic Eucharist," 3.

in transubstantiation.[13] Zwingli's extended version became the most irreconcilable as Luther countered consubstantiation, and other reformers either supported him or retreated to the conventional Catholic view of real presence, while Calvin refuted both. Luther interpreted "Take, eat; this is my body" while Zwingli interpreted it alongside Christ's command "do this in my remembrance," invoking symbolism and nullifying the physical presence of Christ.[14]

Still preoccupied with the crippling fear of punishment and hell, Luther wanted to dissociate the Eucharist from Christ's repetitive sacrifice at Mass. He proposed, in turn, that the believer can benefit from grace and the forgiveness of sin through consubstantiation.[15] We can disagree with the man but cannot deny that he was a visionary his theology was influenced mainly by his anxieties. Much as I might commend Luther, I believe that scientifically and philosophically Zwingli was ahead of his time and was the prophet we did not know we needed. It is as though Zwingli knew there would be times where his theology would come in handy when we needed to justify the absence of the Eucharist altogether due to lockdown restrictions (alcohol ban and elevation of the host) and still call ourselves Christians who are justified by faith in good standing. We need both Luther and Zwingli for our times. They differed in their time but prove to be beneficial to ours.

Semiotic Poiesis: Sacramental Signs and Religious Phenomena

Prompted by the Reformation, in 1652 the Council of Trent, being empathetic to the pleas of the Reformation, added a new challenge: no cup sharing. A close look at Luther and most of his contemporaries' initial objections will show that during the pandemic those are thoughts we would have to consider ourselves, namely, the absence of wine and sharing of a cup and what happens to the body of Christ and the laity doctrine.

The material dependence on the literal wine/water and bread becomes the source of discontent because when they are absent, that contradiction calls for a re-engagement with dogma. Luther held the opinion that the two cannot be separated; as the Holy Spirit works inwardly, there

13. Maunder and Bettenson, *Documents of the Christian Church*, 82.

14. Llorente and Feldmeth, "Zwingli on the Symbolic Eucharist," 8.

15. Llorente and Feldmeth, "Zwingli on the Symbolic Eucharist," 9.

needs to be a literal outward sign; "the Lord's supper exemplifies the general rule that, while God certainly deals with inwardly through the Holy Spirit, who works faith in our hearts, he does it by the instrumentality of the external world and sacramental signs, through which the blessings won by Christ on the cross are distributed."[16] Semiotically, this ideological posture raises a few questions about sign processing, signified, and signifier; therefore, there needs to be a sociology of knowledge conducted on the poetics of ritual performance. As Yelle argues, a semiotic approach contributes to elucidating religious phenomena.[17] Yelle further argues that although cultural performance is to some degree symbolic, meaning is not reducible to the purely utilitarian in ritual behavior; the symbolism arguably predominates, to the extent that such behavior may appear to serve no pragmatic objective.[18] This is why it is essential to ascribe meaning and practical purpose to behavior and signs lest they lead to the inference of just being ritualistic.

Even with a pragmatic objective, signs exude aesthetic performance that requires a domain for expression closely linked to their essential meaning or predicates. The field for expression is where we locate and manufacture the rhetorical function for repetition (i.e., the Eucharist, Mass, and Easter pilgrimage). From a semiotic point of view, according to Murphy, there is a repertoire of cultural meanings, a taxonomy, that pre-exists the act of creation (i.e., dogma).[19] The domain for performance and the taxonomy of importance intersect and collapse at this endogamous and exogamous juncture, where the two camps, with no pun intended, marry each other, leading to an inescapable cycle of empirical analysis and theoretical reasoning. This is the intellectual rapture we are chasing with this argument, to ask whether the performative feature can be mailable and what grounds constitute that change.

How then do we describe the event of the sacrament when one or more of the collective or performative features required is absent (alcohol ban, sharing of the cup, no Mass)? When does the feature become performative active (transubstantiation), only demonstrative (consubstantiation), or representational (Zwingli; John 6:63? In her *What Is an Event?*, Wagner-Pacifici details the three events and provides an understanding

16. Gerrish, "Discerning the Body," 379.

17. Yelle, *Semiotics of Religion*, 1.

18. Yelle, *Semiotics of Religion*, 3.

19. Murphy, "Elements of a Semiotic Theory of Religion," 50.

of the eventful forms as I will briefly discuss them below. This is my attempt to demonstrate through a dialectical argument that both Zwingli and Luther present the metaphorical exogamous and endogamous complex accumulation of signs through semiotic constructs to show that during the pandemic they both would have been right; a case for mutability will be proved as the logical synthesis.

On active performative features of events, Wagner-Pacifici notes that events are mobilized and constituted by speech or performative equivalents (i.e., Luke 22:19, "He took some bread and gave thanks to God for it. Then he broke it into pieces and gave it to the disciples, saying, 'This is my body, which is given for you. Do this in remembrance of me'").[20] Jesus associated speech through performance and memory with a particular event. Through the utterances of those words, a social world for this particular religious phenomenon through a specific set of signs is conditioned and evoked through repetition. This active performative feature only forms a quorum when (1) there is an authorized speaker (i.e., clergy), (2) procedural and conceptual order (dogma or Scripture), and (3) legitimate place and time that corresponds with the social order of the active performative feature (church service). The first instance seems uncompromising in my view; therefore, we shall not consider at this stage the contingent realities of the three performatives.

Wagner-Pacifici's analytical reference is the theory of performative speech acts by the language philosopher J. L. Austin in his notable work *How to Do Things with Words*. This theoretical framework argues that "performative speech acts are those that change the social world in and through their utterances."[21] Austin's conceptual framework evolved to be more complex when it began to incorporate all forms of speech and not only performative ones, which distinguished a more precise vocabulary for the performative speech as:

> Locutions ("the act of 'saying something' in [the] full, normal sense"), illocutions ("performance of an act in saying something as opposed to the performance of an act of saying something"); and perlocutions ("what we bring about or achieve by saying something, such as convincing, persuading, deterring, and even, say, surprising or misleading").[22]

20. Wagner-Pacifici, *What Is an Event?*, 20.

21. Wagner-Pacifici, *What Is an Event?*, 20.

22. Prochasson, "Qu'est-ce qu'un evenement Politique," 141–63.

According to Wagner-Pacifici, Austin's initial categorization of illocutionary only consisted of five primary classifications of speech: verdictives (findings, acquittals), expositives (affirmations, concessions), exercitives (orders, commands, openings), behabitives (apologies, protests, felicitations), and commissives (vows, promises).[23]

Typologies often overlap and interject one another, and the performative speech acts are no different as we will see that they usually work against themselves because realities can be contingent upon conditioning, and meaning is mailable. The possibility for change, according to Wagner-Pacifici, is that social agents performing performatives depend on other agents acknowledging or heeding the speech acts, and such acts can never be guaranteed (i.e., during the liturgy, the congregation can choose what and what not to respond to as a matter of faith).[24] Another example is that a priest cannot serve Holy Communion in the absence of the congregation, as was the case during hard lockdown. The first instance, which is performative speech, requires presence and a social world for the repetitive acts to retain their meaning, demonstrated mathematically in the form of a simultaneous equation below:

> verdictives (findings) + expositives (affirmations) =
> exercitives (orders) + commissives (vows)

My argument, therefore, is that the collectives that share the same variable can be explained as follows as deduced from the equation: the clergy, from *findings* (dogma), requests for the congregation to join in the liturgy, and through *affirmations*, the clergy executes *orders*, and the community commits to the act through *vows*. The social order of the sacrament is retained in these conditions of possibility. The variables exist simultaneously but are also mutually exclusive; therefore, verdictives and expositives can function independently of exercitives and commissives since they are the same variant. This is, in essence, what I perceive was Luther's argument as he proposed that Christ is present "with, in, and under the elements," not only simultaneously but mutually.

In the film *Dead Poets Society*, one of the main protagonists says something impactful: "I am laughing near you, not at you." This makes me think about the multi-evidential nature of events and how they occur "near," "inside," "here," and "there." Proximity designation plays and places importance on the second part of performative acts and speech,

23. Wagner-Pacifici, *What Is an Event?*, 20.

24. Wagner-Pacifici, *What Is an Event?*, 21.

demonstratives. Wagner-Pacifici locates demonstratives as proximal, relational, and distal entities that are distinguishable through speech acts such as "this," "that," "those," "these," and speech pronouns like "I" and "you," known from deictic as "shifters" or "floaters."[25] The flexible nature of these deictics is incumbent upon the subject uttering them.

The episto-politics of semiotics dictate that we situate events within a given context to align them to a specific social order or words. We do this while cognizant that these contexts, like the deictics that produce them, shift and float. They expand and contract; "the very concept of indexicality assumes a subject position that is oriented and aligned toward or away from other subjects, deriving its location and direction relationally from them and vice versa."[26]

By way of Zwingli, "The flesh is of no avail" (John 6:63)" means that Christ cannot exist simultaneously as the bread during the Eucharist while also sitting at the right hand of the Father in heaven. An examination of corporeality and flesh in the book and theology of John is necessary to deduce Zwingli's argument. A reader-response stance is beneficial to the reading of John as Johannine theology is heavily embedded with symbolism. In my view, Zwingli's reading of John seems positivistic, generating a belief that only operates within the confines of experimental knowledge. John himself opens his gospel with a scandalous statement that "the Word became flesh," which would prove to be John's deictic climate and symbolic media. We find through the reading of John a play on symbolism that is empathetic to the cognitive dimensions of the subject on the narrative receiving end. According to Lee, "flesh" in John is presented as the vehicle of God's self-revelation and communication. It is within the contingency of human existence that God speaks.[27] The Word becomes "flesh"; in other words, God speaks within the human condition's transitoriness, transience, and perishability.

I want to dissociate Zwingli's view of flesh as corporeal identity during the administration of the sacrament and his reading of John 6:63 through a reading of Mayria Rivera's *Poetics of the Flesh* to argue for elemental flesh instead. It is through christological incarnation that we see that flesh and signs are interconnected in John, as Lee explains that this is where God's glory is revealed and at the same time becomes the ultimate

25. Wagner-Pacifici, *What Is an Event?*, 23.

26. Wagner-Pacifici, *What Is an Event?*, 23.

27. Lee, *Flesh and Glory*, 57.

paradox of God's communication.[28] They pierced his flesh (now Gods' glory is attached to a dead body); the Word becomes flesh (immanence); the flesh is of no avail (passion and resurrection narratives).

The pronouncement "there is nobody [*soma*], only flesh [*sarx*]" creates conditions of possibility to collapse the conflation of these two circuitous elements. Rivera notes that while the body is simply a corpse in John, the flesh is unstable and complex.[29] The flesh is what the Word became (*egeneto*), but also what is born (*gegennemenon*) of the flesh is flesh and what is born equally of the Spirit is spirit. This is not a fixed boundary because those born of flesh are simultaneously called to be born of the Spirit, evoking the elemental dimensions of life; flesh, or his flesh, is also bread. The bread is the flesh that Word became. Rivera argues that we should be wary of replacing the images and metaphors for a message deemed more critical because that dismisses the poetics of the text, whose impact is in the intricate relations between common material elements and metaphysical assertions.[30] Rivera's thesis is for both Luther's consubstantiation (with, in, and under the elements) and Zwingli's symbolism (corporeality).

Concluding Remarks: Administration of Sacraments during the Pandemic

Eucharistic theology is clear on one thing: the sacrament's essence is not malleable in nature, even if the social worlds are performed in change. The starting point of these engagements does not begin with Luther and Zwingli; they are just a pathway. The Fourth Lateran Council in 1215 aimed against Cathar and Waldensian heretics and began to proclaim that "[Christ's] body and blood are truly contained in the sacrament of the altar *under the appearances* of bread and wine the bread being transubstantiated into his body and the wine into his blood by divine power."[31] Theologians would later then want to distinguish between sign and symbol, whether it was the literal body we are chewing and blood we are drinking.

28. Lee, *Flesh and Glory*, 57.

29. Rivera, *Poetics*, 21.

30. Rivera, *Poetics*, 22.

31. Burnett, *Debating the Sacraments*, 51.

The thesis of substantial conversion has been argued and modified. However, the interest of this article is to ask what happens when one or more of the performative elements required for the performance to be complete is absent or unattainable. Most Protestant churches were affected by lockdown restrictions in observing the two most essential ordinances, baptism and Holy Communion; these visible signs that call for faith in action are the most visible and the highest expression of the grace of God. These two signs are elements of the formula of salvation, and the pandemic threatened their instituted power.

It seems that under the constraints of lockdown, the responsible and life-saving way for believers to engage in this performative speech and act without the consecration of the priest and the social world that legitimized them was to turn to confessional faith as the interim practice. This is possible if we believe that, verdictives (findings) + expositives (affirmations) = exercitives (orders) + commissives (vows). While the former variable is absent during a hard lockdown in a pandemic, the believer evokes the second variable. The believer would then reminisce on the exercitives and commit through faith verbally to the commissives (i.e., recite a confession).

The multi-evidentiality of events ("near," "here," "there") creates a gear-shifting mechanism where in the absence of elements, the powers of indexicality can be evoked so that while not there, the believer can still be near. By way of Wagner-Pacifici, "Semiotic systems that establish spatial and temporal binaries, boundaries, rhythms, and coordinates and those that develop networks and genealogies of kinship provide the mechanisms by which we reconfigure our senses of the reasonable and the possible paths, orientations, alignments, and feelings of belonging and solidarity."[32] This is why we believe in the communion of saints and the ecumenical church. In the absence of substantiated elements, confession must prevail. This view culminates in the representational feature in the politics semiotics, which only prevails if:

> conditions for performative active are impossible (pandemic, hard lockdown restrictions), and demonstrative elements expressed simultaneously can exist mutually verdictives (findings) + expositives (affirmations) = exercitives (orders) + commissives (vows); therefore, the conceptual and cognitive work required for the representation feature can be initiated.

32. Wagner-Pacifici, *What Is an Event?*, 25.

The operative logic of all these semiotic structures is the very foundation of the religious phenomena of ritualistic practices and performance. It is, therefore, the conclusion of this paper that during the pandemic, neither Luther nor Zwingli were wrong; both strategies are applicable only if we apply them in the formula I have provided above. We draw from both arguments about carnality, corporeality, and elemental flesh a poetic force that emerges from the world to express what Rivera calls the "Relational": what the world makes and expresses itself.[33]

The disputation of 1529 between Luther and Zwingli is a pathway of radically reimagining and doing Eucharistic theology in a manner that is faithful to incarnational Christology. The manifold arguments I have presented can be summed up as follows: The pandemic presented us with a unique challenge to Eucharistic theology. Wordly flesh, fleshy words, and elemental flesh all encompass the imagery equivalences of the intertwining of the material and spiritual. On this stance, I stand and offer my synthesis as: "flesh is distinct from the body, and even more clearly than spirit, in both cases, the distinctions keep flesh human and thus blessed."[34] In the absence of elements, confession prevails.

Bibliography

Beto, George John. "The Marburg Colloquy of 1529: A Textual Study." *Concordia Theological Monthly* 16/1 (1945) 8.

Burnett, Amy Nelson. *Debating the Sacraments: Print and Authority in the Early Reformation*. Oxford: Oxford University Press, 2018.

Chung, Kim, Esther. *Inventing Authority: The Use of the Church Fathers in Reformation Debates over the Eucharist*. Waco, TX: Baylor University Press, 2011.

Gerrish, B. A. "Discerning the Body, Sign and Reality in Luther's Controversy with the Swiss". *Journal of Religion* 68/3 (1988) 377–395. doi:10.1086/487875.

Lee, Dorothy A. *Flesh and Glory: Symbolism. Gender and Theology in the Gospel of John* New York: Herder and Herder, 2002.

Llorente, Glenn Pates, and Nathan Feldmeth. "Zwingli on the Symbolic Eucharist." 2012. https://www.academia.edu/12552658/Zwingli_on_the_Symbolic_Eucharist.

Luther, Martin. *The Babylonian Captivity of the Church*. Fig Books, 1970.

Maunder, Chris, and Henry Bettenson. *Documents of the Christian Church*. Oxford: Oxford University Press, 2011.

McKim, Donald K. *The Cambridge Companion to Martin Luther*. Reprint. Cambridge, Cambridge University Press, 2003.

Murphy, Tim. "Elements of a Semiotic Theory of Religion". *Method & Amp; Theory in the Study of Religion* 15/1 (2003) 48–67. doi:10.1163/15700680360549411.

33. Rivera, *Poetics*, 3.

34. Rivera, *Poetics*, 49.

Nmah, Patrick E. "Luther and Zwingli's Eucharistic Controversy: A Reflection on Nigerian Christianity." *Unizik Journal of Arts and Humanities* 14/2 (2014) 120–39. doi:10.4314/ujah. v14i2.6.

Enns, Paul P. *The Moody Handbook of Theology*. Chicago: Moody, 2008.

Prochasson, Christophe. "Qu'est-ce qu'un evenement Politique?" *Divinatio* 39–40 (2015) 141–63.

Rivera, Mayra. *Poetics of the Flesh*. Durham, NC: Duke University Press, 2015.

Sahlins, Marshall D. "The Return of the Event, Again: With Reflections on the Beginnings of the Great Fijian War of 1843 to 1855 between the Kingdoms of Bau and Rewa." In *Clio in Oceania: Toward a Historical Anthropology*, edited by Aletta Biersack, 37–99. Washington, DC: Smithsonian Institution Press, 1991.

Wagner-Pacifici, Robin. *What Is an Event*? Chicago: University of Chicago Press, 2017.

Yelle, Robert A. *Semiotics of Religion: Signs of the Sacred in History*. London: Bloomsbury, 2013.

Index

www.ingramcontent.com/pod-product-compliance
Lightning Source LLC
LaVergne TN
LVHW020539100826
845148LV00010B/1534